RUNNING
FROM THE
DEVIL

C DAVID CASH

NEWMAN SPRINGS PUBLISHING
320 Broad Street
Red Bank, NJ 07701

First originally published by Newman Springs Publishing 2022

ISBN 978-1-68498-306-3 (Paperback)
ISBN 978-1-68498-307-0 (Digital)

Printed in the United States of America

To Angela, Lavada, and Cynthia, my three wonderful sisters.

He dwells in desolate cities, lives in Abandoned
Houses that are destined to become ruins.
—Job 15:28

CONTENTS

INTRODUCTION

"**Y**OU SHOULD WRITE A BOOK," I WOULD HEAR THIS OFTEN, and I agreed. My problem was starting the book. I would work at it, gather information about my adventures, write something, and see how someone liked it. My one or two friends, as time went on, would read what I had written and respond with "You should write a book." I am sure people hear this all the time. I believed it. Big deal, what am I going to do? Write a book! Millions of people have thought that and never even try. I could join that crowd. Millions have started a book, and that's it. How can I write a book that someone would read, much less buy? Not just sell but be a *New York Times best seller*.

At first, I blamed it on not having a new computer, so I purchased a nice laptop with money from the first COVID stimulus check. Nothing happened. No motivation: maybe leftover depression. Something I am going to have to deal with. I wrote short stories and sharpened my skills. I enjoyed writing, something new I discovered. So what was the problem? Taking the first step on a long journey. The second problem was a memory that just did not work all that well. Excellent life. Definitely enough for an exciting best seller.

God Almighty himself solved that problem. Jesus told me to write this book. You may say, "Yeah, sure." There is a lot that led up to me saying that. If you are a *true believer*, you may understand. If not, call me crazy. After you read the book, you may become a *true believer*. You may shake your head and say, "I don't know about that." Let yourself believe. This is a true story. Not cleaned up. I did not add or hold out. I stayed positive. Because I was told to just write the truth. Simple. No outside influence, no mental distractions. Everything you have ever done is stored in your brain, just stored way back and hard to find... I believe that, and *that* is what I have used in this book.

Right out of the gate, I do not know anything about writing a book. I have not taken a class or read a book about writing a book. First and most important, this will be a true story. Many of my facts can still be verified. I have changed names, times, and places to protect some people. For many places or exact times, I do my best to get right. It is very close or exact. Somebody out there today will say they saw it differently. Just like the tomb when Jesus rose. This is the way I saw it. The results are the same. The story remains true.

I will try to breeze through the younger years. I must go there because of my st-st-stuttering. My mother who would often punish me for no reason, could be the reason for my extreme st-st-stuttering early in life. I can't say this enough: my dad was a *saint*.

The first chapter is important. You must know me to understand and enjoy the book.

This book has drugs and drinking. I did not write it so you would like it. I did not write it to sell. My main purpose is a true story. It will not *attract* Christians or non-Christians. I don't know.

In chapter 1, I will tell you about praying for *wisdom*. I prayed extremely hard for *wisdom*. I will warn you to be careful what you pray for. When God decides to answer your prayer, *he will let you know! And...you may be in for a rough ride!* Of course, I did not see this till decades later.

I stopped praying for *wisdom* after chapter 2.

The ultimate situation to achieve *wisdom* is in the unexplored, unknown, unfamiliar, distant, and new.

CHAPTER 1

Growing Up in Chamblee, Georgia

Thanks Cowboy Belt

This is the most important chapter. I need to introduce myself and let you get to know me. Without reading and understanding David, you will not believe my true story. To really enjoy my book, you have to understand what I am made of. After that, you will enjoy this book.

The earliest memories I have of my family are living in an old house down a dusty gravel road. The backyard was vines and bushes. A house across the street burning to the ground worried me. The kids who lived there were my size. I wondered if the friends I played with were burned up. No one cared if I was worried. Finally, a fireman said, "It's a good thing this happened during the day. No one was hurt."

A few times when Mom was asleep, I went across the road and played with those kids. Leaving the side yard was against the rules.

It was tough getting to my friends because of the ditches. I was so little. Their house was not directly across from us. It was a little to the right, which made it easier to sneak across. It was a big adventure for me. Big adventure! Being in the road or across the road meant a whipping. I never got caught. Then the house burned down.

I got a rusty nail stuck in my head from a makeshift see-saw Angela and I were playing on. It was in the side yard. It was so funny. I was under the board "adjusting" or "fixing" the seesaw when Angela decided to get on it. Ouch.

Angela and I were hungry in the morning. One morning, Dad was home. We looked for some food. Nothing. We decided to cook something. We put the bottom of a bag of Cheerios into a pan. Just the Cheerios. Not the Cheerios dust. It was not much. We added some water. After that, Angela and I put it on the stove. We didn't know about turning something on. We thought we were cooking. While bringing it back to the table, Mom walked in, wearing her housecoat. I figured we were in trouble. Mom looked around. Water and Cheerios were on the floor, stove, and table. Angela and I were standing beside the table. On top of the table sat the pan with some Cheerios and a little water.

Mom asked sleepily, "What are you two doing?"

My quick-thinking sister answered, "Making you and Dad some breakfast."

Slow me yelled out, "We were hungry!" Sisters learn mean looks early.

Mom was so nice when she said, "You two go out and play. I will clean this up."

I promise you we never went hungry. We were not starving. There was plenty of food in the refrigerator and out of reach. Dad worked all the time. Mom soon had a job at a place that made packaging. She brought home a bunch of small different-size boxes for us to play with.

Treasure hunting under the house, I found an almost empty old peanut butter jar. I worked and worked. Finally, I got the scratched-up lid off. I scraped the peanut butter out of the jar and ate every bit of it. It was so good.

There was no furniture inside the house. No toys. It was bad. Kids know. We did not live in that house very long.

When I was eight years old, my uncle Billy drove us down the gravel road and showed me the house. It was abandoned, and the roof was in need of repair, where a large tree limb had fallen on the house. The house and yard looked too small. I recognized the front porch and dirt driveway. This was it. We were parked next to the remains of the burned-down house.

I thought we lived in the country. We were facing Interstate 85. This old *abandoned house* is on the edge of Chamblee and what is today Metropolitan Atlanta. A five-foot chain-link fence ran along about fifty yards from the access road and parallel behind my old house. The fence was covered with vines and bushes, like I remembered my old backyard.

Like I mentioned, we did not live in that house very long. It was a five-mile drive to the next place we lived. A basement. It was the lower floor of a two-story rental house in downtown Chamblee. The top floor was street level. We had chickens. This house was on Chamblee Dunwoody Road. Before long, we moved upstairs in that same house. Upstairs had more room. It had more sunshine. This was something to be proud of, living *upstairs*. Being level with the road. We lived upstairs for a good while.

I will live on Chamblee Dunwoody Road for a couple of years. Chamblee Hospital is on the same road. Just turn right out of our driveway. Go a mile The hospital is in Downtown Chamblee. That is where I was born. Turn left out of our driveway, go two miles on Chamblee Dunwoody Road, and you will arrive at Chamblee High School. Yep, you guessed it. My high school. As long as we are doing this, turn right and go two blocks. Great-grandmother Purcell has a nice home with about an acre of land. Angela and I were dropped off there sometimes. I was known as Jonnie Mae's boy. There were always a lot of people at Grandmother Purcell's house.

I didn't talk much, because I stuttered. First and second cousins would ask my name. I would run off. They would ask, "What's your name, Da-Da-Da-Da-David?" This could be where I started being alone.

You have met Angela. She is older than me by a year and a half. Lavada is two years younger. Cindy, my youngest sister by eight years, doesn't come along until times are better. My mother goes by the name Johnnie Mae. She is not the most loving mother. She can cook, sew, and keep a clean house. My father, Charles, is a *saint*—a loving father, true Christian, and worker of a man. I go by David, which is my middle name.

My grandmother, whom I love dearly, is Ma. We pronounce her name as *Maw*. Mom's mother. Ma knows that Mother is very mean to me. She has told her daughter to quit being so mean to David. Mom pays no attention to Ma. Ma pays attention to me. I get special privileges. I can go into the huge basement of Ma's house. That is an honor. I respect the privilege. I keep a picture of Ma in my office today. Pa (Paw) died twenty-five years before Ma.

Less than a year after moving into the upstairs house, my father became employed at General Motors, working on the assembly line. Not long after that, we bought a home with two bedrooms, one bathroom, a kitchen, and a living room. I was so happy. I was five years old and ready to settle down. Our home had a cement block garage. It also had a good-size backyard for a garden with some peach trees and plum trees. The front yard had one nice maple tree. Home.

Dad took me everywhere with him—parts store, hardware store, side jobs, to work on someone's car, to run to get milk. I was his helper. He did things for me.

I will back up just a little. You gotta hear this. It won't take long. I was four years old, almost five, living upstairs. I had a belt that said "Cowboy" on the back of it. I found it in Ma's house, in the basement. The buckle must have fallen off, because it had been repaired with screws. Now it was torn up again. Ma said I could have it. Ma was like that. When I got home, Mom told me to throw it away. Mom was like that. Mom gave me a thin shiny black lady's belt to wear. Mom said firmly, "Just wear it. No one will notice." My pants were way too big, which was really okay, but now a girl's belt. It even had sparkles.

I wore the lady's belt outside behind and down below the upstairs house. I had the cowboy belt in my huge pocket. Dad walked out of the old rickety shed that we used as a chicken coup when we lived downstairs. Dad asked, "What's going on son?" I was tired of being laughed at for stuttering. I did not mind the big pants. I could carry a lot of things in my pockets.

I was worried Dad would be mad. We were taught not to complain. Be thankful. The less you have, the more thankful you are supposed to be. I just shook my head. I wanted to run away like I always did.

My father said, "Whatever it is, we can fix it." I said, "Okay." I showed him the lady's belt I was wearing. He did not laugh at me! He did not smile. That stuck in my memory. I had been laughed at so much. This belt was the limit. Dad knew the stuttering had been giving me a rough time.

I pulled the cowboy belt out of my pocket. I asked, "Ca-ca-ca-ca-ca-can yo-yo-yo-yo-yo-you fi-fi-fix this?" Dad took the cowboy belt, looked at it, and said, "I have an idea. Why don't you hop in the car, and I'll tell your mom we'll be right back?"

What a relief! We went to the shoe-repair shop. Johnny, a skinny old Black man with white hair and who was always talking about Jesus, wrapped the belt around my waist. He told me what a great man of the Lord my father was. Later that day, we picked up the belt. It had a new buckle! The belt had been polished, so now it was darker. Before, the leather was dry and light in color. Now it has soaked up all the fine leather cream. Fine-looking belt. I couldn't say anything, so I shook Johnny's hand.

Cowboy was the first word I learned to read, spell, and write. I decided to do another word. Southern was on a railroad bridge we would often pass under. The bridge was next to the GM plant. So the second word I could read, spell, and write was *Southern*. I could read, spell, and write over twenty words when I started school. Thanks, Cowboy Belt.

By the time we moved into our home, I was learning about measuring, handing Dad the correct tool, and checking air pressure. I was a good assistant, picking up things at a carpenter job and putting things up. I would keep busy. If I stayed home, Mom would put me in the kitchen doing dishes or scrubbing something.

We kept a one-acre garden beside Ma's house for four years—from first thru fifth grade. We skipped a year. Three days a week during the growing season, Mom would pick me up from school and drop me off at the garden. Hoe the dirt, especially up around the corn; rework and rake clean an area; reseed, post, and string for beans; and always pull weeds. Of course pick the vegetables. Never-ending cycle. I knew what to do. No shade. Three hours.

Sometimes, when Dad got off work, he would join me. Other times, Mom or Dad would pull up when my time was up and take me home.

I did not mind doing this. I was proud of my garden. I always have a mason jar of iced water.

Sometimes, at the end of a long hot three hours, Mom would pull up, get out of the car, and, I could tell, would think, *Oh no*. She would start off, "What have you been doing?" I could not answer. I would get hung up on the first word—*pulling*. I looked down at the ground. "Pu-pu…," I'd say. After that, the word totally hung up, and I could not talk. I could not say, "Pulling weeds."

Then Mom would say, "Look at me." So I would look at her a little. She demanded, "Answer me."

I would change my words, "Working in the garden." "Wo-wo-wo-wo-wo-wo-wooorrr…worrr…wooorrrkkkiii…wooorrrkkkii-innnggg. Wooorrking iii-in th-th-th-th-th-the ga—"

"You've been playing."

I would look at my shoes, one shoe on top of the other. "N-n-n-n-n-n-n-no, ma'am," I would say really softly. I was glad the word *ma'am* popped right out.

Mom was furious. "Don't you talk back to me."

I was thinking, *I am in trouble. Here it comes.*

Mom would always say this, "When we get home, your father will hear about this. Now get in the car."

That type of incident happened often.

You would not believe how many weeds I pulled that day. I was a weed-pulling machine. You see, I was alone doing something the family needed. I felt something. You know what I mean?

Now sometimes, my mother would drive up with iced tea with lots of ice. She would bring an extra jar of iced tea. She might even be early! We would walk around and look at the plants. She really enjoyed doing that. It was our best time together. Mom would say, "Just look at all the work you have done. I don't see a single weed anywhere. David, you already have the posts in for all these beans. You have really done a good job."

I was so happy to walk in the huge garden with my mother. Yes, I enjoyed it when Dad came to pick me up. He let me sit down while he did some of my work. He would gather the tools and load them. You know how much I love Dad. That praise from Mother was wonderful. It was rare. I needed it.

Every time I got home from the big garden, dinner was ready. We ate together as a family. We always had every meal together. We laughed together. It always seemed like there was something funny to laugh about.

We had another small garden at home. Tomatoes, squash, cucumbers, and more beans. Some years I even planted watermelon and cantaloupe. I always converted the garden at home into all turnip greens in the late summer. Mom and my sisters canned the vegetables. We gave a lot of the vegetables away to aunts and uncles. The needy. Our family ate well with fresh or canned vegetables. We had fresh tomatoes at every meal.

I will get the *mean mom* over with. I shared a bedroom with Angela and Lavada. I slept on a top bunk. Mom or Dad would usually have to tell us to calm down and go to sleep. Every once in a while, Mom would come in and *pop* me with a belt. That would shut us up. She said something to me that was very embarrassing one time when she hit me with the belt. She crossed a line. She said in a regular voice, "Stop playing with yourself." Everybody could hear it, and then she popped me with the belt. Mom said that in front of my sisters. The embarrassment was so painful. We do not even say *dang* in our house. We turn the

TV down for beer and cigarette commercials. We are such good kids.

She never brought the belt in again. Dad told me my mother was sick. I used it as a positive thing to understand the worst in people later in life. I also realized, later in life of course, my mother remained sick. I did not want to carry this sickness with me. It is sad. Some people will let the past control their present. If you hear an adult repeatedly talk about their mother, father, or childhood, no one cares to hear it. Yet they keep talking of a bad childhood. That person carries a sickness with them. They can stop.

CINDY

One morning, I was up before everybody and out the front door with my bow and one arrow. There is a space in front of the garage the size of a car window I wanted to hit. I leaned back and released the arrow, what looked like, straight up. Cindy, my little sister who thinks I am the greatest thing in the world, waddled out. She was one year and a few months old, I don't know for sure. Still in diapers. Cindy ran out the back screen door and stood on my spot. She was looking the other way. In my mind, the arrow just flipped. I pictured the arrow going through her head. I yelled, "Cindy." She turned around and stood there for a second. The arrow was on its way down now, picking up speed. Cindy smiled real big when she saw me and quickly ran/waddled toward me. The arrow hit right behind her. I picked Cindy up and hug her so much. She pushed me away and started laughing and laughing, and then she hugged me.

I enjoyed going to church. I went to North Peachtree Baptist Church *every time the doors were open*. I was in RAs, Royal Ambassadors. I went to different church camps. We even had basketball and roller skating at the church gym. I drew the line at the choir. No.

I needed money for church camp and different programs. Well, school things, I wanted to pay for those. By the time I was twelve, I was cutting a few yards and getting paid. This grew into twelve places. With twelve places, I bought my own lawn mower. I also kept a schedule and gave 10 percent to the church. I asked Dad to let me put gas in the truck. He put his foot down and said, "*No.* You are a good young man. I will take care of this." Well, I poured gas from my five-gallon can into his truck without him knowing about it from time to time. I learned that trick from Dad.

Dad and I did a lot of work on Uncle Harold's cabin in Highlands, North Carolina. For two years, we worked on the cabin that faced Whiteside Mountain. We had endless work to do. I still took off. Endless trails, creeks, and waterfalls. I found an old bridge over a large stream I could stand on and watch the trout go under me by the hundreds.

The best regular woods were at Grandfather Cash's house. I spent a lot of time there. Lots of visits. A week every summer. I was blessed with good Christian aunts and uncles.

I learned about construction because Dad took jobs to make money. On weekends or after work, he would be adding on rooms or helping with any type of construction, tearing off damage and building back again. Roofing houses was one of our specialties. Dad even taught me about cement. He was good. Starting from a driveway, we poured a set of steps that curved around a large tree. The steps then curved back to line and matched up with the cement deck below. A beautiful work of art. It was very professional. My father could do anything as far as construction. He always said, "You just have to put your mind to it."

The two of us never went fishing or to a ball game together. Our favorite pastime was firewood—cutting, splitting, and stacking firewood; cutting the tree down; picking the tree out to cut down; putting that big knotted log on the fire…anything to do with firewood.

Something else we did together was help people. We did it all the time as far back as I can remember. I would go with my father to deliver food, firewood, and coal to needy families. We would go to the hospital together. Those were some tough calls. So sad, many times. There was a time when I was with my father and he was helping a single woman. When the lady offered him tea and he could not stop working, Dad said, "Son, would you get the tea from the kind lady for me?" I have helped him patch a roof in the rain, put plastic over drafty windows at night, rush out to fix someone's car, or fix a flat at night. It seemed like a lot of people needed help on cold winter nights.

We walked in one freezing cold home where there was no food. The children were under a pile of blankets in the middle of the day. We got them some heat going and food in the house. A few times, it would be for prayers for a sad situation, along with repairs or food.

It would usually start with my father waking me up, saying, "David, wake up, son. Get dressed. I need your help." I guessed we were on a call list at church. Maybe some people just called Dad.

When I was sixteen, my father asked me to go to a funeral with him. It was of a person I did not know. I did not know anybody at the small funeral. I was asked to pray with some people. Dad was busy holding hands and praying with someone else. I am sure I was asked, because I was Charles Cash's son. I said the most beautiful sincere prayer and later some comforting words. It sort of surprised me. Dad was not surprised. Anyway, helping people.

At fifteen, I was already driving Dad's three-speed truck. He would let me drive through Atlanta and in the mountains with him. I had a job at Chamblee Fence. I was always loading and driving the superheavy-duty six-wheel, eight-speed (four-speed transmission with two-speed axle) trucks around the property. Also, down to fill up or short distance alone. Chamblee Fence had two of these trucks and three heavy-duty four-wheel trucks. I had the newest six-wheel loaded on a Monday morning. We were slammed. Mr. James Clark, the owner of Chamblee Fence, walked up and asked me, "David, can you drive?" I answered, "Mr. Clark, I am fifteen years old." James Clark came back with "I didn't ask how old you are. I asked if you could drive." I quickly responded, "Yes, sir." He told me to get in the truck and drive. I already had the job information from loading. It was a big job, seventy miles south. I felt someone get in the back as I was turning the key. A young man jumped in the passenger's seat. Mr. Clark hit the side of *my* truck and yelled "Let's go!"

Jumping to 1969. The world had gone crazy—long hair, sexual revolution, drugs everywhere, and the hippie scene was big. Peace, love, and Vietnam. The year 1969 is also the year I decided do not drink or smoke pot at all. I no longer wanted to even be around either one.

I started getting drunk when I worked at Chamblee Fence. My boss "Red" would buy Glen Thigpen and me both a pint of cherry vodka on payday. We were very responsible. Bahaha. I looked forward to getting drunk and sharing it with friends. I was fifteen. Later, at sixteen years old and right after turning seventeen, my superneighbor who was back from Vietnam would buy me whatever I asked, usually just a twelve-pack beer.

My first marijuana. I purchased two joints from a friend in homeroom. I tried it alone for the first time and went to the mall. I loved it. Soon enough, I was passing a joint or pipe around. Buying a lid. Getting drunk and stoned. I did not stutter when I drank. Nothing wrong with getting high.

Late in 1968, I left that path. I am very healthy, and I understand the trap of drugs and alcohol. My neighbor is an alcoholic. He gets drunk a lot. I want to be like my dad, respected. I do not want to be cool. I do not want to be around those people anymore. My decision was made. I do not want anything to do with drugs or drinking. *Ever.* I am going the direct opposite. My desire in life is to be more like Jesus.

The decision was made. The year 1969 was a great year. I was living good. If you can remember, I broke my neck that year. I was not a drinker or using drugs. I most definitely never wanted them in my life.

I pray a lot now. I pray for wisdom. I started over a year ago. The only thing I have continually prayed for. I am being quite serious. David, in the book of Psalms, speaks of wisdom. Solomon, his son, prayed for wisdom. Now I pray for wisdom every day. Careful what you pray for!

I have become a deep thinker. I am a loner a lot of the time. I am beginning to see how Jesus hurt. When my father told me, "Set your eyes on the higher light," I set my goals higher. I look for Christ. I want to be more like Jesus. I read the Bible every day to help me stay on track. I may go to Vietnam. I can get killed. I can be a loser. The next Billy Graham. I may get married and have half a dozen children.

Grand first-chapter finish. I owe it to you. Some of that was boring. Introducing you to me. That will be the last of boredom in this book. Hang *on*. Yahoo.

As you know, I am seventeen and in perfect health. I lift weights at school and home. Allen Brunner is the hundred-yard-dash champion at Chamblee High School, a large school of, I believe, three thousand students. Allen is my friend. I just beat him in the hundred-yard dash, after the last track meet. Allen challenged me. I am the broad-jump man. Running and standing broad jump, 440-relay third leg. I was a winner. Invisible player. Not the hundred-yard dash, which is exciting. Everybody is shouting. The complete race is run right in front of the stands. We had large cement stands.

Allen and I are always in the same homeroom and share many classes. Always physical education. Allen was popular, funny, always getting into trouble. Big trouble, like running a new Mustang into a house. Bused out the bricks and blocks. Left a hole shaped like a car in front of a nice house. Less than a mile from where I lived. Fame.

Back to the hundred-yard-dash challenge. The stands were emptying out. All the equipment was put away. Nice cool night. No hurry to go home. I had changed back to my regular clothes except for my tennis shoes. I was jogging around the track in deep thought or something. I noticed Allen was standing across the field on the starting line of the one-hundred-yard dash. That was odd, so I started walking across the field toward him, wondering why he was still here.

When I was a little over halfway across the field, Allen asked, "David Cash, do you believe you are faster than me? Right now the hundred-yard dash?" Well, Allen, being Allen, said it loud enough for me and everyone in the stands to hear it. The people who were left in the stands all stopped. The few people on the field heard what Allen asked. Allen loved this kind of attention. I did not like attention.

I felt great. I came right out with plenty loud "I believe I am faster than you, Allen. I would be glad to race you." I jogged over, wondering where this bravado came from. As I was getting close, I had to say, "One-hundred-yard dash, *right now.*"

The people in the stands—men, women, and children—stood right where they were. About twenty-five people. Some of them recognized us. The people on the field gathered and talked. One person jogged over to start the race. Allen said loudly, "No way. Let's get this over with." I asked, "Why did you challenge me?" He came back with "David, well, you are fast. If I am going to say that I am the fastest, I want to be a hundred-percent sure." I quickly said loudly, "Let's go, Allen, second-fastest guy." We started laughing until the "official" stopped us so he could start the race.

That night, I flew. Allen got the jump. We went neck and neck about twenty yards, and I left him behind. I was six or seven yards ahead at the finish line. I ran past the finish line and turned around. Allen was so winded. He was gasping for breath. He finally caught his breath; looked up at me; and, between breaths, said, "I knew it."

Allen stands up in homeroom the next Monday morning as our classmates are being seated. The class is over half full. Allen tells everyone about the race. Made him even more famous.

I have worked two summers at Chamblee Fence. Heavy-duty work. Pushing wheelbarrows full of concrete up hills in the woods. Spinning out of the heaviest gauge fence. Using posthole diggers. Wire cutters all day. Switching between left and right hands. Building strong forearms and upper body. My forearms are like steel. Biceps like rock, impressive, just saying. The rope climb at school in record time. My physical condition at the time of the accident is one of the reasons I can use my arms and hands and walk today.

I have often imagined how my life would have turned out without the next chapter.

CHAPTER 2

Murrells Inlet, South Carolina, May 31, 1969

I Know I'm Going To Die

GEORGE, MY SOON-TO-BE BROTHER-IN-LAW, IS A TERRIFIC guy. This is our big family getting together to celebrate the upcoming marriage.

His sisters picked out a nice place for a picnic, a day of swimming and fun at the beach. We went to a place only the locals knew about. Their biggest concern was crowded beaches, this being Memorial Day weekend. We were away from the holiday mob. The small town of Murrells Inlet was miles away. The place was perfect with three picnic tables and palm trees for shade. The water was a beautiful clear aqua blue with a bright-white sandy bottom. We had the area all to ourselves. The nearest people were far away and out of sight.

Eleven, maybe twelve, people were at our beach picnic that day. George was with some of his immediate family, in addition to Angela, Lavada, and myself. There was also Joel, a close friend of George's.

The area George's sisters have chosen is like a small inlet or cove. This inlet is fed by a delicate wide and shallow estuary, which is feeding clear water into our peaceful little bay. The area is noticeably picturesque. Two great blue herons in the estuary are standing perfectly still, waiting for lunch. An osprey is in the pines with its nest. The beach where we are swimming is right below the picnic tables and where we are parked. A unique or rare place.

The water is shallow for about twenty yards out and then begins to quickly slope deeper along with the water, becoming a darker blue. I can see the sandy bottom very clearly, standing up near the cars. After that, the bottom drops off and appears deep aqua and after that dark blue all the way to the other side.

The other side has a small strip of sand beach along a seawall. The seawall is about six and a half feet tall. It runs the length of the inlet and partway into the estuary. The water along the strip of sand next to the seawall appears to be dark sapphire blue in color and very deep. That is the crystal clear water running from the estuary river.

This bay-like area was maybe sixty or seventy-plus yards wide. I got out of the car, and I couldn't wait to swim across. It was one of the first things I do. When I swam to the other side of the inlet, I began diving down. I never reached the bottom. At twelve feet, I could not even see the bottom. I swam back to the shallow side and started goofing off with everybody.

So many fish. Holding my breath, I would float facedown and just look at the fish. Of course, I needed to move away from everyone to do this. Inhaling a maximum deep breath, I can relax, float, on top of the water, and hold it for two minutes and fifteen seconds.

George and Joel were on to this and started attacking me.

Okay, game on.

When they least expected it, I would grab their legs and flip them or throw a Frisbee full of water into their face. Over and over. For some reason (my incredible physical condition), I was far away when they found Underwater Rocket Man David. Yahoo, yahoo! We were all having so much fun.

Frisbees were all the rage back then. Everybody kept good Frisbees in their car. We could all catch behind our head, back, and legs. Jumping or running. Any respectable seventeen-year-old could throw the Frisbee in several different ways. The heavier Frisbee was best for the windy beach and for distance. All Frisbees float.

We had two Frisbees going. Someone threw one of our heavy-duty Frisbees across the inlet. It went up, over, and past the seawall. No big deal.

I swam across the inlet and walked a fair distance down the narrow beach. That was next to the seawall, toward the estuary. That was where the seawall was lower.

I effortlessly jumped up on the wall.

It was a grassy area beyond the seawall. That grassy area was flush with the top of the seawall. The grassy area was large.

I saw the disk walk out, grab it, and return back to the wall, an area across from where everyone was in the water. I threw it back.

Next, I walked slowly along the top of the seawall to where I had been swimming earlier. I was looking for the best place to dive in and easily found the dive spot I wanted.

Piece-of-cake dive, not much beach to dive over. Looking down, I had some sandy beach at the bottom of the wall. Right after that, the water dropped almost straight off into a dark-blue channel.

I looked across to the other side. No one was paying any attention to me.

Everyone was having a great time.

So I dove in to go join them.

I went down to make the dive and gave the big push off.

Remember I was the standing broad jump man on the track team.

This push off would take me far into the deep water.

Something went horribly wrong. I remember looking forward to the dive with confidence. Looking down at my spot in the water, I even remembered swinging my arms back then and starting to swing them forward as I released upward but mostly outward with full power. The last of my memories for a few seconds! My brain had erased the *hit* and a bit of time on each side of the *hit*.

With all the force I used to push out, I might have slipped. I just couldn't see it. I did something wrong. I made a bad mistake that day. Round and round, I thought about it. I must have come up short and hit just a few inches into the water. I stopped thinking about what went wrong decades ago.

I am suddenly floating underwater. My eyes are open. I have no air. My lungs are completely empty. The air has been knocked out of me. I immediately think, *I am stunned. I will shake this off. I need air. I am still stunned. I cannot move. This is very real. I know I dove off the seawall. Now I am underwater, and my lungs are totally empty.*

I see my hands floating in front of my face. I cannot move them. I realize that the damage is more than being stunned. The silence sharpens my awareness. I need air. The reflex to suck air in hurts. It is painfully impossible to overrule. My lungs are empty, empty, empty.

I am terrified that I will not be able to overrule the "breathing in" reflex any second.

I have broken my neck. I am paralyzed. I need air. This is too real.

I look past my hands. I can see a lot of fish. Some are swimming along. Some are swimming back and forth. Looking at the fish is a microsecond reprieve from the circumstance I found myself in.

I am deep in the water. I must have hit the edge somehow. The remaining force drove me deep into the water. I am pretty deep. I can almost see the bottom. It looks bleary.

My lungs are in pain. I hope to float to the top. Just not enough time. I will be dead by then.

I think about how very real this is. My body wants to convulse so I will breathe. This is the worst pain I have ever felt. Empty lungs holding no air for a period of time.

I am totally conscious.

I know I am going to die. In this horrible pain.

I am not going to float to the top and be rescued.

I am sinking. My surroundings are slowly becoming darker.

This is how I die. I drowned.

I will not give up. Even though I know I am going to die.

The pain is off the scale. I lock my lungs.

I am one tough *son* of Charles, the greatest man in the world. He taught me, "You can't give up. You don't have that choice."

I can clearly see the bottom now.

A fish comes in close to my left fingers, nibbles, and leaves.

The pain of wanting to inhale water is unbearable.

My final seconds will be choking.

The bottom is closer, and I can tell that I am moving with the current.

The silence is deafening.

Something just happened. I will not inhale. I know it.

I have *prayed*. At first I prayed for help. Now I pray for Dad and the people who will be hurt.

Is the bottom closer? I see sand fall off the side.

With my eyes open, I pray, "Thank you, Jesus, for everything."

A fish is back, looking at my fingers. "Hey there…" I don't know if it is the same fish. That was an actual thought during my final seconds. The fish and my fingers are all I see. I b-l-i-n-k. The fish is still there. The pain is much better. Where did the fish go? I hope the fish is okay. I did not complete that last blink. That has been a while. I remember thinking about the fish. I knew I was going to die.

See notes at the end of the book.

Alive floating on top of the water, not way underwater.

It is bright because the sun is reflecting off the sandy bottom. I am floating on top with my back up and out of the water! Now this is very, very strange. I remember opening my eyes, and just a second before that, I remember feeling the air and sun on my back above the water.

But can I feel it? I don't know. I think I can. I know my back was above the water because I can see the top with my peripheral vision. The back of my head being above water.

What am I doing way over here? Sunlight reflecting off the sandy bottom?

These are rapid thoughts that somewhat diminish as I am floating. I cannot feel the sun and the air on my back?

I see the bright sandy bottom, and soon I see movement.

My head is snatched above the water. It is turned to the right.

I can see the blue sky through the drips of water falling off my forehead. I inhale and manage to grab some air, a half a breath.

Immediately my face, head, along with my whole body, is pushed back under the water.

I do not feel the hand placed on my back to push me under.

I am underwater, fully conscious and ready to live.

My brain is operating in survival mode.

I am back underwater and have some precious air.

As I am being pushed down, my left hand touches my mouth. What luck, maybe not luck, I don't know.

This is definitely *not* heaven.

I open my mouth and barely grab my hand with my lips.

Great idea: I will *bite* it. I use my lips, tongue, and finally teeth. I have no feeling in my hand. I bring my hand all the way into my mouth and bite down.

I am definitely paralyzed. I believe. I do not feel a thing.

I bite until it bleeds and keep on biting.

I will be running out of air soon. I was only able to inhale about half a breath.

I try to bite my hand to the bone. I bite and shake my head. Shaking the head is a bad idea. I am biting my hand at the base of the left thumb. I am wiggling my teeth. I have blood all in my mouth. I keep biting.

Blood more blood.

Whoever pushed me down thought I was goofing off.

They will wonder why I have not come after them for revenge. They may push me down again. We are ruthless.

I see blood everywhere. So much blood. I keep biting in frustration.

I almost make it. I am so close to living. I am going to drown anyway.

Is this my *hell?*

I am almost out of air.

I push my hand, now useless for blood, out of my mouth with my tongue and lips.

I start screaming.

No one sees the blood.

I scream, my lungs totally empty. I am out of air, so I start crying. My eyes are closed tight because I am crying so hard. I have no air again. This time, I brought it upon myself.

I remember this terrible feeling today—how I screamed underwater, ran out of my air, and was in the most horrible familiar pain again.

"How did that work out for you, David?"

"Not too smart." I am giving myself a lecture. I release all my frustration in the scream. "Wish I had not done that."

"Poor choice, that scream." During my lecture to myself, the horrible pain skyrockets as my strength is depleted. I give up.

Someone grabs me, pulls my upper body above water, and turn me over…

It is George's friend, Joel. The same one who pushed me down.

God bless him.

He is wondering why I have not come for revenge.

Joel later said, "I looked at David and could tell that something was wrong. Then I saw all the blood." His statement was also in the police report.

I can breathe. I am being pulled to the shore. I do not feel anything except the back of my head in the water. I hear someone say, "I got him." There are two people helping me. I see them. I speak in a rough voice, saying, "My neck is broken." I feel the new person's hand go under my head. I cannot feel anything else. That hand on the back of my head feels good. A beach towel has been laid out. I am finally on the shore when four more men come to help place me on the large beach towel. "Don't move him!" a lady keeps yelling. "Don't move him. Wait for the ambulance." This lady will not shut up. Somebody finally yells, "Shut the hell up! Nobody's moving him." Some people clap. I would clap if I could.

I keep coming and going. Everything is hazy. I hurt. Nothing normal. Sharp pain. My tailbone hurts! Some of the sharpest pain in my sides. It all goes away. So do I for a minute. I finally stay in reality until the ambulance arrives. I see faces, haze, and sun. It has taken a long time for the ambulance to arrive.

I have a *hero*—a fifteen-year-old lady who is afraid of water. She has taken swimming lessons in high school and hated it. She came away from those lessons even more afraid of water. This woman "respects" water even today. Earlier that day, back in 1969, she would not go out deep, staying in the shallow water to play. On that day, Lavada was standing in the water and saw my back floating across the inlet. She was concerned. Her instincts told her that I was in trouble. Even though Lavada was quite a distance from me, she started heading my way. A lot unfolded in front of her. Lavada watched as I was pushed under! She kept on heading in a straight line. She saw me being pulled to shore. Lavada never stopped. Even when her feet could not touch the ground! Lavada started dog-paddling straight toward me. Lavada still had over half the distance to go. The water would soon be way over her head. Totally unnoticed, she steadily dog-paddled the distance to the opposite shore. Lavada was there, right there, when I needed her. When I saw her face, I knew I was going to be okay. I was not alone. I cannot express how much Lavada did for me that day. When I saw her, I could still see her face and the bright hazy sky behind her. I was glad she was with me. Waiting for the ambulance would have taken twice as long. I was having some phantom pain. Lavada was so concerned and did not know what to do. I saw other faces come and go. My middle sister sat beside me and never left. We waited for the ambulance together.

CHAPTER 3

The Ambulance and the EMT

"I Am Just Having a Hard Time Right Now"

LAVADA HAS TALKED TO ME AND KEPT ME COMPANY.

Now she has informed me the ambulance is here.

She is very protective. No one gets near. She is worried about sand getting on me.

She said, "I am going as soon as this person from the ambulance gets here." That is it. Lavada steps back.

An EMT replaces her.

I am loaded into the ambulance.

On the long ride to the hospital, a lot happens. I cool down. I am so hot lying out in the sun. Way too long. I am getting delirious.

The EMT lady gets the IV going to get some liquids in me.

We immediately hit holiday traffic.

Of all things, the siren does not work.

I keep having the worst pain in my back, just like I was having at the beach. So sharp, like someone had put a sharp rock under me. Then it was like bones were sticking out and hitting something hot. That pain has started fading away. Then a sharp pain showed up inside my tailbone. I was in so much pain after being moved. My neck is suddenly in a huge pain. Like the neck just realized it is broken.

I want to pass out.

The people in the ambulance will not let me sleep or pass out. The lady EMT tells me not to. We are just now getting on a main road. The man in the right seat keeps turning on the siren. It will work and quit.

He says out loud, "Every time it pops the circuit breaker."

I have decided the best thing to do is to go see Grandfather Cash.

He passed away years ago. I was sitting beside him when he died. That's sad.

Grandfather loved grapes and bananas. Biscuits. Homemade applesauce. Boy, oh, Boy. We had the best times.

There he is. There is grandfather walking down the steps of his house. It is just like him to say, "Howdy, howdy, howdy." Well, there he is!

I start to slowly run up the driveway and wave. I am yelling, "Grandfather, Grandfather!" I slow down to a walk and say loudly to Grandfather, "I thought I would come over and visit." As I get closer, I hear myself say, "*What's* going on!"

Someone is shouting, "David... David... David... David, *open your eyes. Now...David!*" Someone opens one of my eyes and shines a flashlight in it.

At first, I squeeze it shut, and then I open my eyes and blink.

Now I have one nasty headache. The bags on each side of my head are pushing, making it worse.

The lady has her face right in my face. She is looking in my eyes.

She whispered, "Thank you, Jesus. Thank you, Jesus. Thank you, Jesus." She backed up and looked at me, smiled, and patted me on the shoulder (I think). She asked the driver how much longer and told him, "The patient just...," and she said numbers. She said, "The patient just abcd and xyz." The man in the right seat explained the siren problem. I will never forget her response. "God, help us. The siren has to break on an ABCXYZ."

I found out later that "ABCXYZ" was a "life-or-death emergency."

The driver would blow his horn. When they used the siren, it would work for three seconds and stop. The driver said it was a bumper-to-bumper traffic jam. The siren finally quit working completely. The man in the front-right seat had been trying to get a police escort. No luck. We were way out in the boonies, near the beach. With holiday traffic.

The EMT beside me was in over her head. She started talking to me. "Where are you from?"

I said, "Miss, I have a terrible headache. Can you pull the bags holding my head still, away just a little?"

She said, "Well, let's take a look at those bags."

I said firmly, *"Do it now. Do it now."*

She did as I so "politely" asked—removed the bags completely and placed them gently back. Much better.

Now my head rested better on the back of my head.

The nurse made sure I was comfortable. "That is the first time in my life to be so mean." I apologized to the nurse. I really apologize. Tears started running down my face.

She said, "David, you are fine. You do not need to apologize."

I explained, "I am just having a hard time right now. I have never yelled at anybody. You have been so nice to me. I really messed up. I messed up the rest of my life." At least, I had quit the tears. "That is no reason to be mean," I explained. "I wanted to use my hand to adjust the bags. Nothing happened. My arms and hands did not move. At the same time, I want to tell you how important it was to move the bags a little."

The EMT started nodding her head, eventually saying, "Of course, you would never yell at me. Do you want to know why?"

This made me so happy, all my troubles went away for just a flash of time. I had to ask, "Tell me why."

She smiled a teary smile. "Because I'm so nice."

How cool is that? I just stared at the roof of the ambulance for a while. Then the headache went away, along with everything in the ambulance. At least my head was comfortable when I came around. The man in the right seat was in the back with me. He was an instructor EMT.

He said, "Mr. Cash, we have a police escort that is going to give us a hand. You are doing great. God bless you, son." I think he said Ms. Lancaster and a bunch of numbers.

Ms. Lancaster was looking into my eyes really closely. She said, "Thank you, Jesus. Thank you, Jesus," under her breath. She responded with a bunch of EMT talk.

I heard the police siren.

You could almost feel the release of tension in the ambulance.

I heard the driver talking to the police escort very casually, sounding unprofessional. "I have a young man seventeen years of age, a diving accident, life or death. Seconds count. You know what to do."

I expected "Seventeen, male, and some ABC WXZ."

Ms. Lancaster pushed the bags up next to my head a little. I saw her praying.

The police had a loud siren. The ambulance locked down their horn. We hit some pretty high speeds.

I was relieved for the EMTs.

The ambulance people were happy for me.

At the hospital, things went like clockwork. I was handled with care.

The bright sunlight hit me as we rolled across into the emergency area. With every little bump, I could hear a soft "Ouch," Careful," or "Oh."

I wanted to say goodbye and "thank you" to the ambulance crew, but I was quickly handed off and rolling down the Ocean View Memorial Hospital hallway.

CHAPTER 4

First Four Weeks in the Hospital

"If He Survives This evening" Dr Yoder

Angela called Mom and Dad as soon as she could find a pay phone. She let them know all that had taken place, including information from the driver of the ambulance.

The person she talked to told Angela I was being taken to Ocean View Memorial Hospital in Garden City. He also provided her with the number to call later and advised, "Give the hospital some time. An hour or more would be best, and it will take us some time to deliver Mr. Cash to the hospital. With what I am seeing here, I would wait at least two hours before calling the hospital."

Angela received this information from the driver of the ambulance while I was being prepared for travel in the back of the vehicle.

The people we were with, George's family, were already sure of which hospital.

Angela remained insistent about talking to the driver of the ambulance and would not agree to leave until she talked to the driver. It may have been the EMT in charge.

Soon after hearing from Angela, my parents went ahead and got on the road. They drove for two hours, stopped, and called the hospital.

My father was immediately given to Dr. Yoder.

The doctor told my father that I might not make it. He added, "Mr. Cash, right now he is struggling. We will do everything we can to keep him alive." The doctor asked for and, of course, received permission to do any procedure.

My father then asked the doctor, "What are his chances? This is my son we are talking about."

Dr. Yoder calmly told Dad, "I could not imagine being in your present situation, Mr. Cash. Right now, he is alive, thinking clearly, and talking. I will do everything I can to see that your son stays that way. Sir, you still need to get here as fast as possible."

Dad told me this story a few times. He had the words memorized.

I met Dr. Yoder when I arrived at the hospital. He had very recently returned from Vietnam. The doctor had a lot of experience in what I needed him for. In a remote hospital like this, I was very fortunate to have this particular doctor. His independent decision-making ability was definitely from dealing with war injuries in a remote location.

This is the diagnosis I heard Dr. Yoder discussing with my father. This is what Dad wrote in his notebook. Dr. Yoder and Dr. JW Purcell agreed with this. They, of course, used more technical terms.

Charles David Cash. Broken neck. The diagnosis performed concluded spinal cord damage in multiple places: spinal cord torn, spinal cord severed, spinal cord cut in multiple places.

Spinal column damage: vertebra number six completely dislodged. Six crushed top and bottom where it exited. Vertebras five and seven crushed together. Crushed completely together five on top of seven, front to back with bone crushing on the side where six exited...

Diagnosis: patent is paralyzed, would remain quadriplegic, paralyzed from the neck down.

My memories are vertebra four, five, and six, with five completely dislodged. I am told today it was five, six, and seven, according to recent X-rays.

The discussion I heard Dr. Yoder repeat as different people inquired about my condition. He would say, "Charles has sustained a traumatic neck injury. If he survives this evening, he will not regain command function, use, or feeling below the neck. My priority is keeping him alive."

My hearing was powerful. My hearing was greatly enhanced because of the loss of all use and feeling below my neck. I overheard the doctor talking outside the door. He would step outside the door to talk. Many times, I didn't exactly know who he was talking to. People tend to talk real low around hospitals. Respectful people do, anyway.

Straight from the ambulance, I was first taken to X-ray and after that an operating room. That is where I was checked in and cleaned up. Being left in the operating room for a short while, I asked a nurse to pick up my hands so I could see them. She picked up my right hand and showed it to me. An IV was attached to my right arm. She told me my left hand was strapped down.

A different doctor had his head down working on the wound where I had bitten my hand. The nurse mentioned he was busy using both of his hands at the moment.

He said some nice things while he worked, "For a person your age, these muscles on this part of your hand are extremely large. This should heal quickly. There was no dirt or sand in the wound. This should heal quickly. You will not be using this hand." The doctor working on my hand seemed like a nice person.

At the same time, Dr. Yoder was at the head of the operating table; he had been setting up to do something.

My father had given permission over the phone to proceed with any surgery. I could tell this doctor was focused and knew exactly how to proceed.

Dr. Yoder started talking. He explained to me that I could not be put to sleep. In fact, I could not take a nap or sleep at all. He was worried about me waking up.

The doctor always told me what he was doing while he was standing behind me or when I could not see him. He also told me he had worked on cases similar to this in Vietnam. He never mentioned Vietnam again. The first thing he had to do was cut two holes in my scalp and drill holes in the bone so he could place a set of tongs in my skull. He was marking the places for the holes.

I was hanging on to every word. I was going to be awake for this. The only place I could feel was my head. That was where the doctor had to drill! They are going to mess up my head. The only good thing I had left.

After a few minutes, he moved around beside me. The doctor was standing over me looking me in the eyes.

"How do you feel now?" he asked.

I said, "I feel okay, okay but sad. The top of my head is real sensitive. I can feel your breath on my hair."

He told me, "We gave you just a little something to help you with the sadness. We can't give you much like I mentioned. We can't take a chance of you getting sleepy. We are also giving you something to assure you do not fall asleep." He then showed me the hand drill he was going to use! It looked like a regular Sears manual heavy-duty hand drill. "I have to use this. It is important to drill as far as I can. It is more important that I do not drill too far. I will drill and measure and check the hole. You will be most aware of what I am doing. There is nothing I can do about that. I can only deaden the skin. Let me know if you get too uncomfortable."

I told him I would.

The doctor went to work.

I will never forget the drilling into my skull.

When he had almost completed the first hole, Dr. Yoder stopped and asked how I was holding up.

I remember telling him I was fine, to just keep going. I wasn't fine at all. I wanted it over with. He knew that I was lying. The hand drilling into the skull took too long. One hole and then the other. He would pause and start.

I came to with a jolt. Everything seemed amplified. I passed out. The doctor had asked a question, and I did not answer. He gave me a shot of something.

The doctor was almost finished. He would pause the hand drilling, drill a little more, on and on. *Erk, erk scratch, crunch, erk.* I could feel it and hear it through my skull. Faster and then real slow. I wanted to shout, "*Stop!*"

When it was finally over, I thought, *You know what, David? Drilling the holes in your skull kept your mind off being paralyzed.*

Stupid thought. I was way too awake.

A few minutes after the drilling stopped, Dr. Yoder walked around from the head of the operating table where he had been working. He looked at me and said, "I know you are glad to get that over with."

I just smiled. Dr. Yoder smiled back, nodded his head, and left. I was thinking, *Well, I don't know about that. I really am* not *ga-ga-ga-ga-glad about anything.*

I used to do that. A fake stutter in my thoughts. Something I'm fa-fa-fa-famous for. Now it is hard to be famous for your thoughts. I'm just k-k-k-k-kidding. I'm not famous.

The doctor had to make a tough decision. I was only out for a few minutes. Dr. Yoder had them "hit me" with something to either wake me up or not. He had to finish drilling the holes he had started *or* stop and go into emergency. "This patient is in dying mode," that is what he discussed/told the nurse.

This was on the clipboard. Dr. Yoder, of course, couldn't keep drilling if I was passed out and ready to give up the ghost.

The problem the nurse had was that if he "hit" me and kept drilling, it would be too much! I would go into a coma.

Dr. Yoder respectfully ignored the nurse. "No choice," was his reason.

Get pressure off the spinal cord above where it had been severed and torn. The spinal cord was being stretched and smashed.

Signals were being sent that were not good. I do not believe "smashed" and "not good" are the correct medical terms.

Dr. Yoder knew it was a risk trying to save me. "The patient is going to die if he doesn't do this now," he said.

He didn't call his lawyer and then proceeded.

No way, he was 100 percent focused. You have to love the guy. Like I said, I was in the middle of nowhere in South Carolina and finding the one doctor willing to go for it. "Just back from Vietnam" kind of doctor.

Things were too real. It was just the nurse and myself. I had a rough ride coming off the drug that Dr. Yoder used to wake me up while he was drilling in my skull. Horrible, I wanted to get up and walk around. Pace back and forth. My skull is vibrating where the doctor worked on it. My neck was killing me. I could not stop swallowing, blinking my eyes, and making sounds in the back of my throat. The wonderful nurse kept washing my face with a cold washcloth and talking to me.

Enough time had passed. Hours, slooow minutes that made up those hours. I was better now. That was too real. I was so awake; my thoughts racing. Awareness of my situation attacked me with the wake-up drug. Now I had a growing headache. I told the nurse. I hate to complain.

The room was kept semidark. The nurse stayed busy. Always writing on the clipboard.

I asked what she was doing. I could only see her head. I could tell by the sound that the nurse was handling the clipboard. Then I heard a loud click of a pen.

I asked her what she was writing down.

She took time and explained everything, along with showing me the form on the clipboard.

I had noticed Dr. Yoder almost always looked at the clipboard before he said anything.

Now instead of writing information on the clipboard at the foot of the bed, the nurse walked up beside me and told me everything she was writing. The nurse, in the first few hours of my arrival at the hospital, asked if there was anything I would like to add to the form on the clipboard.

This practice of asking me if there was anything I would like to add continued twenty-four hours a day for the rest of my stay.

This helped in another way; I used every little thing to break up lying alone and thinking.

I was still in the same room where the holes were drilled—the operating room.

The nurse told me the hospital was not busy. She added grimly, "The holiday weekend is not over." The reason I was still in the operating room was they did not need it.

Sounded like the correct medical tongs needed to get here. Now before the hospital got busy and needed the operating room, Dr. Yoder ordered the Crutchfield tongs as soon as the X-rays were complete. Via fastest way. Express. Next flight. Dr. Yoder constantly checked and followed up every step of the way. Following the package. It made the flight. The flight left on time.

The nurse was sitting in her chair. I couldn't see her. I heard the kind nurse. She definitely needed a break.

I believe it was in the middle of the night. I have no idea of the time. Definitely still getting something to keep me awake. When I was about to ask the nurse about the time, I heard talking way down the hallway. It got closer, and I recognized the voice. It was music to my ears. Dad soon walked in.

The nurse offered the chair to Dad.

He was so kind when he turned it down.

The nurse disappeared into her corner.

When Dad stood beside the bed, I cried. I told him, "I made a big mistake." I cried, "I will never walk, use my hands, or have a wife." I said pretty loud, "I did this to me."

Dad did not try to calm me.

I lowered my voice but not much. I stopped crying. "I have to live like this." I remember stopping to breathe. Then the tears started again. Just the tears. I didn't want to cry. I said, "Dad, this is too real." Then I said, "I hurt you, Dad." I felt better.

Dad and I just talked. We talked and talked.

I said, at school, I would only be remembered as the guy who stuttered. I thought that was funny.

It was just after my father showed up at the hospital, the Crutchfield medical tongs arrived at the airport. The tongs would be delivered to our hospital in forty-five minutes. The doctor was at home asleep. He was at the hospital in a matter of minutes. I was informed that he went home when he was finished earlier, showered, dressed for work, and slept on the sofa.

Later in life, Dad and I would talk about that time at the hospital. The time that he walked into the room, not knowing what to expect. Me talking about life was too real. How he responded, "Yes, I don't like what makes us realize how real life is."

We are waiting for the package from the airport to arrive. Dr. Yoder talked to the nurse after checking the clipboard.

Sometimes, the doctor would ask the nurse to step out the door and talk about what was on the clipboard. I could hear everything the nurse said.

This time the doctor asked my dad to step just outside the door. I could hear every word. The doctor explained what was happening so far to my father. They had to keep me awake. He was showing my father things on the clipboard.

The doctor was starting at the beginning, explaining to my father, "He almost died in the ambulance on the way over here. It was a big scare because the siren did not work They were not equipped for handling a life-and-death situation like that for a long period of time. The EMT staff did an exceptional job keeping him alive. He was in near-death shape when we received him this afternoon. We can't let him go to sleep. We are worried about David slipping into a coma or dying. Another problem we are facing now is that your son is exhausted. He has been through a lot."

Dad thanked the doctor and asked kindly but very firmly, "What else can be done? Do I need to bring something or someone here? Just tell me!"

Dr. Yoder answered my father so simply, "We are doing all we can."

Dr. Yoder always treated my dad with respect. He never talked down to him.

I heard the door open. Dr. Yoder and Dad came back in and went over my X-rays. Using my superhearing, I heard about me dying, keeping me alive, a coma, and such. I could do without all that. I need to choose more wisely as to when I listen in on the doctor.

I could hear Dad's wrist watch when he was beside me.

The nurse was loudly turning pages. I could hear when she crossed her legs, scratched her eyebrows, softly sighed, or moved at all. This place is louder than a steel factory. This super hearing came in very handy. I can't turn it off. I can concentrate or direct my hearing to listen more over here or over there.

The Crutchfield medical tongs arrived. Nothing to it, the doctor had them "installed," checked, and double-checked in a matter of minutes.

I was moved to my room. The ceiling I was to see for the next two months. To the left was a double window. I was told there was a parking lot. I could see a bit of sky out the window.

To my right was a bed that stayed empty. I could see the top of the door open. People's heads would show up. I had a TV located at the regular spot hospitals put TVs.

Above the foot of my bed, a little to the right, there was a clock on the wall. A plain ten-inch clock kept perfect time. The clock was most important because I received my shot of morphine every four hours. Never a minute late. I will talk about that later.

The TV was also very important. Three or four nurses would hide in my room and watch *The Tom Jones Show* when it came on.

As you know, I had not slept since yesterday morning before going to the beach. It had been a long time at the hospital. I was moved to a room next to the nurses' station. It was early morning. I had been in a room without windows. Now I was rolled down the hall to a room. The morning light was throwing me off.

Dr. Yoder went to work immediately! He did not seem to mind work. He mentioned using all this light to make sure the attachment for the pulley and weights were installed properly.

A nurse told me he had checked the bed and demanded a new bed and mattress.

The bed must be tilted exactly, something like, seventeen degrees. He worked on that and moved on.

He attached a cable to the tongs. The cable went through a pulley. This pulley was supported by a heavy-duty attachment on the head of the bed. I had been informed what was going to happen. It was just the doctor, myself, and two nurses. The door was closed with a "Do Not Disturb" sign.

Dr. Yoder stood up and looked at me. He said, "Are you okay?"

I answered, "I'm fine." He smiled. We had this "conversation" a lot.

Then he said, "I am going to start with five pounds." He disappeared/dropped down behind the bed.

I heard and felt some sound; and I then felt, with my head, the weight being placed at the end of the cable. Silence, and that is what five pounds pulling on the tongs clamped in my skull feels like.

Dr. Yoder popped back up. He explained to me, "With weight on the system, I want to go back over and check everything." Dr. Yoder told me everything he was doing. He adjusted the tilt just a tiny bit. He explained it. Measured every angle.

"Perfect," I heard him say. He stepped toward the door and announced that he would be back in forty minutes.

As the doctor was leaving, he spoke to Angela and invited her in to see me.

Angela looked at the tongs and the new equipment. I believe she was a little squeamish. She was given a cloth with ice to hold on the area where the holes were drilled. It felt nice.

I told the nurse that "I do not want any more people in here. Just my sister." The nurse told me the "Do Not Disturb" sign was still up.

Having a weight pulling on my head sort of made me anti-social. That must be it. I couldn't shake hands. Could be the drugs to keep me awake. I had to ask someone to help me if I needed to blow my nose or rub my eyes, even a tickle on my face.

The time with my sister went by way too quickly. She knew it was time to go. I loved having my sister with me. I wanted Angela to stay. Bye, Angela. She was heading back to graduation. Chamblee class of 1969.

The doctor was back. I know what he wanted. "David, we need to go to ten pounds to see if you can stand it. Ten pounds for one hour. We already talked about this."

I said, "Okay."

He dropped out of sight. I could feel him slowly add the additional five pounds.

When Dr. Yoder was back up, he looked at me. His look was a question.

I answered with a question, "Are you sure that was just five more pounds?"

He came right back with a question, "Are you okay?"

I said, "No, I am not okay. The tongs are pulling on my skull…" I was always honest. Dr. Yoder was always asking if I was okay when clearly he had just made me very "not okay."

I was trying to be nice. I didn't think it was working.

The doctor knew everything was going well. He told me, "We were going for the full hour with the ten pounds." It was so funny. I thought, *"We."* I was exhausted, thinking that was funny.

The doctor said he would be close by. I could count on him being back in fifty minutes. He left, and Dad came in. There was always a nurse in the room. She gave Dad some instructions and information.

I did not have much to say. I told Dad to sit down.

He did.

Forty-five minutes later, the nurse said it was time for the doctor, so Dad left and went to their motel for some rest.

Something Was Up

A nurse walked to the foot of my bed and held my ankles.

Two other nurses arrived in the room.

One was the head nurse, and she walked around the foot of my bed and then up the left side after that disappeared behind the bed. She stood on the other side of the weights from where the doctor would be.

The other nurse sat down to my right with the clipboard. She must be writing. I heard a page being turned. I heard her writing. She didn't ask me anything. She got up and was standing on my right side very close to my right arm and shoulder.

The nurse who had been in the room all morning had moved. She was standing over my left shoulder. At this point, she placed her hands on my shoulder and the top of my left arm. I could see her head and upper body being so close.

Dr. Yoder came in. He walked up beside me and said, "David, five more pounds, ten minutes."

I said, "Okay."

He said, "David, I am right beside the weights. I will be managing the weights."

I said, "I understand."

The three nurses around my bed whom I could see made little moves. It appeared to me that my ankles were being held in place. Both shoulders and upper arms were being held in place. I believe. I know. This has been practiced!

The nurse behind me was talking in a low monotone, in the direction of the doctor. Her finger was on the cable. I felt it. I pictured it in my mind. They were both watching the pulley. The doctor had to take his eyes off the pulley to properly manage the weights. He announced his intentions to manage the weights. Her information got louder and more complete when he looked away from the pulley. Dr. Yoder said softly, "Nurse, I see the pulley." She softened her voice and discontinued information.

The fifteen pounds was getting very heavy. Fifteen pounds for ten minutes. I was watching the clock for ten minutes to go by when I heard from behind the bed, "Five more pounds, real quick."

Twenty pounds is some serious weight. I felt it slowly being added.

Dr. Yoder said, "That's full weight. Twenty pounds." I was watching the clock. One minute, fifteen seconds and counting. Then the counting was overwhelmed by this enormous weight. It felt like a bag of cement had been added.

The doctor said, "I added five more pounds."

"Full on."

"I'm all in, David."

"Thirty seconds."

"No more."

I think that is what he said. I felt the weight on my head where the tongs were. I also felt the weight pull at my neck. Well, I didn't feel the weight just pull at my neck. My neck was starting to hurt. Then I felt the rapid increase in pain and thought, *This is escalating rapidly.* This pain was suddenly unbearable.

I said pretty loud, "*My neck is hurting.*"

The doctor and nurse already knew. "I cannot take this."

I felt my neck bones move. I said, kind of yelled, these exact words, "Doctor, my neck just did something." That's what I said. Nothing noteworthy. This is exactly what I said next, "This is too much pain. Dr. Yoder, you will go to hell for this. Too much pain, too much pain. I cannot handle this. This pain is out of control."

"This is a hospital. What is going on?"

"This doctor has made a bad mistake." I could barely hear the doctor over my pain and loud announcements.

Dr. Yoder said, "That's it. David, we have already backed off the first five pounds. We will remove five pounds a minute… David, we are moving you to X-ray now. You will remain at ten pounds."

At that moment, a headache felt very sharp. It seems to want to push the front of my head open. The headache sat on both sides of the front of my skull.

This is what I yelled as we were leaving my room, going down the hall and in X-ray, "Someone call the police. This doctor gave me drugs to keep me awake for his evil pain. Where are the police? Doctor, you are going to jail. There is a special place in hell for you, Doctor. This man needs to be in prison. Doctors don't do this to people. No man is allowed to put a person in this kind of pain. God, please help me. Do something! This is too much. God, let me die, please. Why am I so awake, Doctor? Doctor, you're a sick man. I can't believe you would do this to me. God have mercy on you, Dr. Yoder. This pain is ungodly. You are a sick, evil doctor. You will never hurt anyone else. The police are outside. You can't hurt anyone again." I even threw in "I don't like you anymore."

Most of that talk and shouting was over in ten or twelve minutes. I moved on.

I had never talked like that. So I guess I let him have it. Pretty funny. I couldn't even type this without smiling and my neck hurting.

I remember a nurse while pushing the bed to or from X-ray. I said, "I know you? Are the police here?" She assured me the police were on the way.

I told the doctor the place was surrounded.

My pain was so far off the charts. I could not pass out. I could not curl up.

X-ray was waiting. The doctor appeared beside my bed, pushing along with the nurses. My headache was a side effect of the "on weight, off weight." My neck was still getting worse. Woah, woah, woah, the neck pain was so far out of control. This means it was a good chance, successful. After that, we went to X-ray. I was saying very, very softly, "God Almighty, God, help me," over and over and then "I love you, Jesus," over and over. Then it was just soft "God, help me. I love you, Jesus. God, help me. I love you, Jesus."

The neck felt every pain that ever existed in the world. It was bigger than God or heaven.

A nurse was soaking up my tears. My eyes would fill right back up and overflow.

I was not allowed to pass out just yet.

I was alone in *hell*.

I could see the pain. I could smell the pain.

I thought God would never allow even a small sample of this.

No one cares. Wait a minute. Jesus understands. Where did that thought come from?

I was back in my room. I do not remember much about getting back to my room. Lights in the ceiling of the hallways. People pushing the bed. In this chapter, I have talked about pain enough.

The X-rays were rushed in and showed what the doctor had been hoping to accomplish.

Dr. Yoder looked at the nurse, nodded, and said, "Morphine." The nurse anticipated the instruction. Morphine was immediately shot into the IV that fed into my right arm.

He then said in front of three nurses he had asked to come in from the desk. Dr. Yoder was doing this for me. He had made this arrangement earlier.

He said very firmly, "Every four hours, Mr. Cash is to be given his dosage of morphine. Do not be late." He looked at me. "David, if the morphine is ever late, let me know." Dr. Yoder looked back at the nurses and added, "You are aware of the space 'Time arrived.' This should reflect at least ten minutes before the shot is administered." The doctor asked the nurses if they understood. He thanked them, and that was it.

The morphine was never late. The nurses were always early.

Dr. Yoder looked at me. The pain was much better now as the drug was taking effect.

I said, "Thanks."

Dr. Yoder took a while and said, "Stacking all that weight." He was going to keep talking.

I said, "It worked."

Dr. Yoder smiled kind of strangely. "There was a possibility you may have not made it." He paused and made me feel like a pretty cool guy. He just agreed. "You are right. It worked. Now get some rest."

Then I said, "Doctor, I don't know. You go way into this zone where you are just 'He is going to die, anyway, if I don't do this, and you do this.'"

The doctor said the best thing as he left. "David, you are wise beyond your years." Between that and the world's best drug, I was feeling pretty good.

The nurse wrote all this down. She gave a copy to my dad the next morning.

Remember the nurse who was sitting down writing? Just before all the weight was added to my tongs, she was the one who got up and held down my right shoulder. She was also the nurse who gave me the first dose of morphine. It was her shift to sit with me, to Fill in the pages on the clipboard. She used the front and back of the paper. The nurse even used quotation marks when writing what we said. She just chose to do that on her own.

It had been a long, long day.

As the nurses were leaving, my eyes were closed. I was floating on a white cloud. Zero pain. Soft, soft world, soft blue sky and clouds. I was fine now. The first feeling of the drug was so overwhelming and pleasing nothing else mattered.

The doctor checked on me often. I finally caught up on sleep and got used to the powerful morphine. I still received a wonderful, beautiful, phenomenal euphoric feeling from the drug. Oh yes, I did. I would watch the clock when the time was getting close. The weight pulling on the tongs was up to twenty pounds twenty-four hours a day now.

At ten days, I had some painful "ghost" feeling in my left leg. Notably the upper left leg. I could not feel the ghost pain. I could feel where the pain was. I could feel this through the morphine. Imagine it without the drug. My neck was going through some adjustments I refused to think about. No limit on the pain I could take. *No limit* at all to the pain. I did not feel it.

Being paralyzed the rest of my life. Morphine will make that right. Never having a life. Morphine, soon after receiving it, lets me say, "Okay, I'm cool with that." An hour before the shot, I needed it more than love, more than friendship, more than sky. I needed morphine more than myself. It owns me now. My deal with the drug. I am forever an addict. That deal is done. Next, I must hand over my soul willing someday. To the pleasure and escape. It will happen fast. Oh, I am serious. Drugs do not care if you are in the hospital or living under a bridge.

Somewhere around seven days after, I went to twenty-five pounds of weight on my tongs. Now I was sliding up in bed. Sliding up toward the pulley. I had slid up a little before at twenty pounds.

41

The nurse would get some help and pull me back down every three or four hours. Now it was every hour and a half or so. Tying my legs down at the foot of the bed was not good for circulation.

At about day ten, Dr. Yoder had to see how my neck was adjusting. Time to go to the X-ray lab. Big project. Locking everything down. I believe I was left with fifteen pounds of weight on my tongs. They had a kit for locking the weights.

I was strapped down and rolled to X-ray. All I could see are people's heads. It was timed to be right after a morphine shot. Maybe. I don't know. It worked out that way. I was X-rayed and back in my room in no time.

Later that evening, Dr. Yoder came in and let Dad and myself know he had to add more weight. He planned on going to thirty-five pounds, which will be the maximum weight on the tongs. That will be one week from today. Right now, he is going to add five more pounds, taking the weight thirty pounds. He told me I had lost sixteen pounds. They weighed me when I checked into the hospital, 189 pounds, all muscle (just saying). They could get an exact weight even with all the gear on the bed.

The doctor would be watching my weight. I would check out of Ocean View Memorial Hospital at 118 pounds.

I remember waking up so many times and hoping this was a nightmare. It was very real. I was seventeen and paralyzed. I would be wide awake with my thoughts. Days went by very slowly.

The doctor narrowed the time to receive my medication so it hit exactly on the hour. I watched the clock a lot, leading up to the time. That was my job. I made that my job. Ace clock watcher.

During all this, around day seven, give or take a day. I opened my eyes, and my uncle JW is standing beside the bed.

This is Ma's (pronounced *Maw*) brother. So he is my great-uncle on Mom's side.

Dr. JW Purcell has always looked after me on the big problems. He is a surgeon and well-known in his part of Georgia. He had rescheduled or canceled everything, rented a nice place, brought his family, and planned to stay as long as necessary. Uncle JW Purcell had been in to visit me earlier. I was asleep.

He had been meeting with Dr. Yoder and had come back to see my father, also to see if I was awake.

This was the first time I could say I was happy. Seeing Uncle JW was really something. I felt like staying awake. Michael, his son, came to visit the next day.

Dr. Purcell was ready to have me moved. He was concerned about the ambulance taking me to the closest hospital. He wanted to transport me to a large city hospital that had a spinal cord injury center.

My Vietnam doctor was fine with whatever decision was made. Offered to help with the arrangement.

The two doctors were so honorable, upfront, honest, transparent that they never had a stressful moment. So much respect was shown.

My uncle said after a few days of working with Dr. Yoder that Dr. Yoder was taking care of me quite masterfully. JW gave him very high praise.

Dr. Yoder was very glad to have JW around.

Dr. JW Purcell would sit with me for hours at a time while his family was at the beach. He stayed for six days. All the nurses loved him.

As soon as Dr. Purcell returned home, he started his near-impossible task to get me into Warm Springs Rehabilitation Hospital. He wanted me in as soon as I left this hospital!

JW let Dad get some much-needed rest.

He told me some stories about him and Ma growing up. I only know that he laughed often when he told the escapades. I remember he loved his sister and bits of the stories.

Dad was at the foot of my bed when JW came by to say he was leaving, they needed him back home. I had to hold in the tears.

Dr. Yoder was also able to relax a little with JW here. He took two days off while Dr. Purcell was at the hospital. Dr. Yoder agreed to stay in touch with Dr. Purcell for any changes.

JW was persistent. He put a lot of pressure going up the top of the ladder at Warm Springs when he returned to Covington,

Georgia. He was determined to get me into Warm Springs. I had to be admitted as soon as I was released from Ocean View. The waiting list was, at best, six months! Warm Springs in 1969 was the best.

Uncle JW leaving left an empty place in the room.

Most of the nurses told me something he said or did.

A lot of patchy spots. Where I do not remember much. People came to visit, they told me years later. I did not remember their visit. Everyone understood. Most made it a beach trip. Laughed and thanked me for breaking my neck.

I've been here for two weeks. I had recently had more X-rays, and Dr. Yoder was happy but not thrilled.

He added the final five pounds of weight. Bringing the total to thirty-five pounds! He told me he was going to leave it at thirty-five pounds for twelve hours. Twelve on, twelve off, etc.

I had also lost eight more pounds.

I started feeling some ghost pains in my left upper leg. The pain was making it through the morphine.

Dad stood at the end of the bed. He had to pull me back to the foot of the bed every forty-five minutes when the thirty pounds of weight was on the tongs. If not, the angle on the tongs and pulley would be wrong. It took two nurses or Dad. With thirty pounds, it was every hour.

A shot every four hours, two nurses to pull me to the foot of the bed every forty-five minutes (or Dad). Changing the IV bag and other things. I was open twenty-four hours.

Dad was sleeping about four hours a day in the daytime. It was easier to get help during the day. He stayed with me all night. The man stood most of the time.

I thought about that a lot. I was dependent on people helping me. I couldn't do anything.

Miracle Number Two

Two weeks and one day. Day fifteen.

Dad had left for about thirty minutes and came back. I had thirty pounds of weight. I was staring at the ceiling when I saw the top of the door open.

Dad walked to the foot of the bed. I knew what he saw. My left leg. Instead of lying flat, it was bent at the knee and drawn all the way up.

My foot had moved toward my body. My knee was pointing at the ceiling. This was definitely something new!

We both looked at my leg. Dad walked slowly toward my feet.

Dr. Yoder was called. Dad went ahead and pulled my leg back down and then pulled me back to the foot of the bed. Dr. Yoder and Dad stepped outside the door. The doctor told my father, "It was just a reflex." He asked my father not to get his hopes up and added not to get David's hopes up.

The sight of something possibly coming true. Hope is breathtaking. You and I know I would walk again. My hopes were up! If I had never moved that leg again, you cannot stop *hope*. I was fortunate. I have seen disappointment so many times, especially at Warm Springs, but you can't stop *hope*.

Seeing a mother and father "hope" a teenage daughter can take *one* step. If she takes one tiny step. She will walk again.

Later, they are so proud of their daughter as they laugh together while she rolls beside them in her wheelchair.

Hold fast to *hope*.

I do not know how that leg moved that first time.

The doctor stuck a pin in my foot when I wasn't looking. I did not feel it. My father worked my legs for ten minutes. I did not feel him doing anything. I got my shot of morphine, fell asleep, and woke up; and the leg had moved a little! Dad straightened it back down to pull me down to the foot of the bed...

Here it comes. Same day, day fifteen. I *moved* my left leg. Just a little. I did not move it all the way up.

I thought about moving it. And it moved some. I knew I had moved my foot. I said that was me. I couldn't see that it moved. I could see my feet because of the tilt in the bed. I could not see the foot slide.

Dad saw it. Dr. Yoder was suddenly in the room. He brought a nurse. I moved it a tiny bit. I did not see it. Dr. Yoder looked at me and said, "David, was that you?" Then he was saying something, but I was so tired I could not hear him.

He recognized that he had started talking before I was ready. Dr. Yoder was excited. I had never seen him be anything but being a doctor.

I think my foot moved a lot. Almost three inches. Dr. Yoder pulled my foot back in place.

I said, "Okay, I am ready now."

The doctor and my dad were acting like best friends, pulling me back to the foot of the bed together.

Dr. Yoder asked me to relax. He explained the muscle I was using was the thigh muscle, the strongest muscle in the body.

Now the room had more nurses. The door was open so the nurses could watch the nurses' desk from my room. As you know, it was not too far outside my door, a little ways to the left.

Dr. Yoder was talking to his new best friend Dad.

Dad was listening closely, smiling, and occasionally slightly nodding.

I was not listening. I had a show to do. I couldn't let Uncle JW down. Dad deserved this. Dr. Yoder. I concentrated on the big muscle, not just on moving the foot. Not moving my leg.

I closed my eyes. I ignored all the talk and noise of my super-hearing. Pulling with the strongest muscle. I thought about the place where the pain was coming through the morphine. That was the place I used to pull. That was the thigh. That was the key.

Dr. Yoder said something very important. He knew exactly what was happening.

I concentrated on the location of the phantom pain. I pulled with that pain. The strongest muscle in my body. I opened my eyes and closed them again. Now it seemed easy.

My room got quiet of its own accord. I concentrated on pulling my leg up. The way I would naturally pull it up, with my thigh muscle.

I could hear my sheets move.

The nurses politely did the hospital quiet soft clapping.

I opened my eyes. My leg was all the way up. My knee pointed at the ceiling.

"Totally unexpected" was the quote from Dr. Yoder. That is what he said when he walked up beside me.

Miracle number two. Well, what do you think?

When Dr. Yoder called Uncle JW, he was astounded.

My improvements were incredible.

We all knew my uncle was on the board of directors for many things, to do with hospitals and charities in Georgia… He had some pull. He was a tactful business man. He began collecting favors that were owed to him. At least that is what he said.

Warm Springs Rehabilitation Hospital sent me a very nice letter. It stated that I have the date in early November, at 9:00 a.m. This date was for check-in and orientation, a list of what to bring, and dos and don'ts. They told me, "Check the boxes you have received everything in this package, sign this, and mail it back." The check-in date was early November.

Big gap in time.

This was signed by two people. Stamped and noted.

Dad's insurance is only going to pay for a full-time bed at Ocean View Memorial Hospital for eight weeks, to which Dr. Yoder said was perfect. Perfect as long as I went straight to Physical Therapy Rehabilitation.

I will have to say that there were a few good physical rehab hospitals available. I was mailed some pamphlets. The nurses held up pamphlets which showed me the pictures.

I could have had the pamphlets read to me and chosen one.

Rooms and beds were available.

Dr. JW Purcell would not even talk about it!

He told us not to worry about it and to just throw those papers away. I was going to Warm Springs as soon as I left Ocean View.

At this point, the Ocean View Hospital hired a full-time physical therapist. She did not start for a while. The hospital paid her to come by and show Dad some things! Dad was excited, so he made a checklist. This made a big difference.

The therapists at Warm Springs were impressed when I finally arrived.

This book is getting pretty boring. I also can't stand talking about myself all the time. Lying in bed in a hospital, boring. I know, I was there. Watch out. Here it comes. Soon I could move my left foot! Up and down, pivoting on the ankle! How exciting is that! Just kidding. The story will kick in soon. That was funny. The foot.

I had a lot of pain. Here I am, talking about pain again.

This is where I was to be taken off morphine. More phantom pains. Phantom pains were increasing. The neck was hurting through the morphine. It happened along with my being able to move my leg. I was glad I had something for the pain. The pain had increased. Morphine continued.

Five thirty in the afternoon. One hour and a half after the morphine shot. I have thirty-five pounds of weight on the tongs. Dr. Yoder is at the nurses' desk. I can hear him talking.

I am suddenly looking out the door.

I *shout*.

The doctor runs in.

I can't stop shouting. I can see out the door.

The right tong has popped out. *Pain, pain, pain, blinding pain.*

The full thirty-five pounds is hanging on by just the left tong. I am still shouting. The doctor shouts something to the nurse while he is diving behind the head of the bed.

I hear weights hitting the floor as the doctor is taking them off.

At the same time the nurse gives me another shot of morphine, I recognize it. Two shots in an hour and a half.

While I am out, I stay out for a while.

Dr. Yoder tells me later that the nurses take me by X-ray and set up the operation room while he calls JW.

A small chunk of my skull has snapped off.

Dr. Yoder has a tough-enough job without this.

Part of the bone that holds the tong is missing!

He calls my uncle. They both seek out answers.

I believe this is the conclusion.

Dr. Yoder did everything right. Exceptional.

Forty pounds is a safe limit on that type of tongs. Fifty can be used. Dr. Yoder places thirty-five as his limit. Masterful job actually.

Both doctors direct the call at what to do next.

Solutions. Dr. Yoder will order a larger-bit tong for the right hole. His next call will be to the manufacturer of the Crutchfield tongs. In the meantime, he would drill one sixty-fourth deeper and reduce the weight to twenty pounds until the new bit arrives. If twenty seemed too much, fifteen.

Continued weight is very critical at this point. Twenty is important.

This is a setback. That new bit is important.

Neither doctor is comfortable until new parts arrive. The parts are shipped by a charter flight service. My parts are pulled and carried to the local airport. Sent as the only package on a twin-engine turboprop airplane to the Small Garden City Airport.

Pretty cool and not as expensive as you might think. Pilots will do anything for a reason to fly and gas money. The distribution center shipping manager told us about this pilot.

When I am finally back in my room, the doctor is on edge. He has all his calls forwarded to this nurses' desk.

Twenty pounds of weight, but the doctor is staying close by. The new parts will be here soon; he ordered everything New, plus extra bits and everything the manufacturer suggested. The doctor goes shopping.

Suddenly, Dr. Yoder can hear me shout, not a loud shout. He knows the right tong has slipped out again.

The doctor is busy diving for the weights.

I don't remember much. My head is snatched over again. I see complete nurses instead of just heads. I can almost look out the door. The whole top of my head is bleeding.

I hear the doctor stand up. He says, "I am removing the tongs," and he pulls the left out. It gives no resistance.

I have no tongs in my head.

I hear a nurse. I can no longer see my IV bag. I hear her. She just gave me a shot.

Just then I feel his hand go to the base of the back of my head. The doctor says, "Close your mouth, and breathe through your nose." His other hand goes under my chin. A nurse slides her hand under my head. Her right hand on my forehead.

As soon as the last hand is placed, the doctor is pulling and moving my head over. The nurse is turning my head. That is it.

It is the last thing I remember till Dr. Yoder tells me the parts are at the airport. He is on the phone with someone at the airport when this person "has the plane in sight." The hospital has someone at the airport waiting to pick the package up. All new parts. Delivered by a happy pilot. Glad to help. He says he got here as quickly as possible, brutal headwind.

Everything is back to normal. Do you know how I know it is thirty pounds? I can tell what weight is hanging from my head.

Sorry, I didn't give you a chance to answer.

Dr. Yoder walked in. This time he could look at the clipboard instead of diving for the weights.

He seemed very pleased. This was a rare mood for the fine doctor. He walked beside my bed and asked how I was. I answered, "Okay. The usual." He then said, "I talked with Dr. Purcell. A remarkable man. You already know this. So that is not what I came to talk about. The tongs will not come out of your head again. I believe you trust my word. After discussing what I did to secure a new set of tongs, your uncle JW would like me to add, I will quote, 'I believe it would take a new Chevy truck to pull the new tongs out.'"

Dr. Yoder said my uncle thought I would like that.

Then he said JW wanted me to not worry at all about the new tongs coming out. I was fine with Dr. Yoder's word.

Uncle JW really got the message across. Especially to a seventeen-year-old. New truck!

Three weeks just passed. I watch the clock. I have vivid nightmares.

I get the shot every four hours.

I have visitors who walk into my cloud and leave. I will show them how my leg and foot move. Now I can move my left lower arm at the elbow up one inch, sliding on the sheet. If someone puts it back, I will do it again.

I take a nap at noon. I am afraid of sleep.

I am at thirty-five pounds of weight on the tongs around-the-clock.

Listen to this nightmare, how they start getting long and multilayered because of the amount of morphine.

I dreamed I died and was in darkness forever. I had a suit on. Demons kept jumping out of the darkness and landing on my shoulders. The demons looked like frogs with people's hands, and the feet were people's hands. The face was half frog and half people. With a permanent grin. They would get right in my ears and laugh, get close to my face, and just look at me… Soon they would swing on my feet and drop off into the dark. I would be alone again. I think that is it, darkness with demons; but slowly a little light turned into day.

There are hundreds of thousands of these demons. I am weightless.

As far as I can see, these frog demons are jumping into people and pushing them up through holes in the thick murky low sky. Everything is the color of a foggy day. People are dressed in pajamas, underwear, and regular work clothes, and some are dressed up. All floating about thirty feet off the mostly flat ground. I can see for miles in all directions.

Most people had one or two frog demons crawling on them.

We were spread about fifty feet apart.

The demons were swinging on feet and dropping off all over the place.

I looked behind me. Miles and miles again. Then I was facing that way. It made no difference.

An Oriental lady two people to my right was pushed up through the mushy sky.

One of the frog demons jumped up and landed on my left shoulder. Another one jumped up and looked me in the face with the permanent grin. That one turned and crawled inside me!

The thin cloud below the swampy ground was only five feet above me. The sky or ground above opened. I wanted to go up and get out of here, and I was being pushed up, but I was demon possessed now!

I am waking up from this crazy nightmare. I think I am waking up from sleeping on the sofa at home. I hear something. I can hear, "David, David, someone is here to see you." The nurse is asking if it is okay for a special friend to come in. I am just now realizing I am paralyzed! I say to the nurse, "That is great. Please send them in." I am staring at the same ceiling. I am afraid to fall asleep. The nightmare with the frog things was very real. I was having mostly vivid full-color nightmares when I slept.

Three and a half weeks. Thirty-five pounds of weight on the tongs full-time.

The nurses all visit. I watch Tom Jones with five nurses every time it comes on. One young nurse talks country sexy cutting up with me. "David, when you get out of here, you and me are going straight to bed. You are better-looking than a new four-wheel drive. I can almost taste you now, sweetheart." She is so funny. She is also the biggest Tom Jones fan.

There was another nurse who said she was going to leave her boyfriend for me! She was superhot! Her boyfriend used her car and wrecked it. Then he spilled gas in the trunk, and the whole car smelled like gas. Then he quit his job. I found out she quit. Never saw her again. I know two things for sure: it is tough to get the gas smell out of a car when you spill gasoline in the trunk, and two, a hot girl like that has already forgotten my name.

Nurses would come in and have girl meetings and then ask me what they should do. I always claimed that I was on drugs. I assured them, "Listening was helping me with future girl problems." They agreed that I chose wisely not to give women advice.

In just short of four weeks.

Remember the events. I heard Dr. Yoder in the room.

He asked, as usual, "How are you?"

I gave the most unusual answer. I actually remember this answer and have smiled at it through the years. I said, "I see a roulette wheel, and I see it when my eyes are open and closed."

Dr. Yoder said, "What?"

I answered, "A roulette wheel."

He responded, "That's what I thought you said."

I said, "Doctor, I can't tell if my eyes are open or closed."

A pause. The doctor said, "I was afraid of that."

I could hear the silence.

Then he said nicely but a little loud. "No more morphine. Starting now, that's the way we are going to do this. David, do you understand?"

I answered, "I understand. I understand exactly." It took a few seconds for me to reply, "You just said I can't have any more morphine."

The doctor spoke to me. "Every hour, you can have a teaspoon of iced water." He looked at me. "David, can you see me?"

I answered, "Are my eyes open?"

He answered, "Yes."

I answered, "No, sir, I see the roulette wheel, but I can hear you fine."

Dr. Yoder said, "David, blink your eyes till the wheel goes away... David."

I responded, "Yes, sir."

Dr. Yoder said, "Shut your eyes."

My response was, "Doctor?"

Dr. Yoder, "Yes?"

I asked, "Am I sitting in a chair?"

He answered, "No, open your eyes."

I said, "That is much better. No roulette wheel." I continued, "Okay, I remember everything you talked about, the iced water every hour."

The doctor said, "Yes, what happens is you will start to look forward to the iced water. Your body will respond every hour on the hour to the iced water. The mental obsession is curved. You will find yourself watching the clock for the water just like you were doing for the drug. It will be there on the hour, fresh water with crushed ice in it."

I said, "Doctor, thanks for nothing," and smiled.

He knew what I meant and said, "You are in for a rough ride. Someone will be in the room at all times. The hours that you do not know where you are, we will still make sure you get the water exactly on the hour."

I said, "Thank you. I mean it. That is a lot of trouble, the iced water every hour."

He said, "You're going to beat this, David. Get through this, and it looks good."

I responded, "I will walk right out of here."

The doctor replied, "David, it would not surprise me."

CHAPTER 5

Despair and Hope

I Walked Out Into the Sun

MY FIRST TEASPOON OF WATER WITH CRUSHED ICE

I WAS EXPLAINING TO MY FATHER WHAT I FELT. ALREADY delirious, now sick and fully in withdrawal. No Morphine is constructed from my father's notes.

NO MORPHINE

My life depends on the narcotic. I am doomed. No more opiates. I can live with nightmares and delirium. No longer young, aged by defeat. I fear what will happen when I do not receive my sweetheart's kindness. I cannot bear the thought. Death would be better than life without her. My delirious vision was a traitor. In delirium, I made known I was deranged. If I could just take my words back, we could be together one more time. Too late! My only love was handcuffed and taken away. I am so alone. No one cares. Watching the clock. The time arrives.

I receive my first teaspoon of water with crushed ice. "God, help me!" I pray. I am alone with only regret and agony. My flame is forever gone. My delirium clears as if to see what has happened. I was devoted to her. So infatuated. Instead of feeling comfort and passion, I will be tormented.

I feel heartache, despair, and misery. Thoughts of killing myself immediately are logical. Why wait?

The morphine termination is rapidly noticed by my body. Desperation sets in. The feeling of frantic troubled isolation grows. I romance the thought of her arms around me again. That is all I can think about, just once again. Suddenly, every second is too real. Everything. Clear. Feeling rejected turns to feeling forsaken. I am confused and in pain. The pain that she took away. She used me. Made a fool of me and left. I feel the torture of my brain pushing me further away. Handing me to the master of death. I try to laugh. Instead, I snarl. I pronounce, "Fine, please let me die. Please." I have this pain. Now where is my fix? I need my true love. I know she has abandoned me. I lust after her. But I am nothing. She deserted me because I am worthless. Now give me my poison. I am ready to relinquish this life. Give me my wonderful poison. I can let go and die. I am so alone, but I will not be lonely for long. I will fear no evil. "God, help me," again, I ask.

~

Second or third teaspoon of water with crushed ice. Fourth, I don't know.

I looked around, and everything was fine. The nurse gave me the most delicious teaspoon of iced water. I felt a lot better. This was not so bad.

I saw a person walk in the door I did not recognize. I looked around, and no one seemed to be worried about the person. The person was short, with a hat.

The hat person just walked in the door and looked at my chart, which was on the clipboard at the foot of my bed. Then the person looked up at me. His face was in the shadow of the hat. I assumed it was a man because of the hat.

I asked, "Who are you?" I received no answer.

He put the clipboard down. The guy walked around to the left side of my bed. Then I saw the person's hat out of my left eye.

He came in real close.

I could see his hat up close.

He tried to tell me something.

I closed my eyes. When I closed my eyes, a nightmare started.

Two dogs are sniffing the ground looking for me. One is a German shepherd, and the other is a big black dog. I am standing on flat asphalt.

When the dogs see me, they show me their teeth.

I have to look at the teeth, which are big.

The dogs are growling.

After looking at their teeth, I can finally turn and run.

As I am running, the dogs are so much faster than me. They are catching up, and the big black dog tries to bite my right ankle.

I turn and kick him so hard.

The German shepherd Jumps on my chest and barks as I fall backward. The German shepherd is giving the black dog first bite.

Land on my back and hit my head.

The big black dog is mad and goes for my throat with his huge teeth.

I wake up.

When I open my eyes, I see the ceiling of my hospital room.

Then the man with the hat tries to tell me something. He is going to tell me my little sister is dead. If he doesn't tell me, my little sister will be fine.

I close my eyes. I am on an asphalt hill.

The dogs are sniffing and looking for me again. The dogs are mad because I got away.

My legs will not move, because of fright. I have to look at the dog's teeth.

I see the teeth are huge and dripping with spit. The black dog grows bigger with even longer teeth! He is bigger with muscles and in size. The big black dog jumps fifteen feet straight forward in the air at me. Lands and almost bites me.

Now I can run. But it is uphill. I run like a deer. Then I am jumping over ditches, and I head for the field. The clouds are bowling fast because a storm is coming. This is wonderful. I am running through the field, and the clouds are blowing past. I see a big oak tree ahead. I will run so fast and climb the tree. I look back.

The big black dog grabs my arm and bites down to the bone.

I am in too much pain. I scream.

Then the big black dog shakes my arm, and I try to kick him. He bites the leg that I am using to kick and drags me down a hill to where a lake is, while the other dog bites my neck. The dogs were just playing. I can never outrun them.

I am so sleepy. I barely wake up and open my eyes. The person with the hat tries to tell me something. I don't want my little sister to be dead.

I close my eyes.

The dogs are sniffing the ground. They are so mad because they are hungry and I got away.

I can tell.

The big black one has my blood on his teeth, and it is snarling. The other dog is barking.

I am standing on asphalt, but behind me is cement. Steep slick and shiny cement. This is it. I would have to crawl to get up out of here.

The smaller German shepherd is still big but looks smaller next to the monster black dog.

I am surprised.

The German shepherd draws first blood this time. He runs up and rips my shirt open by dragging his claws across my chest.

It is very painful.

Both dogs are in my face.

I am pushing them away with both of my bloody hands.

The smaller dog clamps my left arm.

The monster with huge teeth bites down on my right shoulder all the way to the bone. He lets go of my shoulder and grabs my right arm and bites it in half.

I am forced back against the cement, cursing the dogs.

The mad dogs stare into my eyes in victory as they bite down and jerk my upper arms.

I love the pain and stare back! Instead of staring, I open my eyes real fast! Wow. How do I do that? It does not matter. I look at the clock. Ten seconds till the hour. This is how to do battle!

The nurse is getting up from her chair.

The hat person is sneaking out the door while the nurse's back is turned.

The water is so good after all that.

Those dogs were real. Just like if you walked up to a stranger's fence and provoked his German shepherd. Dogs can bite in the withdrawal illusions. I could feel the teeth go into my skin.

The guy with the hat was also real looking at first. Regular guy. Not so much later. He shrank and looked a little cartoonish sneaking out behind the nurse.

Where does the brain come up with all these characters? The situations, like the van I am going to tell you about.

Please, God, help me with the pain, that is all my brain thinks about. I always craved morphine. My neck is definitely not liking what is going on. I can't describe a pain where my neck knows it is broken. Even the pain is in pain. The tongs and weight are very sensitive or painful. I don't know if I can get along another minute with those tongs. It gets worse with the nerve endings shooting "ghost pains" in various places. I keep holding my breath. No more powerful opiates for pain. I am in all kinds of trouble.

Anyway, this is how my withdrawal from morphine started. Nightmares become more and more vivid, leading up to my mind staying in another place. A place I would describe as worse than hell. I am gone. Eyes open or closed. Asleep or awake. There is no difference. The nightmares become my reality. As real as today. Full color.

I took a few airplane lessons a year ago. I enjoyed flying a small airplane with an instructor. I have a logbook with the flight time on my desk at home. Now in my nightmare, I had to stop the airplane propeller from running into my father as I taxied. I was too late.

I drive a van that keeps hitting the people at church. I am pushing the brake. I am going so fast that their heads snap off and land in the seat next to me. So bloody with veins and sometimes spinal cord hanging out. Heads keep piling up. Facing different directions. They can talk for about ten seconds to about a minute before they die.

Some would tell me horrible things. One told me about a child who killed itself. Others would sing or recite a poem so beautiful. Others, just random things. I ran over a baby that a lady dropped as I hit the lady. When her head landed in my van, she told me not to worry about it. The baby would be fine. The head below hers was blowing her hair out of his face. It was so real. I ran into twenty-plus people.

Some of them were people I knew from North Peachtree Baptist Church. A new head rolled into the floor, and I picked it up by the hair and put the head on the passenger's seat. I would then roll older heads into the floor to make room for new heads. The whole time going over a hundred miles an hour in the church parking lot. The parking lot was so large it had a convenience store. There were some stop signs. The convenience store was like a huge movie theater lobby. I would think, if I could stop, I would like to go to that store.

I cannot wake up. Nightmares become more and more real, lasting a long time. Three hundred and sixty degrees, I can turn around. I return to the previous nightmare every so often. It's always for the worse. People have died from heart attacks while having or living through intense nightmares during withdrawals. Oh, well, here I go. At least I am in a hospital. Dad and one of my sisters tell me I was having trouble with elephants. I warn them about the elephants. I warn two nurses as well. I do not remember the elephants.

∾

Notes: in a hallucination, anything is possible. To me, it was as real as me sitting here at this laptop. My last nightmare or vision during my ninety hours of withdrawal was a visit to hell. That was it. My trip to hell. I spoke to the devil himself. This trip to hell is in the back of the book. It is not a nice fluffy read about hell.

~

Close to four days had passed. After that, I woke up to the midmorning sunshine coming in my hospital room window. I stayed fully awake for about thirty minutes. Talked to two nurses. Told them I was glad they were not monsters. We laughed. I had my water with crushed ice. Told the one nurse, "Thank you," and I was suddenly very sleepy. Then I went back to a peaceful sleep and woke up about six hours later. It was good to see everybody.

I was not out of the woods yet. The worst was definitely over. That was it for my peaceful sleep. Now I couldn't sleep without immediate nightmares. I wanted morphine. Oh yeah, iced water every hour, a must. I had to have the iced water. What I really wanted was morphine.

I had flashbacks of the withdrawal life like nightmares until I was twenty years old or so.

When I came around after being out for four days, I wanted to see what I was able to move. Dad and Dr. Yoder had to see. Lavada was up there. Nurses kept stopping by.

I could move a few more inches with my left hand. Big news. I moved my right leg some. That was it. I was so happy.

I tried to get out of bed some of the time in my delirium. Moving everything possible. Left leg and arm. Right arm getting in on the action. My right foot moved the sheet once. Not a lot. I did not get very far! (Funny.) It appeared that I was giving it everything I could a few times. Dad made notes of it...

My father never stopped working my legs while I was out. I had four weeks until Dad's insurance ran out at this hospital.

I am exhausted, but every time I try to take a nap and close my eyes, I am being chased or something is going wrong. I finally

have a nightmare, stayed in too long and slept. If I get to screaming, I must wake up or someone needs to wake me up. The nightmares are still too vivid. Mad animals can still hunt me down and
chew on me. I keep falling off a ship and going through the propeller. Glad I get to wake up. Time for my iced water. The nurse
comes in right on time.

My father is not super-superhuman. Dad cannot go any longer. He has been on his feet for four days and nights. He is getting
about four hours of sleep a day.

A man at General Motors, where Dad works, loans our family a house for as long as we need it. Mother has slept all day. She
has made a big deal of telling everyone she is going to take care of
her son tonight and give Charles some rest.

So Dad sits on the porch to be real quiet.

Mom has slept all day. She has no trouble doing that.

Dad makes sure she is asleep.

Even the nurses have had enough of me, not really.

So Mom and Dad show up at about seven o'clock in the evening of the day after I came to. It is still light outside.

The weight on the tongs is back to twenty-five pounds. I
have no painkiller! I am miserable. Miserable. Miserable.

Mom is supposed to stay with me tonight. Give me water
every hour. Keep me company. Be prepared to wake me quickly if I
start screaming. Just watch over me. She must move my legs when
she gives me the water. Very important for circulation.

Dr. Yoder talked to Mom in the waiting room. He talked to
her for about fifteen minutes before Dad left. He told me the next
day that he emphasized the importance of talking or reading to
me, that I was in a lot of pain and this was going to be a very bad
night for me.

"The water had to be there. David will be watching the clock.
I told your mother. Just get a nurse if you get to where you think
you may fall asleep."

I could see how exhausted my father was. Guilt is what I was
feeling. I was miserable. Mom gave me the eight o'clock iced water.
Dad said he was going to run on. He had to check everything.

Mom and I told him everything was fine. A nurse came in, and Mom made a big deal about staying.

The nurse told her what a fine Mother she was.

Dad and Lavada left with the nurse and Mom in the room.

Mom was talking about bla, bla, bla to the nurse.

The nurse was smiling, standing in front of mother, and asked me, "Is anything you would like to add?" talking about the clipboard.

Mom could hear me. I said, "I am very worried about tonight. Look in on me."

The nurse said, "I will write that down." She wrote it down, looked at me, and nodded. The nurse finished up and left.

The clock hit nine o'clock. I asked for the iced water. Mother was ready to get the water. Very nice. "A good combination of ice to water," I told Mom.

My dear mother went right straight back to sitting down, so I couldn't see her.

My neck hurt. My neck hurt. I was craving morphine. I made it a point to ask Mother about church and the neighbors, especially the people who had sent me letters and cards. This was excellent. I missed everyone.

Mom got offtrack telling me about problems with our next-door neighbor. Bla, bla, bla.

Sorry, I didn't care about the neighbor problem. I was friends with the neighbors' kids.

Mom was getting short with her answers, and eventually, I could tell she was mad because I did not want to talk bad about the neighbor. So to stay awake, I told Mom how much I missed her biscuits. She liked this.

She said, "You can make them as good as I can now."

I said, "That's my goal, to walk in the kitchen and make some biscuits."

Mom said, "Your father can tell the difference."

It was only 9:25 a.m. when Mom said something about it being so bright in the house. It was hard to get any rest today. Just before Mom started snoring she mentioned the chair was uncomfortable. Mom was "sawing logs." I knew this was going to happen. So I was alone. I would not close my eyes.

I made it till the fifteen-minute mark till I got the iced water. I kept trying to touch my chin over and over. When I brought the left arm up bending at the elbow, I was turning my hand and pointing my finger at my chin. Close. My back left shoulder blade responded with a sharp pain. Something new.

I would work on my right leg. Six more minutes till I could have some iced water. I would try to move my right ankle while I watched the clock. It moved! Wow. My right ankle just moved. I thought it moved. My right foot swiveled on the ankle. One minute. Time for my iced water.

"Mom, Mom, can I get my iced water?"

Mom said, "Hush up, and go to sleep."

I shouted at her, "Mom!"

She quickly came back and said, "Hush now. Goasleep." Next thing I heard was her soft snoring again.

I am so alone. The minutes crawl by. I feel the twenty-five pounds pulling on my skull. I want to rip my neck out. Well, well, well—10:07. There we go—10:10.

Mom is definitely getting a good night's sleep.

I am afraid to go to sleep. I cannot fall asleep. Scared of sleep. Terrified.

I will not shout loud enough to get the attention of the nurses at the nurses' station or down the hall. Embarrass Mom.

Procedure is to hit the emergency switch before walking in my room. Brings in half the hospital. Rings the doctor's phone, puts him on alert. I don't want to embarrass my mother. She will wake up and say she was not asleep.

I can't think. Morphine sounds good. My dream scream is not a full-blown scream. I will need to really scream when that door is closed. Not always someone at the station at night. Simple things like pushing the "Call" button, I wish.

It is now 10:14. I now have a headache. I am in a bad fix. My neck is killing me. The new muscle under the left shoulder blade had to pick now. I feel the phantom pains. They are not being curbed by morphine.

"Please, God, help me. Jesus, can you come sit with me?" I pray out loud.

I have to do something. Try to distract myself. The hardest thing to do when I am in pain.

One, two, and three: "Guess I will run down to the store." I imagine. "No, it is kinda late. I will just grab something out of the fridge." I am so funny. I will be positive. "Yes, David, let's talk about walking. Okay, David, I like walking. Walking gets you places. I like to walk up mountain trails. Very good, David. Stairways and sidewalks are also good places to walk. David, a hallway, like right here at the hospital. Very good, David. Walking is much better than not walking." I am finally okay. Talking to myself. Avoiding panic mainly. Pain, pain, pain. If I can distract myself from the pain for just a little while. That is nice.

The time is 10:28. The door opens. The nurse who was in earlier walks in. Seeing the situation, she gets me a teaspoon of iced water. When I have finished the wonderful iced water, she said softly, "I must apologize. Your message just hit me."

I said, "Don't worry. She will not wake up."

The nurse went over to Mom and asked if she would like to lie down on the bed. I could hear Mother crawl up in the bed that had remained vacant the whole time I had been here. The nurse went out and received permission to remain in my room. That nurse had some pretty good stories; she could be funny. Her combination of ice and water was most excellent. She said it was a top secret recipe.

Mom soaked up praise the next morning. Dad was so happy to be back. He knew something was wrong, so I told him. Dad was not surprised, but knew I had to let him know because of future arrangements. The hospital staff knew because of the disruption it caused that night. Pulling a nurse from another area to cover for my nurse. The nurses had different shift times. The chaos that it caused.

My life was wonderful! I am drug-free. Seven days! If I was out of this place and had the ability, I would not be drug-free. If I had the choice of morphine or walking, I would quickly choose morphine.

Day seven after the iced water started. The doctor and I talked, and everything was okay to stop every hour of iced water. Every dream suddenly stopped being real. Full screen, color, 360 degrees, real people, talking and shouting, and actual pain. Long dreams. Now brief black-and-white stupid stuff. Regular amount of people muted color. All at once. It was like God went into my brain and flipped a switch. Let me have a few nights of sleep. Now I am sleeping well, looking forward to sleeping.

I can move my right leg all the way up! It is difficult and awkward. My right side is not right. The right hand, not good, tiny bit of thumb movement is it. No feeling. With my left hand, I can kinda make a fist. Okay, it kinda takes some imagination to see a fist. My left shoulder and upper arm are doing okay. My left leg is doing very well. The X-rays are good. I weigh 134!

I need something every day. Yes, I still need my fix. My true love.

The physical therapist is giving me workouts every day. Dad is her assistant. Her goal: I walk out of this hospital when I am discharged! I do not care about the pain. That is a lie. The workout distracts me from all my troubles. I thank Jesus a lot for what is happening in my room today. Everyday workouts. Days mix together.

I have been fitted for a neck brace. It will be here soon.

The weight on my tongs is only fifteen pounds.

With the workout, my weight has dropped pretty fast. I weigh 126 pounds.

Two weeks and three days to go.

The workouts are brutal.

Fifteen days to go.

The neck brace arrives.

Fifteen pounds going to ten pounds.

The physical therapist and Dad go crazy over the neck brace. The doctor gives them the okay to put it on me for workouts.

Needless to say, workouts went beyond anything we had done before.

A few days after the neck brace arrives, Dr. Yoder takes the tongs out.

With the help of two nurses, I sit up. It does not last long. I can't sit up without getting dizzy. It take a day and a half for me to stay up without getting dizzy.

I have new major pain. *Both* of my shoulder blades stick straight out. The serratus muscles that hold the shoulder blade in are just about gone. The serratus muscles are being stretched. Very sharp pain on both sides of my back where the shoulder blade usually is and above where it should be. A new test in how much pain I can handle.

My workouts are taking most of the day. I sleep because I am so tired. I sleep to escape pain.

Wonderful news. Warm Springs has given me the perfect check-in day.

I will go home for two weeks. After that, I will check in to Warm Springs.

It was Uncle JW, Dr. Purcell, who approved the date.

A long-term bed was made available.

The physical therapist was leaving soon. A job she wanted in another state came through. It seemed like everybody was fine. She was here exactly when I needed her. Thank you, Jesus, again. She made sure that I stood up and took a few steps.

After standing a few times, I leaned away from the bed. Dad let go of me. Then I let go of the bed rail. I asked for her and Dad to hold under my arms. I walked out into the hall with them holding me.

I said, "That's enough." When the nurses saw me, I asked, "Can both of you let go of me?" It felt very odd to be standing in the hall.

I walked!

Five small steps. Just me and a nurse pushing my IV. I was exhausted. I needed a wheelchair. I went the same distance as one regular step, and I did not go straight. Pretty happy with that.

I am learning to sit up on my own.

My right arm and hand are useless. Bad news, I can only move my right thumb a quarter inch more. I am not sure it moved any *more*. The therapist orders a brace before she leaves so I will not have "a monkey thumb." The brace goes up my right forearm. It can be used to connect my arm to my belt. My right arm will not be flopping around and getting in trouble.

I cannot sit up on my own.

The IV comes out soon. I get to eat regular food soon.

I order a McDonald's quarter pounder with cheese, fries, and a chocolate shake. Back then, in 1969, it was good food.

Guess what. Not only does someone have to help me hold it, to put the hamburger in my mouth. It tastes terrible. Rather, no taste. Like stuffing a paper towel in my mouth! Chocolate shake, horrid!

My taste buds do not work! I have to eat baby food. I do not want to tell you this. Someone has to feed me. I could not hold the hamburger, much less a spoon. I have to eat enough calories to take out the IV.

No one is in the room.

I cannot leave the bed without help. The main reason is I cannot sit up without help. So I have never tried. I am still working on sitting up. When I finally sit up on my own, I am fine for a second. My bottom slides off the edge of the bed. I think I am fine.

It is only a few inches to the floor. The bed has been dropped down to the lowest level.

My weak legs can't handle it. They buckle.

The door is open, and a nurse is right there where I can see her. She is looking at me.

So I say, "*Help.*"

I see her running in as I fold up on the floor.

I woke up in bed.

Okay. Do you remember in chapter 2? At six weeks, I remember something. Well, this is when I remember the complete vision, the part where I almost went to heaven.

I worked on getting out of bed and moving to a chair. Exhausting. Great strength builder. From the chair to the bed. The hardest part was still sitting up. Walked to the door.

I took my first shower. Baths in the bed were finally a thing of the past.

One of the nurses brought some new clothes for me to wear at home. Her church had purchased them. Earlier, the nurse had made my measurements for the purchase. Three sets of under-clothes freshly washed. Two shirts and pants washed and pressed.

Dad helped me get dressed. Wheelchair to the door. I was able to walk outside. I walked out into the *sun*. The sunshine on my very white skin felt hot. I told Dad that I was ready to go to the beach. Not that funny. The clothes felt strange. Not complaining. Just saying.

Being outside, I was suddenly so exhausted I could not stand up… My father held me. A nurse rushed the wheelchair twelve feet out the door to me.

I had a lot to do. I would get sleepy by walking around. I weighed 118 pounds. I would only take fifteen-minute naps. I had a lot to do. I had to check out tomorrow. I could walk two more steps each time. Eating was a problem. I couldn't hold a fork or spoon. Dad and I had been practicing getting in and out of a car. I could drive. Kind of!

I looked strange. I did not care. I loved it. I am six feet one and 118 pounds. My right hand was in an open metal brace strapped to my side. My right foot pointed to the right. Both shoulder blades stuck straight back. Easy to see. They pushed my shirt back. The four-post neck brace kept my chin and back of the head in place. I walked very slowly with a lot of effort.

I checked out of the hospital.

Dr. Yoder was waiting for me in his office. He stood up when I reached his door. We shook hands left-handed. My right hand did not work.

The fine doctor invited me to take a seat.

I chose to stand.

He understood.

I was taken aback at the first item Dr. Yoder wished to mention. I didn't want to hear it.

He said, "David, I need to apologize about the morphine."

I wished he had not said that word.

The doctor went on, "The pain would have killed you. I had no other choice."

I could only respond, "I understand and I agree. You made some tough choices." I then added, "We went through a lot. You have nothing to apologize for."

Dr. Yoder, in the voice I am so used to, said, "I would like for you to accept my apology, if you would. David, it's not just the episode of a month ago. There are some long-term issues and matters you will be dealing with." He could not be more clear. We had discussed my present painful addiction, his breaching the amount and far exceeding what any patient had received in that period of time. The doctor told me himself he had never heard of such an amount. Dr. Yoder looked me straight in both eyes.

I replied, "Yes, of course, Dr. Yoder, I do understand, and I will respectfully accept your apology." As we were shaking hands, the Great Dr. Yoder thanked me.

He went on to say that he was sending something to Warm Springs about the amount of morphine I received in that short period of time.

With that out of the way, I asked Dr. Yoder while I was standing in front of him, "What were the chances of me walking again when I came in here?"

He came back very fast with "None, absolutely zero." He added, "It is actually still something, even with myself being witness, I would still today say, could not transpire."

The doctor and I talked about how we both did not see me walking out. Just weeks ago even with the unexplainable progress, we did not foresee David Cash walking and getting into a car. We both, in reality, still saw me rolling out to the car in a wheelchair.

Suddenly, there were no words. We just said our farewells.

CHAPTER 6

Two Weeks at Home

So Content With Being Alive and Standing

HOME FOR A COUPLE OF WEEKS. IT WAS GREAT TO SEE THE house. With the five front steps which I had already thought about, I went in the back door. No steps.

What a shocking sight for people who had seen me two months ago. Some neighbors would actually say, "What the 'hello' happened to you?" A lot of visitors came by the house in a short amount of time.

On Sunday, I was looking forward to church. Carrying my cushion to sit on. That same cushion went with me everywhere. I could not lean back in church because of my shoulder blades. Soon as the service was over, I stood up. It was easier to stand. I liked standing.

The $384 in a savings account at C&S Bank was empty. I had saved money cutting grass for money at ten years old. I have told you about how much I worked. Most of the money was from Chamblee Fence. The account was opened with only $5 when I was nine years old. I rode my bike to Chamblee Plaza and deposited $2 many times. I had the passbook filled up.

Back in the hospital, I had told Dad to take the money.

He was sitting beside me. It was a week in the hospital. I could hear my dad counting his money.

I said, "Dad, you have four ones and two other bills. You just counted the money in your billfold."

He said, "You are right."

I went ahead and said, "It is the way you count them. You counted four bills quickly and the other two slowly. By the way, yesterday, you had six ones, a five, two tens, and a twenty. You counted it three times, so I am sure."

Dad responded, "Yes, son, that is correct. How do you do that?"

My answer was, "My hearing and thought processing are very enhanced with nothing below the neck. I have been keeping it top secret."

Dad said, "I understand. The top secret part."

I added, "The FBI will snatch me right up." My first joke in a week. That is when I said, "Dad, grab the money in my savings account. Just between us."

He responded, "I hate to do that."

I said, "Dad, please go into the bank, and move it over to your checking account. I want to pitch it in."

"Okay. I will, David. I don't have much choice. I was going to ask you about that money."

I said, "I know you were. Let's talk about interest. Fifty percent seems fair."

Dad was quick. "Okay, I will pay you back. Later on, next month sometime, maybe." I know it's an old joke, paying ridiculous interest. I believe it was my second joke that terrible week!

My father put a knob on the steering wheel of a Plymouth Valiant. I could use that to help with driving. Push-button transmission selection on the left.

I drove to the bank hoping my father had left, maybe, ten dollars or something. The teller at the Chamblee Plaza bank remembered when I opened the account. She told me C&S requires the account to be closed if there were zero funds in it. I am pretty sure I remember her name, Robin. So Robin told me about "Mr. Cash" coming by and keeping everyone at the bank up to date with my recovery. He was so excited to tell us good news. "We would all watch him in line to hear what he had to say." I told Robin, "Dad told me about the twenty dollars this bank collected and gave him." It was in the form of a handwritten gift certificate from the Phillips 66 Gas Station across the street.

North Peachtree Baptist Church had a special collection and purchased a new set of tires for our car. A man who worked at General Motors gave my family the use of a very nice house in Ocean View. So much was given. I was broke when I left the bank that day. So many people gave!

I wanted to go see some friends. I had an afternoon and evening planned with a girlfriend. My plan *now* was to go to Murphy Candler Park. Not too exciting.

How about this? I was getting in the car at home.

George walked up to me, handed me a twenty-dollar bill. Yep, he stuffed a twenty in my hand and said, "Don't tell anyone about this."

I was running late. I believe George timed it that way. So I had to get in the car, saying, "You just saved my life."

George just waved me away and turned around.

I could not wait to see my grandmother Ma (pronounced *Maw*). I was so fortunate to have a good down-to-earth grandmother who is alive.

Jimbo brought her over. (My uncle Jim was a little slow mentally.)

On the first day, she brought me some very nice new clothes. She told me my mother had given her the sizes of the new clothes I bought home from the hospital.

I had worked up a big appetite. You can bet I had figured out how to manage a McQuarter Pounder by now. I kept a towel in the car to put over me.

For dinner the first Sunday, Mom cooked up one of my favorites roast beef, turnip greens, and black-eyed peas. Corn bread.

Mom is the world's best cook. I am not kidding. Mom can cook this type of food. That is where she shines.

I am going to figure this out. Big Sunday dinner at home. There has to be a way.

Mom was told not to do this. Because I cannot use a fork and spoon.

I see her point. And thank her.

She has already made me a plate. A reasonable portion of each dish.

I get a towel and put it over me. I break off a piece of corn bread and manage to get a bite. Not the Southern way to eat corn bread. I go ahead and ask Dad to cut the "fall apart tender" roast beef into bite-size pieces. He leaves the fork stuck in a piece and asks if that is okay. I can only say, "We'll see."

It is so funny now. The whole family wants to help. I have to pick up the fork and feed myself; I cannot do that! I don't know.

The clock is ticking. My fork is stuck in the roast beef. This may work.

I move my left hand to the fork.

Angela is to my left. She almost reaches over.

I believe I will use my right hand to help a little. I have taken off the brace. The right hand is useless, but it can help completely close the fingers of the left hand, guide under the fork or something.

Great, I am feeling pretty, almost, okay about getting the roast beef to my mouth.

I move the right hand up and start it across the plate. I lift it some more to make sure it does not touch any food. Feeling good. I lift my right hand up and flip the plate of food over on the table. Of course, my full glass of iced tea goes with it.

My little finger is caught under the edge of the plate, and I do not feel it.

Nice and loud.

Food, tea, and ice everywhere.

Everyone jumps.

Angela shouts.

Mom and my sisters have it cleaned up in no time. We all sit back down.

I have a roast beef sandwich. Great meal.

Dad helps me eat some black-eyed peas and corn bread that evening.

We will cook out hamburgers the next Sunday.

After my wave of visitors, I was mostly alone the rest of the days I was home. I recall just standing in the front, on the cement parking area at the top of our driveway, a lot.

My butt was so skinny I could not sit just anywhere. Then the shoulder blades were sticking out, and some places were worse than others to sit. Porch swing, front porch, picnic table, old-style folding chair, piano stool, and so on. Nope, skinny butt, bones sticking out. I carried a cushion around.

I could not drink out of a glass, open most car doors, button a shirt, tie my shoes, get the billfold out of my back pocket, shake hands, and so on. I never felt sorry for myself after the shock of that first day, never.

I was amazed that I was home now. I recall standing, like I just mentioned, in front of the house, thinking about what just happened. I was alive and standing. It would hit me. The two simplest things.

Then hang in here with me. A bird would go off singing, just like always in our neighborhood. My hearing was fantastic.

Okay, now I would be standing while listening to the bird. The bird would stop, and then another bird would answer a mile or so away.

That would be it. I was so happy. To be alive, standing in front of the house. I would start crying because I was that happy. I kept a handkerchief in my left pocket. I could quickly clean up my face. I always carried a handkerchief from the time I was five.

I cried being so happy, maybe three times while I was home those two weeks. Two of the times were in the front yard. One time, I was parked at church. No one ever caught me crying or with tears. Oh, I teared up when I saw Ma. Tearing up doesn't count. I am talking, *boom*, tears. No ugly face, just tears. Tablespoon of them. Time, about thirty seconds.

So content with being alive and standing. I could not handle the sheer satisfaction of standing. When it became a pleasure, a gift, a gladness. You see there is no word.

I would cry because I was just that happy. I would thank Jesus and all.

Don't, for a second, get me wrong here. The miracles happened. That is the only reason that I am standing.

The tears were from being that truly happy. Wow.

Thanks for listening, *again*. One more thing. Man, did it feel good to bust out those tears! Good old soft ironed and folded handkerchief. Oh, boy, feeling good.

I had my suitcase packed. I was going to be dropped off at Warm Springs, the best physical therapy hospital in the country. Dad's Blue Cross Blue Shield insurance was good for six months for this type of treatment. I would be an inpatient at the hospital in Warm Springs, Georgia, for the next six months exactly.

CHAPTER 7

Warm Springs Rehabilitation Hospital

I Felt at Home, More Than Home.

Honestly, I do not like going back in my memories to Warm Springs. While I was at the wonderful place, I would have never thought that. This may be cut short.

A well-handled check-in had me promptly set up in my room.

Before our arrival, my parents had the information of exactly where and when they were to leave. They departed, gone, out of here. Mom was asking stupid questions. See you later.

My folks left very early in the day.

I was soon involved in an informative orientation. I was here at last. Oddly enough, I felt right at home.

I was surprised when it was lunch. The day flew by. I was wondering what I was going to eat and how I was going to eat. I recall walking into a nice dining room with a buffet line. White table clothes.

The color of my name tag was the information; I was new and checked in today.

A local young lady dressed in a light-blue-and-white trim shift dress-type uniform walked up beside me in the buffet line. She told me she would be assisting me until I was finished with lunch.

When we arrived at the food line, she grabbed a tray, and I followed her down the line.

I decided to go for a fried chicken leg and told my assistant that it could be something I could hold to eat.

She told me not to worry that I should choose whatever I liked. She picked out a dessert I was looking at. Told me it was something special.

I went for whatever I wanted. Mashed potatoes. Gravy. Black-eyed peas. Corn bread muffins with butter. Some sweet potatoes in a separate little dish…

My assistant picked up a long tie around the neck and back apron to cover me. Once at the table, I noticed the nice ice-size fork handles.

She did something like wrapped the end of the chicken leg and then wrapped that around my left thumb and two fingers.

I still dropped it.

Guess what, Ms. Blue and White picked up the leg off the floor in an unnoticeable swift move, carried it away, came back with a big chicken breast, pulled it apart, and fed it to me.

She asked me to relax and fed me the rest of the meal.

About a third of the people in the dining room were being fed. Very low profile.

I noticed a lady kept a cup in one hand.

We placed a corn bread muffin in my left hand to hang on to. I didn't have to pick it up. I could hold it and take an occasional bite. She even kept it buttered to perfection. We used the napkin exactly when I was thinking about it. Sweet tea, all I had to do was look at it.

I was at home more than when I was at home.

She was so good at feeding people that we could talk and I could just take a bite naturally. I was able to relax and ask important questions. She was all smiles answering and adding extra information I would need. No hurry.

My tea and ice were refilled. Extra food was offered to be brought to the table.

The food was excellent.

I was to have an assistant for all three meals until the therapist in charge of my case filled out a certain form and signed it. I was to sign the form as well.

So much to do.

Warm Springs had my bed chosen. My high school records along with some questionnaires that had been filled out. It was important to match patients with compatible roommates. The rooms are very big. Four beds to a room. In my room, three beds are for the long term. In the fourth bed, patients came and stayed for a short term (hardly ever used, never in some rooms).

Sidney Lucas

My longest-term roommate was Sidney Lucas.

I recently found out Sidney died in 2019.

Sidney lost his left arm just below the shoulder. Lost both legs above his knees. Yep, a triple amputee. My best friend at Warm Springs. I could not have made it without Sidney! The addiction thing. He could really understand. No one has ever understood my painful addiction. Like my friend Sidney.

Sidney and I would borrow someone's car. Never had a problem getting a car. Not once.

We had to escape. Sneak out.

Buy a six-pack, sometimes twelve. Sidney got drunk on three beers because he didn't have much body.

We would ride to the lake, drink, and talk. Sometimes, we would ride around.

We had to sneak back inside our building and to our room.

Ms. Martinez

When I was assigned my physical therapist, I was blessed with Ms. Martinez.

She wore a white dress uniform with a black band on her cap and some other emblem meaning she was a "supertherapist." She was the "highest-ranking" therapist per her education. She was hired as the head therapist as well.

Ms. Martinez was 100 percent prepared for me. The first minute we met, while introductions were being made, Ms. Martinez had my right arm and hand on a table looking at it.

"Hello, I am Ms. Martinez. David, come in, sit down, place your right arm on the table, with the hand palm down."

She had other well-qualified therapists work with me because of the long hours.

Ms. Martinez was the absolute best.

They were all good. The pay here at Warm Springs for physical therapists was very high. The qualifications were tough. The hours were brutal. The waiting list to get a job here was long.

Martinez was of Latin American descent and went to school in the US. She was about five feet and two or three inches. Very good features. Of course perfect health.

Translation: beautiful and smart.

Martinez went to work as we talked. Introductions out of the way, she got started.

The first day was work and pain while she told me what my schedule would be.

I could tell Ms. Martinez was excited about her job. She was especially happy to get my case. Martinez said something that just hit me that first day, "You should have come straight here from the hospital. What damage has been done, that is behind us now. We will do as much work as possible every day. On the one day you do not have to get up and go to these rooms, I will have instructions for you." She didn't look at me for a comment. It was just said.

She kept working on me and making notes. That explains Ms. Martinez better than I can try to explain her.

Ten hours of work in a day was not that unusual. I had twelve-hour days!

It included hours of work or recovery waiting on the next painful item on your schedule.

It may be stressful, like fifty minutes of learning to write with my left hand.

Recovery was waiting in a room with other people waiting for their next pain or visiting patients who were stuck in their rooms. Many times, there would be people crying or tears running down their face, just waiting for the next workout.

The pain was horrible at first. Absolutely, no screaming, shouting in pain, or crying out loudly in the workout or therapy rooms. So many warnings, and you would be sent home. The occasional slip was very understood.

I was there when a man about fifty years old in a wheelchair kept yelling. We all talked to him. He said it hurt too much. The physical therapist backed away on how far they pushed him, and he still yelled. He was assigned Ms. Martinez. She pleaded with him to stop yelling. I was in the room with him a lot. How inconsiderate. Not just a cry or low painful ouch. I mean, "Ow, ow, ow, ow, ow. Oh, oh, oh, oh, ow, ow, ow, ow." I could hear him down the hall. Being in the same room was impossible.

They even tried working on him in his room with the door shut. No good.

The therapist could not handle it, and you could still hear him.

Finally, Martinez had the paperwork and told the old man she would give him one more chance. She had him dropped off, in his wheelchair, in the young people's workout room for about an hour and then with the young kids as they waited in the room for the next workout.

When she brought him in for evaluation, she kindly mentioned the young children and told him not to scream out.

He agreed.

She started to give him the final evaluation workout. She stopped at the points where it would be zero to the very lowest pain level.

Old Man still screamed, "Ow, ow, ow, ow!"

She asked, "What is it?"

He said, "It hurts."

Ms. Martinez told him, "Mr. Grey, no, it does not. You are lying. I only moved your arms a small amount. You can do that yourself. You lied to me about the pain. You are screaming and yelling, disturbing the patients here. I have wasted too much time trying to help you. Warm Springs can do nothing for you. You are no longer a patient here. Reapplication will not be looked at, only returned. You will not return to your room. You will be moved to guest quarters with privileges until a family member arrives to check you out of this facility."

Martinez had a witness in the room, of course. She also discontinued looking at him after saying, "You are lying."

She told me about it. Plus the backstory.

Mr. Grey sat at home in his wheelchair for two years after a car wreck left him paralyzed from the waist down. Insurance covered in home or full-time physical therapy. He was bitter. Pushed away all help. Relatives had enough of him.

He had to do this now or never. He could no longer push his wheelchair, get on and off a toilet, and reach the items in the kitchen. He was recently released from the hospital because of infected bed sores.

Mr. Grey's mobility was horrid. Worst she had seen at Warm Springs for his type break.

He could be 100 percent functional in a wheelchair, probably even use crutches. Easily drive a car. Have a long life with his family. Go on vacations or anything.

She said, "David, you will meet a lot of perfectly healthy Mr. Greys in your life."

I said, "I know, and you and I want to help them."

She agreed. A few minutes later, Ms. Martinez said, "You can't help someone that doesn't want to be helped."

The whole time we were talking, she was working with me. Ms. Martinez might be pushing her full weight up on top of my right foot with me on my back. She was pushing down and twisting while I was trying to feel the weight or trying to push up. I was hoping to feel pain in my right side.

I couldn't get the strength of my left side of my legs too far ahead of the right. My right foot pointed right when I walked. We kept working on that. The weak right foot just wanted to point right.

Electric Shock Therapy

Five days a week, three times a day. One treatment on Saturday.

Only Ms. Martinez would do these treatments. It had it to be perfect.

On Saturday, if it was her day off, Martinez would come into work wearing regular clothes, do one treatment, and leave.

Every muscle she was working on had to be worked and shocked. Very small detail work looking to shock every muscle in each finger. We were excited when I could twitch a small muscle of which I had not moved since my accident.

At first, it took a long time to find the exact spot to shock.

Also, early on, I had no feeling in the area I was being shocked.

Later as the feeling came back, I would put my head down and cry, or the tears would roll out because of the ongoing pain. The pain from one shock or burn would continue as she would burn the next spot and on. My tears would pour out the complete continued time.

At first, Martinez had to find the spots to shock each visit. I would watch and see the muscle jump.

Soon enough, pink spots marked the places to shock me. Then red marks.

One morning, she shocked one of the red marks, and I said a loud, "Ow, sorry." We stared at each other. She shocked the next one. Man, that hurt.

Feeling had come back to an area that we were shocking. As the days went on, the red spots became burn marks. Ms. Martinez would take the end of the probe and touch the burn marks, three times a day and once on Saturday. This is when I started putting a towel in my lap to catch the tears.

I knew when it was almost over. So I would start blinking away the tears. Ready to pick the towel up and wipe my face so I could wait for fifteen to twenty minutes with the other patients. Waiting between treatments or workouts. That is it for the whole first two months.

My right hand does not work, but the muscles are strong!

Learning to use my left hand to eat was hard. I learned how to put food on the fork with my left hand. Then I was learning to eat with a fork and spoon. I would learn to write with my left hand. Every day, I practiced for fifty minutes. Now it was also six days a week. I must make the left arm and hand dominant.

My legs *couldn't* get too far ahead of each other. I was working on the right leg and foot a lot to catch up.

Totally different with the hands. The lower right arm and especially my right hand were not doing good. I must at this point go to my left arm and hand.

I would start working on throwing a ball left-handed, lifting weights, and working my left arm and hand.

My therapist explained, if someone tossed me my keys, I should naturally reach out with my left hand and catch them. Same thing with an ink pen. I would be reaching for it with my left hand.

I would throw a beautiful left-handed spiral with a football.

I hated that left-hand class at first. So stressful. A month later, much better. Still stress, stress, stress. Two months later, I had a strong left arm and my handwriting was okay. So stressful learning to do everything with my left hand. Zip up my pants. I could use my right hand. But it would not clamp a zipper.

Three months, I had a very dominant powerful left arm and a strong handshake. Nice handwriting with my left hand. Oh yes, I could throw a spiral football. And pitch the baseball. I was glad

I could write with my left hand. My right hand was still slow in recovering. I couldn't write with my right hand. I couldn't zip up my zipper with my right hand.

I would pitch a ball with anybody. Throw the football or Frisbee. All with my left hand.

I had a place to hit with my left hand. Five four-inch foam mattresses stacked against the wall with two workout matts hanging over the top third of them, very important.

Striking harder and harder.

Flip them over and move them around.

Harder and harder. *Wham, wham, bam, wap.* More and more natural. More powerful.

Making it the left shoulder, left arm, and left hand, my first choice for every chore. Big or small. My right hand could hold a fork. I worked with them for the same amount of time!

I loved this place. I had a new work schedule.

Younger patients were awesome. They talked to each other. Bob would say, "John, did I hear you yell, '*Ouch*, ouch, ouch'?"

John would say, "You misunderstood me. I shouted, 'Halleluiah,' because I was so happy."

Or Bob would say, "Is that hurting you when she is pushing your arm that far back?"

John would say, "I didn't even notice. Even if a tractor tire ran over that shoulder, I would think it was a fly."

John would say, "Bob, is that you crying?"

Bob would say, "I am crying, John. I am only so happy to be at workout this early."

The younger residents would talk in low to natural voices to each other. They naturally become friends, I guess.

The courage I saw in the kids who were around ten years old was unbelievable. Some have survived a car wreck. Lost family members. The environment of Warm Springs every day was what kept me going seven days a week in the beginning. Young people from all over the country were at Warm Springs.

Ms. Martinez kept me late most days. A lot of my day was broken into forty-five- and fifty-five-minute tasks. Exhausting.

Like learning to eat if I could not do it. The battle was real. If I did not learn right, I would pick up a weird thing or habit that I could not change. I would swing my head down "unconsciously" the rest of my life. Stick my tongue out a little. I just wanted some food. This therapist was perfect. I worked with her and never broke her rules. She pointed to a person she tried to help one evening while we were at dinner. It was so sad to look at, to have a "glitch" that could have been fixed. I mean as long as I was there and it was on the list of things to do. I have six months. Two months were gone.

BRENDA

I made many friends. End of every day was a big social event. One girl my age who had recovered from polio would come flying down the hall almost every day. Always so happy. Blond hair, blue eyes. Never will walk. She just wanted to talk. I give her all of my time.

There were 50 percent girls at Warm Springs.

But this girl was special. She contracted polio when she was a baby. She has never walked. She can use a wheelchair like no one else.

She had a crush on me. Here is the story.

She asked me if it was okay if she had a crush on me the first time she came into my room.

I asked, "Well, do I have to buy you a house or ring?"

She laughed and said, "No, can we maybe just hold hands sometime?"

I said, "I am so shy, and my face is already red. I don't know your name."

Blond and Blue Eyes said, "Brenda" Then she rolled up and grabbed my right hand. Guess what. Brenda kissed my hand, held it up to her lips, looked over it, and smiled.

I had to ask, "Brenda, is this the way you introduce yourself to all the guys?"

"Never, silly. I just decided we are going to skip the first week. I have not had a boyfriend in a year. He was trying to grow a mustache. So I broke up. I asked the nurse, and she gave me my happy pill thirty minutes ago. I was afraid of you. Now I look like a, you know.

I said, "Brenda, I am honored. You took a happy pill for me?"

She still had my hand. Guess what. She kissed my hand again! Her blue eyes got bigger, and Brenda nodded yes.

I announced, "We are boyfriend and girlfriend no other, as long as we're both here, okay, deal?"

Brenda is smart. She had the perfect answer, "Kiss on it." Sparkle blue eyes.

Made my day. Nice sweet kiss.

That was my girlfriend. She left in three and a half weeks.

I met crazy people. Life was too much for some of them.

I would visit the crazy ones often. A friend would die, and the bed would be empty. It has been fifty years. I still think about them.

It was a very rough last three months.

I had six friends die on me in the last two months I was at Warm Springs. It is because I knew the most patients.

HENRY

Henry was a quadriplegic. He was going to have his spinal cord cut a little higher up. He had horrible full-body spasms.

After the surgery, he was to be in a wheelchair and possibly be able to go home. His two boys were excited. His church was praying.

I met Henry the second day at Warm Springs. We became friends that day.

Henry was on the same floor straight down the hall, out my door to the right.

His bed was set up where he could look down the hall when he wasn't having spasms. When the nurses "flipped" him over to avoid bedsores, he looked the other way in the room. Henry's bed was against the wall.

He was really messed up, getting worse; he knew it.

I was thinking, *How could Henry get any worse?* When the doctors are planning to cut the spinal cord, in order to stop the spasms, that is pretty bad.

The day before that surgery, Henry told me he was worried. This man never complained! So I stayed with him between workouts and whenever.

We talked till Henry fell asleep the night before the surgery. He asked the nurse for something strong.

He was in a new bed for about two weeks after the surgery. Now it is away from the wall. No spasms. He was like a different person.

A custom wheelchair with the latest electronics was being assembled in New York.

The therapist could finally work on him.

Ramps were going to be installed at his home.

Two week later.

Henry asked for me, no one else.

I sat with him and his wife.

He just stared at his wife and quit breathing… She was folding a handkerchief over and over, smoothing it out, talking.

I told her, "Cora, it's okay now."

She stopped with the folding, put both hands on top of the handkerchief, stopped talking, closed her eyes, and nodded a little. I said, "I will leave you alone. I have to get the nurse. Are you going to be okay?"

She said, "I don't know, David. Please hurry back."

I promised I would.

She was twisting the handkerchief.

I already knew their story. Grew up in the same neighborhood. Went to the same medium-size Baptist Church. Married at twenty years old.

Henry had a good Job that meant a promotion and a transfer to a different state.

Cora said it was all she ever knew. Henry and the boys.

Henry loved motorcycles.

His broken neck was not all that bad. It was very high in the spinal column.

Henry lived longer than expected.

Laura

One day, Laura, so beautiful. Stunning, actually, even while lying in bed. Only thirty-two years old. Three little girls. A very wealthy repulsive husband.

Laura very recently had a blood clot: aneurysm. Hit her right at the base of her skull.

Our doors were across from each other. I walked in to visit the new patent with three beautiful blonde girls. Her bed was rolled up against the wall. This was a bad sign.

When I first saw Laura, she was lying on her side.

Again, *strikingly gorgeous blonde lady.*

Her husband was on the phone.

Laura spoke very slowly. "Please stay. Have a chair."

Her personal nurse told me the aneurysm hit suddenly only a week ago. She was at home and fell down a few steps when it happened. Laura had come from the hospital to here.

I told Laura's nurse I was a patient across the hall, that I would like to see if I could help.

Laura's husband hung up the phone and asked the nurse, "Who the hell is that?"

She responded, "This is a patient. He is part of the welcoming group."

Her husband looked at me and made another phone call.

Laura's nurse placed a chair close to Laura's face. The nurse motioned for me to sit down.

I sat in the chair.

The girls came to me one at a time. Told me their names, how old they were, and something about school or what was going on with Mother. So polite. They leaned a head on my arm or relaxed and asked me questions.

When "Father" hung up, the girls sort of jumped.

The nurse gathered them up, and the girls were out the door.

The husband stood up and announced, "I hope this does not give them nightmares."

The husband left. He never even looked Laura's way.

I was sitting so close I could hear Laura breathe. Both eyes were pouring tears.

I grabbed a handful of Kleenex and took care of her tears.

What to do?

Put my hand on her head? I don't know. I did that without much thought.

I know from experience it feels good.

I stayed with Laura for a couple of hours. It was on a Sunday. She talked so slowly.

Warm Springs nurses came and went.

It was about time for the restaurant to close, so I told Laura I had to leave.

She asked me to come back.

The next evening. It was night after dinner, late training, and a shower. I walked over.

Laura was awake. She said she had been trying to "yell" my name. Laura could not yell above a whisper. She did most of the talking.

I went over and listened to her every night for six nights.

The next day, the "Do Not Disturb" sign was on her door.

Laura's nurse came into my room as soon as I was finished for the day. She asked me to come over quickly.

I had seen her nurse only once since the first day.

A chair was placed close to Laura's face. The way I would place the chair when visiting Laura. I would always return it back.

The nurse told me, "Please say the prayers Laura told me you prayed. Laura wanted that."

Laura could no longer talk. She was breathing. Her eyes were closed.

I was told the blood clot moved. She would die soon.

So I started praying and talking to Laura. I began to pray.

When I paused, Laura's nurse whispered, "Mr. David, would you place your hand on her hair and head, please, sir?"

I felt it best to first go about placing my hand on Laura's hair. After that, I answered, "Yes, of course. That is how we always prayed." This felt more natural. Her nurse seemed to relax a little. She had taken care of the last detail for a dear friend.

Laura died only an hour later. I did not think it would be that soon.

No one expected her to die so quickly.

I got up.

A Warms Springs nurse, along with her personal nurse, were sitting in the room.

Like I mentioned, her dying that soon was unexpected.

I believe her nurse friend must have felt it.

Her husband and family were on the way.

I thought it best to stand up immediately, move the chair out of the way, and leave the room. Laura's nurse found me the next day.

We walked outside and sat down beside each other.

I asked her name. The nurse was Latino and hard to understand. She answered, "Yes, of course. My name is Dolores."

She was wearing an all-black dress and shoes, and a hat with veil and gloves. She held my hand and told me about Laura. So sad the ending. Dolores added, "Laura told me about this the day she died, early that morning. She told me she saw Jesus standing right next to you when you sat down. Laura saw him reach beside you when you placed your hand on her head. Laura felt both hands. Jesus only stayed a minute. She felt his hand lift. Laura said, 'Jesus looked at me and walked toward the door.'"

I told Dolores to stop. She was talking faster and faster.

I asked, "When?"

Dolores continued, "David, that was early yesterday. I talked about the girls after that. But it made Laura sad. We sat quietly. I left when I returned the door was closed. I was not allowed in. That was yesterday. You were gone all day."

Now Dolores was crying.

That's the story. I wanted to ask, "Are you sure about that? If Laura saw Jesus standing beside me, why didn't she tell me? Laura and I talked for over an hour."

The last time I talked with Laura. Looking back, Laura said for the first time that night, "I love you, David! You have been so good staying up, listening to me babble on. When we meet in heaven, I can walk, we can dance, and you can throw a football across the planets."

It was a good conservation. Completely different. Laura talked slowly as ever. I remember being way too happy listening to her talk about heaven and Laura being awake in a good way.

I do not see any reason for her nurse's need to lie.

Back at Warm Springs, I thought Laura may have dreamt about it.

Today, I believe Jesus was in the room, and Laura was ready to go home with him.

At the end of the book, I will tell you about Laura's vile husband.

When patients are dying at Warm Springs, they can't send them anywhere, like a hospital. The patient is already here.

After about the second month or so, I found out about the beer store that would deliver beer to your car. No ID was ever asked. Just drive up out back. Someone would walk down the steps, take your order, and bring it right out. This had been going on at that location for over thirty years. It was located at another place before that when the county was dry.

I was always the driver when we snuck out at night. No security. Great stories. Sidney always went. Like I said, a car was never a problem. Someone usually had a car with hand controls added. We tore up one set, minor damage. The owner was in the passenger seat. Almost drowned everybody. So funny.

I got a lot of history when the old-timers came in for all kinds of problems. We had a very illegal poker game every so often. Stakes were way too high for me.

I was there when the police busted one of the games! This was in 1969!

Some of the pots were getting into five or six thousand dollars. The police did not arrest anyone for this game. Scared me! Three police walked in.

One of them said something about the violation of a certain charge. County and state. Gambling on these premises on and on.

The officer in charge said, "Okay, that's enough. I have a good mind to arrest every one of you." Then the officer said, "Now get that mess cleaned up."

Everyone quickly looked at their cards, played what they had, and the winner pulled in his about $1,500 pot.

Seven players and as many of us watching. All in wheelchairs but me.

The officer looked at me and asked what I was doing here.

Sidney spoke up. "He is one of us."

The cop then said, "I don't have time for this. No more gambling! Are we clear?"

The guys at the table were putting their money away—in shirt pockets, wheelchair pockets, and billfolds. All were saying, "Yes, sir. You got my word on it. I promise. You are a good man."

The police looked at each other. The one who spoke first said, "I guess that's about it."

Another officer asked one of the guys, "Merrell, are you still collecting old cars?"

Merrell answered, "Thanks for asking, Ricky. I love my cars. I just built a very nice metal building for them. My son and I live in a full house attached in the back. I enjoy looking at my cars. My son loves working on them."

Ricky asked, "How many cars do you have?"

Everybody was listening.

Merrell's quick answer was, "All put together and running, thirty-six. Sixteen of them are Ford Model As. Five Model Ts. I also have a 1940 Studebaker truck with only three thousand and four hundred fifteen miles on it, a 1929 Buick, and it is like new, a perfect 1924 Cadillac. My new prized possession, a 1911 Thomas Flyer. Have you heard enough?"

Ricky asked, "What do you drive?"

Merrell said, "The shop here at Warm Springs just added hand controls to a new '69 Impala for me. I get a new Chevy every two years. That is why I am here. It is ready for me to pick up."

I had heard enough! I asked Merrell, "Merrell, excuse me, I am just very curious. "Where is all this money coming from?"

Merrell answered, "None of your business, but everyone knows I had a good lawyer."

I asked, "That's it?"

He said, "You're a nosey feller. No, my lawyer made me invest in Exxon stock and a few others, with a lot of the money. I quit feeling sorry for myself, stopped drinking, started buying and sell-ing old cars with the rest of the money. No junkyard, a nice oper-ation. I keep the best cars for myself. Well, enough money can change my mind. I have been known to sell my most prized cars."

Merrell ran ads in the back of all the car magazines like *Hot Rod* and *Car and Driver*.

Anyway, Merrell's son ran his operation now, which had about twenty employees, stripping the cars for parts and selling the bodies for race cars.

Merrell was a nobody, a drunk carpenter before his accident.

I met a lot of very successful people at Warm Springs. I met the best people at Warm Springs. Back to the police.

Before the police left, the Cop in charge blamed a couple of guys for causing all the trouble. Told them they had better not be caught playing poker here again. Had one man arrested after calling back into the office, just not in handcuffs. Hard to roll a wheelchair in handcuffs.

I don't know what that was all about, didn't ask.

It was a lot of work. Plenty of time to study. A great social life. Six months at Warm Springs changed me.

Rough Checkout Interview

When I was checking out of Warm Springs, I was required to see a psychiatrist before I could leave and be free of hospitals after eight months. The doctor had most of my records. I was sitting across from him. It was a nice office, so I was looking around.

The doctor said, "Charles David Cash, you go by David, is that correct?"

"Yes, sir, that is correct. I prefer to be called by my middle name, David."

I had learned the doctors here liked long answers also to treat pauses with a "Yes, sir."

"Very well, David, I am just reviewing your records from Ocean View Memorial Hospital."

"Yes, sir."

"I see you were diagnosed 'paralyzed, originally no chance of recovery.'"

"Yes, sir."

"Give me a minute please. I would like to look through these papers. Dr. Yoder has made some interesting notes."

"Yes, sir."

About ten minutes passed.

The doctor with a slight British accent just blurted out, "My God, son."

"Yes, sir."

"In just three and a half weeks, you get a hundred and forty-eight injections of morphine." He paused.

So I said, "Yes, sir, I believe so."

He then said this to me, "David, you have a serious drug addiction problem." It struck me like a knife. I knew it. It still cut me pretty deep.

The psychiatrist went on. He did not notice my pain. "I have never seen this amount of morphine given in such a short period of time."

Mr. Cash…" The doctor went on to discuss the future problems I would have, how my addiction would never go away. In fact, a worse addiction with time. Thoughts of morphine or the desires could "attack" or my addiction could make me have strong cravings at any time. Even when I retired with grandchildren! "A case like yours, with this large dosage of morphine every four hours, then to continue the same dosage six times a day for nearly a month, David, son, I have never seen anything quite like this."

I wanted to say firmly, "Shut up. All I can think about is morphine. It is all I want, you stupid doctor. Don't you think I already know a little about this subject?" I also wanted to say, "Please stop saying the word *morphine*."

More importantly, I wanted to check out of the hospital, so I just sat there and listened. The doctor was looking at me.

I said, "Yes, sir." I decided to add, "Thank you."

I sat.

The doctor turned the pages of the report he should have read six months ago. The letterhead was Ocean View Memorial Hospital.

Of course, this is the information Dr. Yoder told me he was sending to Warm Spring, specifically about the amount of *morphine* administered under his care.

The doctor looked at me and asked, "Is this all correct?"

I said, "I have not read the letter. Dr. Yoder only told me he would send one about the amount of *morphine* I received." I went on to add, "I do know of one difference. Something I agreed to earlier. Although, I am not sure if it is your conclusion or in the letter."

He looked at me and asked, "Of course, what is it?"

"Yes, sir, the number 'a hundred and forty-eight' is incorrect. I am not sure about the exact amount of time. I know I discussed this with a nurse. Well, two nurses looked it up… Sir, it was easy to track the exact number of shots of morphine. Probably three or four different ways. The morphine was on its separate log as well. The number of shots was easy to confirm. When I asked, it was not a problem. I had a hundred and sixty-two injections of morphine. The amount of time was closer to four weeks. I believe, a day maybe a day and a half short of four weeks."

His response was spoken more to the letter from Dr. Yoder than to me. Without looking at me, he said, "The amount of morphine you received in such a short period of time is inconceivable. I have read the report from your doctor. I still find it an unthinkable act. Totally unacceptable."

I was thinking, "With all the time I had here, insurance money at hand, the best place in the world to help me with my addiction, right here at Warm Springs—*why did you just now read the letter?*"

Dr. Yoder sent the letter because he had wanted help provided here.

This psychiatrist made the worst mistake. He knew it.

I stayed in his office a full hour while he asked about my plans. The doctor tried to make the tension lesser. I was stressed out, ready to get out of there. He completed the regular exit interview and signed me out.

I was done. Six months. Warm Springs was an incredible place.

High School and a Job

I RETURNED TO CHAMBLEE HIGH SCHOOL FOR FOUR AND A half months of my senior year. This is what I had to do to graduate. All I need was English. Back then, it was something you had to take in your senior year. It was nothing to catch up and pass. After what I have been through, I was just saying, what was so hard about any of this?

I signed up for the distributive education work program, along with just the minimum classes. I did this while still at Warm Springs. Now I could leave early and go to work. I needed money. I had to stay in school till eleven o'clock. I must take a minimum of three classes. Next thing was to get a job!

I was not looking forward to school. A waste of time. I had better things to do.

I checked out of Warm Springs on a Friday, got a job on Saturday, and went to school on Monday.

It was an adult going backward in a time capsule to become a student. I was again shy. Now I was very bored. School was no longer challenging. My first-day plan—the back corner and invisible just do my time in each class.

After a few weeks, I was beginning to fit back in, sorta.

Page Gibson, my best friend, was there. He was glad to see me. What was left of me. I was sort of weird looking. Page did not hold back. He made some good jokes about it. "David, you need to lay off the drugs. Great weight loss program."

I told myself, "Lighten up, David. This is Page Gibson." Page let me know I wasn't weird; I was a minicelebrity.

I asked, "How many is mini? Is there girl value?"

Page assured me, "Many girls!" Of course, Page was lying, or I misunderstood. It was "mini girls." We laughed about that but did not wear it out. Haha, move on. My friends were there. Charlene from Cross Keys. We stayed in touch. Doug Cofield greeted me back. "I thought you were dead." So funny.

Page really helped me and did not even know how much. I needed a friend, badly. Looking back, I see it. I wish I could find him now and tell him.

He introduced me to Beth Farver.

I was now complete with a girlfriend going to the same school to hang out with. No idea at the time I would get married to Beth. I also had no idea Charlene at Cross Keys was going to break up with me. I wasn't the same person she dated when we first met.

Right out of Warm Springs, I had to get a job.

Ma (*Maw*) wanted to take me to get some new shoes. I had no dress shoes for job hunting. Jimbo drove us. It was my first day home from Warm Springs.

First stop was Kinney Shoes on Buford Highway.

As good fortune would have it, the store manager, Mr. Williams waited on us.

Ma asked him if he would hire me and told him what a fine boy I was and what I had been through. Mr. Williams could not turn Ma down, so when Ma asked directly, "Will you give my grandson a job?" he answered, "I don't see why not." He looked at me and said, "I don't know if I should be hiring you or your grandmother here." We all had a good laugh. He stood up and shook my hand and introduced himself as "Ray Williams" and then said, "Come in on Saturday morning at nine o'clock."

I said, "Thank you, Mr. Williams. My name is David Cash. I will see you Saturday."

I was hired before I said anything!

Mr. Williams gave me the employee discount on the shoes I soon tried on.

CHAPTER 9

Work and Living Fast

I Learned Way More Than I Bargained For

Working and going to Chamblee High School. I dropped a class which was against the rules. You had to have three classes. No one cared. I just walked in the school office, asked if I could drop a class. I said, "I have five months of makeup work, with four months to go."

The lady did the paperwork. She said, "That is a lot of makeup work. Okay, you are good."

Now I was only taking two classes. I was dropping the class so I could work full-time. After checking out of Warm Springs, there were only four months of school remaining. All I needed to graduate was senior English. I had become so independent at Warm Springs that high school was slow and hard to handle.

I was wrong. It was good to see the other students and friends.

I had trouble with adults and teachers. I forgot I was a student. Not an equal.

After studying the senior English book, I was finished and ready to graduate. On one of my weekends home from Warm

Springs, I drove to the high school and purchased a used twelfth-year English book.

When I returned to school, my English teacher showed me six makeup tests and told me to go to the library during her class and study for each test. When I have passed all the makeup tests, only then could I return to class.

I had to say, "Yes, thank you, I would like to take all six tests today, to avoid missing any further classes."

She answered after a minute's pause, "David, I would have to grade each test before I gave you the next one. I can't give all six texts to you."

After her long answer, I said, "Okay." After she graded my first two tests, I received a quick A on both.

She handed me the other four tests and said, "Just complete these in the library today. I returned a couple of hours later with all four tests completed, and she said, 'David Cash, I understand you have been in the hospital eight months recovering from a broken neck?'"

I answered, "Yes."

She responded, "I was very rude. I look forward to having you in my class."

I wanted to ask for the final exam! I had already tried that.

I was soon dating Beth Farver. She was a lot of fun. I still to this day think about Beth. Love her and love her laugh. Beth liked me just like I was. Her parents hated me with a passion. What is this? I am drawn to women whose parents are going to hate me? This relationship was doomed. We were headed for marriage and divorce.

I passed senior English and graduated from Chamblee High class of '70. The week after graduation, I became assistant manager of the High Volume Kinney Shoes Store. I know, *Wow*. Longer hours. It was a good work experience. Two week later, I started going to Atlanta Baptist College summer classes. The campus was close by. My schedule was fine. Working all the time and going to school seemed normal.

I was living on the side of our house. Dad had turned the carport into a nice bedroom with a closet and windows. He did this construction project soon after Cindy, my youngest sister, was born. It was the best bedroom for me. It was big, away from the other bedrooms so I could study late at night. My addiction is still every day. I will quit talking about it. It's bad.

Well, back to Beth, work, and college. I could be myself around Beth, which I was not around much with my schedule. She did not try to change me. I was smoking pot and drinking just a little. Beth did not care. She could go where she wanted for weeks. I did not care. We would finally get together and find out that we liked each other.

Average marijuana was junk back then. Mexican, lots of stems and seeds. You didn't get wasted like the pot today. Just a little high.

Campus life was great. I enjoyed everything about college.

Work was always something new—a new contest, new manager, or district manager. New ways to track inventory or payroll systems. Computers were being introduced and always upgraded at the main office. We had new forms and instructions. EDP sales tickets. I remember those. Electronic data processing. The newest thing.

I was always the best at this or that at work. I had to win every contest. I won a color TV. Color TV was a luxury in 1971. I came in first place in a district-wide shoe-polish-sales contest. I sold the nice color television to the manager of the store.

I was robbed at gunpoint one night. The store was on Buford Highway just north of Atlanta. It was a freestanding store, not in a mall. Right at closing, two men came in looking for some dress shoes. They had been watching the store. I had not made the bank drop. The robbers robbed us of the bank drop, and I cleaned out the safe and gave them all the money... I was looking down the barrel of a large-caliber revolver. So I did what I was told, which included being the last one forced to lie down on my stomach in the back room with two other employees. The robbers' faces were not covered. We were all duct-taped, our hands behind our back and our feet together.

They promised to kill us if we tried to get up. The robbers then said not to talk.

Next thing, we heard the front door open and close. We all waited about a half a minute and started talking real low. The robbers were gone.

Not very often, but sometimes, Beth would drop by work. I would always stop. The customer would say something. I would excuse myself by saying, "This will take a minute. Please understand." I would give the customer to another salesperson. Beth never took second place. I would do this for special people. My father, grandmother, and Beth, maybe a few others.

Beth was my girlfriend now, and best friend. We loved to laugh. Beth had a sense of humor that took brains. Wonderful and so smart. We both had our own lives. We may get married one day. Too early to tell. The more her mother and dad hated me, the more likely it became. Right now, we are very busy. Where would life really take us?

Back at home. I had been home from Warm Springs for about eight or nine months. My mom told Dad I had to go! I was being kicked out. This came as a shock. I was in my room studying with a friend from college, Alvin Conyers. He was studying to become a missionary. He did go to Africa for the rest of his life as a hardworking missionary. Alvin was a great missionary. He died of a heart attack as a missionary later in life.

Back to being kicked out of my home. I was using Al's superbrain to help me. He was good at explaining things I did not understand. I wanted to go to school and learn something to help people. Similar to what Alvin was studying. Alvin's home environment was bad. Alcoholic, nonworking Dad. Horribly dirty house.

Toward the end, we were laughing, talking, and studying for the exams. I wanted to make a top grade. About ten minutes earlier, I had walked up through the utility room into the kitchen and pulled two Cokes out of the refrigerator. This may have been the straw that snapped a nerve. When we finished the Cokes, Alvin was going home. We were done studying. The books were everywhere. I felt good about the exam tomorrow morning. Alvin felt good about having a new friend and a clean place to study.

Meanwhile, Mom told Dad to kick me out of the house. The only time we stayed up this late to study. Probably 11:00 p.m.

No warning. Dad walked just inside the door. He told me I had to leave *now*! He said, "Son, I hate to do this, but it is either you go or your mother will leave." Dad had left doors open in the house so the conversation could be heard. He nodded his head to signal such.

I said, "It is fine, Dad. I will come over tomorrow afternoon and pick up all my things."

Alvin caught on quickly and said in an even tone, "You can stay at my house tonight, David. We have an extra bedroom. Mom will make us breakfast in the morning."

Dad said, "Thank you, son. It was nice seeing you, Alvin."

Alvin and I gathered as much as we could that night. We packed my car and quickly left.

Alvin lived in a two-bedroom, cement-block dump with his parents. His mother worked. She was a grammar school teacher. I believe his poor old alcoholic father was on benefits. That night, I slept on a nasty sofa in a junky room. I made sure to bring a pillow and a sheet. I had taken a shower at home before Al came over to my house to study. So glad I did.

Being around my regular family made Al feel better about himself. He was very respectful of my family. He always cleaned up something before he left. We studied on the back porch sometimes. He wanted to feel like part of a normal family while he studied. He spoke to Mom and Lavada very, very respectfully. Cindy thought he was the nicest person. Dad checked his oil, changed plugs, and took care of keeping up his car for him in the afternoon while we studied. Alvin had never had a real dad. Al tried to pay. So funny. Dad said, "Only if David fails the next test." Al would come over and start raking the leaves or sweeping the driveway while waiting on me to come home from work. Lavada would bring him iced tea. Fact is when I was kicked out that night. It really crushed Alvin. I saw he was hurt.

I have never used the bathroom at Al's home. I would not want to eat breakfast at Al's. The dirty dishes are piled across the kitchen. Al and I got up early and left. The exam was early, and it went smoothly. It was my last exam, so I have no afternoon classes. In the back of my mind, I knew it would be my last quarter at Atlanta Baptist College.

I knew exactly where to go after the exam. NorthGate Arms Apartments. A big banner was out on the road, some kind of special. The banner had in the largest letters "Ready for Immediate Occupancy." Leasing an apartment was too easy. I had a key to my new home. No one wanted that apartment because of *the great view* of Interstate 85. I mean my apartment was just before the exit ramp. Very loud horns and trucks downshifting for the exit ramp. No noise or exhaust rules back then.

My new home had a fresh paint job. *Brand-new* dark-green carpet. I was proud of this. I rented it before I looked at it. Scared someone might take it while I was looking at the apartment. Three out of four in this building were available. *And* with this great view! *Haha.* I had to pay the first and last month's rent, plus one hundred extra dollars because I was under twenty-one.

As soon as the half-minute grand tour was over, my next stop was the mattress store. I knew what I wanted and how much money I could spend. I did not have time to shop, only buy. I had to make it to Dad's to pick up my things. I went to a huge furniture warehouse place. Largest in the southeast.

I walked in. I was next, and a saleslady looked past me, so I asked her "Can I get something delivered today?" I believe she was trying to greet the family behind me. They got out of the old van with different-colored doors. She told me no. So I went to leave.

A man—in a very nice suit, built like a football player— came from behind the sales counter and asked what I needed. I said, "A queen mattress set. I may buy the rails, also. I need a rather firm mattress set. I live right off the expressway. NorthGate Apartments."

The man asked me to walk straight back to the mattresses.

I said, "Okay, but I hate that I do not have much time."

He picked up his pace, walked fast, and introduced himself as Mark. Mark stopped and showed me the rather firm ones. I mentioned my budget. I thought it was a nice high number. I knew what I wanted.

He said, "I have just the perfect one." Mark pointed to a white mattress set.

I said, "I will take it. But the delivery is important."

He came back surprisingly and offered, "We have a dining set with four chairs we can throw on there. They are on sale and sitting by the dock door. We can be on our way in forty minutes."

He was reading my mind. I was curious and asked, "What does it look like?" He saw I was in a hurry, so he answered in a fast rhythm, "Rectangle with rounded edges. Real veneer oak top. It has a small leaf. You may want six chairs."

I asked the obvious question, "How much?"

"A hundred and thirty-seven dollars."

I asked another question, "With six chairs?"

"Yes, it is the loss leader for this weekend."

It was fine. I said, "Well, okay, thank you. I must have one of those with six chairs." But I must ask one more question, "Any more loss leaders?"

He shook his head. As he said, "No, SIR. I will get the men loading. We are headed that way with a living room set. Yours will be on the back, so you will be the first delivery." He then asked, "How old are you?"

I wondered why the saleslady brushed me off. I smiled and answered, "Eighteen, sir."

He shook my hand. He had a powerful handshake to go along with the football player's physique. He crushed my right hand. I could actually hear the breaking noise. I usually tried to stick out my left hand. Mark sure felt it.

He scrunched his eyes and immediately let go.

I said, "That's okay."

Mark said, "Are you sure?"

I nodded and answered, "Absolutely."

Mark did not believe me. Mark stared me straight in the eyes for a few seconds. I am very sure Mark was thinking, "How did that not hurt?'

I could just tell. He said, "Thank you for your business, Mr. Cash."

For some reason, I thought that my furniture shopping experience was worth putting in this book. I took and aced an exam, signed my first legal document by leasing an apartment, and made a major purchase.

The day was not over. When I paid for this, it took forever. I needed to be at my apartment for the delivery. The truck was only five minutes behind me when I finally finished paying and arrived "home"! Unbelievably, the table and chairs were of good quality. The delivery guys said I was working with *the* big shot. The table and chairs were strictly off-limits. Could not be sold until Saturday at 9:00 a.m. That is why my payment took forever. The mattress set I received was heavily discounted. He also upgraded me to a better mattress set. He sent along a card that said, "We are very sorry our salesperson said *no*. We try not to use that word at this store." The chairs and table were self-assembly. Oh no, the deliverymen took care of assembling all six chairs and made sure none of them wobbled. The men assembled the table and added an accent pottery vase, *free*. Very nice. Talk about fast.

I emptied my car while they worked on the assembly. These guys were done in no time. I only had six one-dollar bills in my billfold, so I gave four dollars to the deliverymen. Of course, the delivery guys tried to give it back (just once), said the *big man* already took care of them.

That mattress got me hooked on good mattresses for life. I walked out behind the deliverymen. I was headed over to Dad's. I needed some clothes, mainly, and the rest of my things. I was going to ask Dad if I could borrow ten dollars. I was down below twenty in my checking account. Along with two one-dollar bills and less than a dollar in change.

It was getting dark in a few hours. I had to be at work tomorrow. Every Saturday, I was scheduled for a full day—from 9:00

a.m. till 9:00 p.m. I know, and have to accept, full-time school is now just too much. Today, I spent all my savings. That was also my electric and phone deposit that bought the table and chairs. Water was included in my rent! I got paid tomorrow. A hundred percent of that check was spent.

Dad made me take sixty dollars. I would not take it. Just ten. He stuck the fifty I refused in my shirt pocket as I was backing up and saying bye. The muscles that hold my shoulder blades in were hurting, sharp pain. I should stop. I do not like to complain, even in this book. The next day was going to be painful.

That night, when I finally finished a good waffle house meal and picked up some food, milk, and cereal, etc., I went home and emptied my car. Clothes, portable record player, some books. My homemade nightstand, the electric alarm clock, and more worthless things. After a shower (note: buy shower curtain), I was ready to sleep. I had a lamp I grabbed at the furniture store and purchased. It was on my nightstand, so I sat on my bed. In my new home.

Less than twenty-four hours ago, I was at home with two of my sisters, my father, and my mother. I was not happy about this "being kicked out."

I wanted to be with my sisters and my dad.

My sisters would come to my door and tell me good night. I liked hearing about what each one was going through at church and school.

They were proud of me. Going to Atlanta Baptist College. Making good grades.

I did something Mom did not like. One time I drank too much at a work party. I was wrong. I knew *it*. Promised never again. As long as I lived in this house, there was no drinking anytime. I liked that rule.

I was fine living at home in the side room. Getting up early for school. Coming in late from work. I had felt safer at home because of morphine addiction. I made some friends at school. I felt almost normal.

Well, I was kicked out, anyway. There I was, sitting on my new mattress. The floor model lamp came with a three-way light bulb. I admired my lamp with the stolen bulb. The lady at the counter told me I could not buy the floor model. I told her, "Mark is my salesman. I…"

Before I could say anything more, the lady said, "Yes, my mistake. I will add the lamp to your ticket, and we will give you the 'floor model discount.'" She was straight-faced supercheery nice in a flash.

Again, I sure missed Lavada and Cindy telling me good night. I already missed those two. It had been a busy day. I did not feel good. I guess I was so tired. Feeling lonely, I walked around the apartment, sat at my table, did stuff. I mean, Mom and Dad could have asked me to leave. Oh well, I was not used to being lonely. Nobody to talk to. They could have asked me. Mom was a minipolitician. She would tell her side of some made-up story first. She was right. After being away for eight months, I was not the same David. Pull yourself together, *you redneck.*

I did not sleep much last night at Al's house. I was in a lot of pain, so I returned to sit on my new bed. My muscles under my shoulder blades was hurting very badly; it was a sharp pain. Plus, I definitely hurt my neck that day, all the moving.

There was something new. My right hand was sending me some serious damage signals. I turned it, palm down. The right side of my hand, around the last two fingers, was black and purple and as big as a small avocado.

The handshake at the furniture store did more damage than I realized. Yep, how many times was I warned about something like this happening? I continued to damage my hand while moving in. I couldn't feel on the right side of that hand. Something was very busted for it to hurt. At least I quit feeling sorry for myself.

Eighteen with an Apartment

I collected a bunch of "friends" who lived at home with their parents. People would be waiting for me to get home. This was not good. My front door was easy to open when locked. So my "friends" would be in my apartment. They just wanted a place to smoke pot and drink beer. I needed to sleep. I wanted to work and read. Even though I was not in college anymore, I liked to study, not smoke pot and drink every night. I did not need to be around a lot of drinking and pot smoking. This was not good. I was drinking way too much. I knew it.

Some of them I liked. We were good friends. I really didn't know most of the other people that well. Some of them were okay.

One night after a concert, I wound up with a dozen people sleeping on the floor. I put a good lock on my bedroom door and kept the phone in there. Steppenwolf, Led Zeppelin, the Doors, Pink Floyd, Jimi Hendrix, but mainly the Who were played over and over.

Dwain Alman came by the apartment with some friends when I was at work! He left me a signed album, but someone stole it two weeks later. It was an album I had purchased that he signed.

Ten days after the mattress purchase, my right hand was in bad shape. I had fine advice from my "friends" at the apartment: "Sue the furniture store," "That will be David's furniture," "That hand is your ticket," "My dad is a lawyer he wants you to call him." The best advice award went to, "You will get more money if you lose a few fingers." I was sick of these people. They were thinking how much of a nicer place I was going to have so they could bum off me there. These mama's boys started stealing beer from their home and bringing it to my apartment. To be my best friend. Maybe I would buy them a new car when I get rich.

I was off my dad's insurance after I moved out. I did not qualify for Kinney Shoes lousy insurance because of my age. A lady, a good-looking "hot" grandmother, at work told me I had to do something. She noticed I was writing left-handed. I was still good at that. Her name was Tracy. She was the manager of the ladies' "Casual Circle" clothes department. Yep, Kinney Shoes freestanding stores had great ladies' clothing. She asked for my hand and inspected it.

Tracy shook her head. "David, when did this happen? Never mind. You have to learn to take care of yourself." She ordered me, "Go in back and sit down. Do not catch a customer."

I told her, "I can't go to a doctor. All I have is thirty-five dollars. This next paycheck is for tires. I can't drive any longer on my tires. They are not safe. I am going to have a blowout." I said sadly, "I can't go to a doctor until I can pay."

She said, "I thought I told you to go sit down." She made a call and somehow had me on the way to a Dr. Williams right then. Dr. Williams was her nephew. He loved his aunt. Aunt Tracy practically raised him, helped send him to medical school.

The X-ray on my right hand showed I needed some immediate work done. Dr. William asked me to wait while he saw the other patients. I went to McDonald's for a Coke and came back. Dr. Williams and his nurse were still getting ready for me. He took a long time working on the hand. I was sitting in a chair with my hand and arm on an operating bench or table. I couldn't see what they're doing, because of a small curtain device attached to the table.

The doctor explained, "You could not feel anything is the only reason you could have possibly lived with that damage. The pain would have driven anyone else in long ago." The wonderful doctor stayed late with his nurse. He also provided me with some medication to take. He put a nice splint on my hand.

His secretary, whom I had not met, had left at her regular time. She had the bill made out. Thirty-five dollars.

I said and asked, "Thank You! Why are you being so kind?"

He answered with a smile, "Tracy has been telling me about you. I finally meet you live. I get to meet Mr. David Cash. When she called earlier, she asked me to help you out. I would like to do that."

My eyes moistened. I used my always available handkerchief with my left hand to dry them. He gave me some pills thirty minutes before we started. Maybe that was it.

It is because I was young. Life was not this kind. I wanted to clear that up.

First thing every morning, I thought about getting kicked out of my "home" and quitting college. I was building up some hate. I could not stop. Until I drove up to the house to get some clothes that I had failed to pick up. The house looked so small. I felt too big in the house as soon as I walked in. I grabbed the clothes out of the tiny closet and spoke to Dad. He was the only one there. I left because of a tight schedule. I did not go by the house again for a long time. The hate I was building up, I stopped—100 percent over. *No hate.* I was not doing myself any good. Move on. It felt so good. I loved everyone in my family. I had outgrown the house. I totally hold no grudge against my mother. Love my mother. My family. My home.

Later on, I won the color TV I mentioned. It was for selling the most shoe-care products in the district. Fancy name for "shoe polish." A guy in another store had other people putting their shoe-polish sales on his number.

So I responded! In the weekly newsletter that went to all the stores in the district. There were enough copies to be passed around. In the "Assistant Manager's Corner," I posted, "I will take on the whole store! Shoe Polish Contest Rules do not apply. I AM SERIOUS!"

It was great. I was cheered to be the winner. It stopped the cheating. I worked every hour my store was open. Now I had to win.

Plus the real reason, I needed something to sit on. And I did win. I sold the color TV to the store manager.

Guess where I went the next day to purchase a sofa. Yes, the furniture store where I had previously been. I walked up to the sales counter and asked for Mark and told them my name. He came out with a huge smile. Big left-handed handshake.

I said rather loudly, "I hate to bother you, Mark. I want to personally thank you for the above-and-beyond service. You and the delivery team provided the last time I was here." Every clerk was listening.

Mark said equally loudly, "It was our pleasure, Mr. Cash. You did not drop by to only exchange pleasantries. You came as a customer today, Mr. Cash?"

I answered in my regular tone, "I am here now because I won a sales contest. I must have a sofa. I know what I want. Close is good enough. I would like to buy it and go, not walk around."

Mark laughed, walked away from the counter (to the disappointment of all the eavesdropping clerks), and said, "Why am I not surprised?" A random salesman was walking by. "Jerry will take care of you." Mark did not walk off.

I handed Jerry a picture I had sketched. "This is it, three removable back cushions, low-cushioned arms. Not a huge sofa. But not small. My carpet is dark green. So I like dark red. But if all you have is brown or tan, okay? A print with bamboo leaves on dark red."

They both started shaking their heads when I started with the bamboo leaves. I said, "Red." The head shaking continued. "I like brown or tan."

Jerry said, "This is a picture of Master Craft."

Mark said, "That is what I was thinking."

I said, "When can it be delivered?"

Jerry sort of answered, "Give me a minute." Jerry walked over to the counter.

I asked Mark, "Mark, just between you and me. Do you have any of those loss leaders?"

Mark held up one finger and walked over beside Jerry. The two of them began having a lively conversation. A few head nods, the universal finger-to-the-lips secret sign. Mark patted Jerry on the back and returned with a flier. "Yes, as a matter of fact, we do. Folding chairs. Black metal with cushion seats and backs. Limit 4." He showed me the flier. The fabric was either muted camo, truck tire tracks, or fall leaves.

I said, "Just two, Mark."

Mark said, "Very good, David."

Jerry walked up. "Your sofa is being loaded in about ten minutes. You will be first. So expect delivery in under one hour." The guys would be in and out fast. I caught them leaving. The other delivery was near Lenox Square. They wanted to beat traffic. This small delivery was fine. It was the same two men. They were glad to help.

I said, "Amazing!"

Mark informed Jerry of the additional two folding chairs. I was to be surprised at which pattern.

Jerry said, "Oh, two folding chairs. I don't know. May not have enough room. This will take too much time, all the walking and lifting, They are right by the loading dock and all. Well, still, you know, reaching over." He was laughing and jogging away.

Mark said, "I told Jerry if he arranged shipping, I would get the invoice." Mark offered me a job.

I thanked him and explained I wanted out of retail.

He added, "If you change your mind," and handed me his card.

I got the floor model discount! Yes, Mark took care of me with a discount, as well as the fast delivery. When I paid, I thanked Jesus out loud. Down here in the South, when somebody says, "Thank you, Jesus," you will hear: a lot of "Amens" or another "Thank you, Jesus." I heard that. Plus "Praise his *name*" and "Hallelujah."

The sofa was a wheat color with a sort of small squiggly tweed print. Two solid lighter color matching accent cushions. Very rich looking. I got the muted-camouflage-print chairs. I will mention those later. Four would have said, "Redneck." Two, "Very cool."

The sofa was so important. I had no place to sit before. I could not comfortably sit on the wooden chairs. The bed I had to lean back against the wall with pillows. With my feet up.

I was about to kick everybody out. *Everybody*. No one cared. Nobody. I needed to read. Study. Work. I was older or something. Not in years. Don't get me wrong. I liked to have fun. This was not fun.

LEXI AND BUTCH

A week or so after I received my new sofa, a married couple, Butch and Lexi, *called* me. They were here for a concert. It was a Saturday night. I was sound asleep after thirteen or so hours of work. I had learned a way to jam the door from the inside. Plus, I put a sign up on the door, the same color as the door, "NOT WELCOME." I couldn't change the lock, because of the apartment rules.

Back to the phone call. They called and asked to come over. Butch was given my phone number and told me a person's name. I did not remember until Butch said, "He told me to tell you, 'I need to bring twelve Millers in glass bottles.'" I knew who he was talking about. How could I forget? I responded, "Is the secret code ice cold." Butch responded, "Pretty sure." I said, "Do you know where I live?" He went over directions. I said I would be standing on my porch, looking for your truck. He thanked me and asked me if it was okay if he brought a case of Miller in a bottle instead of half a case. I explained we would have to drink twelve.

They also bought some groceries. Sandwich things. Breakfast items. Snacks. No one ever did that before. Everybody always asked, "Got anything to eat around here?" I had to keep bread and peanut butter in my room. My fault for being kind, thinking kindness would be returned. I learned that people take, take, take, and forget.

I guess they were there for about three and half weeks. It was over a month! I was not really sure how long they stayed. Butch was twenty-two. Lexi was twenty-one. They were low on funds. I liked the heck out of the couple. They were a little too much into "God is in the earth, sky, and your soul or whatever."

Well, I needed help! I asked Butch to clear out the freeloaders in exchange for a place to stay. Lexi answered for him, "Say no more." Butch was just back from Vietnam. He ran everybody off. Fixed the lock on my front door with new parts. I never had one ounce of problems again. Most friends believed I moved. I parked in a different lot for a week.

They never bothered me at work. Lexi cooked breakfast for me every morning. Work, sleep, work, sleep—I hit it hard for about the first ten days after those two arrived. Pulled ahead on the money situation.

I gave Lexi money to buy the supplies for the apartment. I left extra funds in the cabinet above the fridge. Lexi kept the apartment spotless and supershiny, washed my sheets, made up my bed, folded the towels and everything, and ironed my clothes. She rearranged cabinets. Bought things I personally needed with the money. She bought a coffee table and an end table at a garage sale. Soon a lamp showed up.

One night, I walked in, and Lexi and Butch were sitting at the table and asked if I needed anything.

I said, "What's up?"

"Nothin'."

I walked over to the fridge and saw twelve new bottles of Miller. I said, "Can I get you one Butch?"

"Sure."

I was thinking "Odd." I grabbed two and sat down on a cushion!

We all laughed. They were so proud of the six cushions they had purchased and tied on to the six dining chairs.

The little things back then made us happy. We celebrated. We went out the front door and came back in to see how I could have missed them. They told the story of finding the cushions. Lexi talked about me sitting down on a cushion and the look on my face. Life was *good*. The beer tasted colder.

Lexi kept plenty of supplies soap, shampoo, paper towels, everything. Butch washed and waxed my car while I was at work. Changed the oil. I kept all the tools in my trunk. I kept some shirts that were too big in the trunk of my car. Butch adopted them. Butch washed my car all the time. Windows on the inside of my car were perfectly clean. Even kept gas in it. I bought him a pair of shoes and her two pairs of shoes with my discount. Lexi had a girl-friend drop by for what was supposed to be five days. Butch told me Brandi was from very wealthy family. Lexi was from just a very rich family. Brandi was on the way home to get back in school. She had left a boyfriend who was from a superrich family, not wealthy. Brandi's parents were "control freaks," as Lexi repeatedly said.

Brandi

Brandi was Lexi's friend. When she walked in. I felt it. She was pretty. *Except*. Her permanent snob face, along with the medium-length blonde haircut. Her having two arms and the way she walked were a big turnoff. Brandi was upset with the apartments not being nicer.

I made a joke about the view the apartment had, "A view so wonderful you could hear it."

That made her mad at me for not doing something about the apartment situation.

I guess! She was used to men jumping.

She did not want to check into a hotel. Brandi was worried her father would find her in Atlanta.

I could not crack her shell. I had no chance. Brandi was a *snob*. So I just cut up and told sarcastic jokes. Later that same night, we were laughing together till we cried.

When we were laughing, telling jokes, and drinking beer, we were putting our arms around each other. Brandi was so far out of my league, no chance. I like her hair. Nice length. Mighty fine walk.

Supershy me. I kissed Brandi on the cheek! She made me.

I was up earlier eating breakfast with everyone. Lexi made canned biscuits, white gravy, eggs, and coffee.

I left to take a shower.

Brandi was washing dishes. She was now the only one there. It was eleven thirty, and I was headed to work.

I said, "Buy, honey."

She just said, "Buy, sweetheart." She had both her hands wet, over the kitchen sink, so she turned her right face toward me and said, "Give me a kiss me on my cheek please. My hands are wet. Look."

We had been up late the evening before. She was cleaning up last night and this morning's dishes. So I kissed her on her right cheek.

She said, "Thank you, I will be thinking about you today. Bye-bye, hurry home."

"Okay, I already miss you," I said, smiling, as I walked out the door.

The four of us listened to music and read. So comfortable being together. I had to go to bed and get a certain amount of sleep.

They could stay up. We played cards and talked. They bought California Red wine, which I really enjoyed, but it triggered my addiction. I drank beer. Not a lot. I had to work? Well, actually, I took off the third day Brandi was here, and I spent the day with her. Yep, I went in ready to bargain for the day off. Al Wilkins, the manager, took any trade in his favor. Cases of Budweiser. Two days working for one day off. He could have taken me to the cleaners for that day off. I showed up for work. Al said, "What are you doing here? You are off today." Al had traded with me two weeks ago. I called Brandi and headed home. We went shopping all day.

Brandi's "family" owned aircraft, luxury hotels, large amounts of real estate along the Shenandoah Valley, and commercial coastal properties, controlling stock in shipping companies on and on.

She will continue attending Ivy League schools. She never had to worry.

Had no chance with Brandi. None. *Zero*. Barely even temporary friend zone. I was just a short-time, funny, soon-to-be-forgotten guy. So I did not even try. I was still underweight. My shoulder blades stuck straight back in the evening. I fought addiction every day. I was a nineteen-year-old shoe salesman.

Renting an apartment with green carpet. Mr. Nice Guy. You could hear the cars on the interstate from my apartment. You could *hear car radios*!

She could choose her man to date and throw him away. It would be Mr. Good-Looking. Well-traveled. Family money. Foreign car. I had a foreign car! A cheap used four-speed Buick Opel. Hers *was* a Mercedes, and it was the latest model.

Lexi and Butch had some friends over. Brandi knew them. They were also heading back to Stanford, Yale, Princeton, or Harvard.

High-end yuppies. Weekend hippies. Ivy League college students. Lots of money. New cars. The BMW was the latest thing. Nice homes.

I figured I was going to be out of place in my place.

This is a funny good story.

Brandi said, "I hear these most intelligent things sometimes, like wisdom from an older person." I wondered what she was going to say. Well, she continued, "I look over, and it is David talking, so wise for his age."

I was thinking, *David who?* Just kidding. I was about to be attacked. This is what they lived for—step on people "lower than them."

One of their friends, Fifty-Dollar Haircut Stephen, jumped on that and asked, "Well, David, share with me some of your great words of wisdom."

His full intent was to put me on the spot. Even a second of silence would make him the winner. To answer with "words of wisdom" was out of the question. I said, "That's okay, Stephen. You wouldn't understand." A second of silence.

His friend said, "Ouch."

More silence.

Stephen came back and said, "Well done, nice, very nice." He laughed and announced, "Don't mess with this guy."

We had been smoking okay Mexican weed. Then Stephen was laughing harder than everybody. Not at the joke now. It was contagious laughter. It was more beer, wine, and jokes.

I rolled a couple of more joints.

One of the other guys put himself in charge of the music. My records and portable record player. He kept saying, "I've got to get this one."

Stephen would say, "You would like to purchase this album. It sounds like you are going to walk out with David's albums." There were two other guys who had some of the best jokes. Nonstop, fresh jokes. One of the guys did a standup routine.

Stephen fell backward in his chair and hit the outside door, slid down, and couldn't get up, because he was laughing so hard. Tears were rolling out of my eyes. I did fit in. I did not feel out of place. I felt out of place with people my age.

I finally had to go to bed and said good night. They decided to go out. As they were going out the door, I heard, through my bedroom wall, Butch asking Stephen, "Stephen, do you want some words of wisdom?" Stephen answered, "Don't do drugs."

Great comeback, killer funny.

Brandi was on the sofa sleeping when I was rushing out the living room for work the next morning.

She woke up and said, "I missed you last night."

I looked over. "You just made my day."

She said, "Good."

I had to get the store open, so I just said, "Buy Brandi," and I opened the front door.

Then I heard, "I'm going to steal your bed when you walk out."

I just said, "Sounds good. It's all yours."

I have told you I had the best mattress. With my messed-up neck and those painful shoulder blades, I had to have it. Plus, it was impossible to carry the load I had to carry without a good mattress and a good night's sleep. Remember I kept my bedroom door locked. No one ever walked into my bedroom uninvited! I didn't bother with the locked door after Butch ran everyone off.

This never happened: the good guy never gets the girl. The good guy always comes in last. The jerk wins. Mr. Tall and Handsome gets the girl. A *nice guy* only wins if he has money. Except this time. Also, I can't write the lovey, lovey stuff very well. I love you. I love you too. Things. I will write it just like it happened. Okay.

Remember the day I left work, Al was working for me? Brandi and I went shopping. It will come up in a little bit, the shopping trip.

A little of what we talked about while on the shopping trip.

We both felt it, *love*, and we talked about it. Also discussed what happened when we first met. She told me she had this thought right out the gate. "Love doesn't care if he is young and poor."

I said, "I am not poor." I was barely nineteen. Brandi was not telling. Twenty-one I found out.

She corrected that statement, "David, even if you had a million dollars, you would still be poor to my father and mother."

When Brandi asked Lexi about whose place. Lexi said, "David is nineteen, but I believe he is older. Like a thousand. Dude is a bit weird. He is so funny, do anything for you. If you can get him to talk, He has been through some shit for his age."

Brandi told me these were her thoughts she had about me after the first day: "I want to be alone with David," "I can't wait for David to wake up," "What time does he get off work?" Brandi remembered looking at me from across the room the first time she saw me. "I felt something beyond wonderful." She was sorry for being snobby; it was her defense kicking in. We had our magical kiss at Phipps Plaza that day we went shopping.

When I found out Brandi was in love with me, I couldn't believe it. I told her, "Yes, I love you. I was only afraid you looked down at me. You are all I think about."

Brandi told me, "I don't look up or down at you. When I look at you or I am with you, I have this feeling that I have never felt before. I am starved for your presence, your touch, and your voice. I can't be away from you."

Do You Believe in Love?

I came in late as usual that last night Brandi was to be here… After a long shower, I was in bed, asleep. I had worked fourteen hours.

I took two showers every day—a long shower at night when I got home and a shower in the morning after I did my exercise; that is also when I shaved. Brandi was going to leave the next day. I was almost glad she was leaving. Not really. The chemistry was too much.

She was two years older. She was probably getting sick of me.

I was skinny and constantly broke. Not poor!

It was nice of her to even talk to me. Sorta. She could play me like a cheap guitar and toss me in the dumpster.

I was in *love*, way, way over my head. I had to let go. It hurt. Now I loved Brandi so much it hurt. Stupid me.

Early in the morning, I had to be at work. The auditor was going to be there. We had to finish up. My promise to Brandi was I would be home at six tomorrow to see her off. Something went through my head at work today; she agreed to stay till 6:00 p.m., to leave for Virginia! Thinking about the next day and seeing Brandi for the last time made for a long day.

Brandi came into my bedroom while I was asleep. She sat on a cushion seat folding chair. I kept those two chairs in my bedroom. Black metal with muted camo fabric. You know the story. Well, I paid good money for that kind of *luxury*.

Brandi was wearing a below-the-knee white silky terry cloth robe. I woke up when she turned on the three-way light bulb too low. The lamp was on my homemade nightstand. She handed me a glass of iced water wrapped in a paper towel.

I drank about half of it. "Thanks, I needed that." I gave it back and moved to sit on the side of the bed near Brandi. I had my T-shirt and boxers on. The light was fine, and she smelled wonderful. I said, "You smell wonderful, Brandi."

She said, "I know."

Brandi and I can talk about anything. We started talking. Brandi looked at me while she talked (she mentioned she recently had her period and she was on the pill). I did not have anything to say, but I was definitely awake, and I knew where this was going. Brandi told me she had not been with anyone since she broke up with her boyfriend three months ago. I had to stop myself from blurting out, "I love you." Brandi had a lot more to talk about. She went on to say I never tried to impress her.

I could finally talk. I said, "What about the pair of tennis shoes?"

She said, "David, you are so funny. I paid for those."

I said, "Hear me out, Brandi. We went to the most expensive stores. Lenox Square and the brand-new Phipps Plaza." I motioned for my water, drank some, and continued, "I noticed your tennis shoes were worn. You purchased four pairs of shoes and an outfit to go with each pair." I was starting to laugh. "I did *not* take you to Kinney Shoes. I was kinda maybe trying to impress you."

Brandi started laughing and leaned over and kissed me on the cheek. Then we kissed a very nice real kiss. It stopped because Brandi was sitting in the chair. Still we were both opening our eyes, amazed.

Back to the conversation. "Nope, you knew exactly what I needed to do before I went home. I feel better about a lot of things. Spending a whole day with you, David, I forgot everything except us." I started to say something but had no words. We sat silent for a minute. Brandi said, "You notice little things. You worry about me being okay when I see my mother again, how my heart is healing after breaking up."

I said something very true, "Brandi, that is a two-way street. When you asked, 'When was the last time you saw your dad?' I was so happy you asked. You even said, 'David, you are too nice to people. you must stop it.' Coming from you, I finally need to do something about people running over me."

She told me a little about growing up. Private schools. Traveling. Her father was hated at board meetings and dinners. Even at church. Tracing their lineage back to the Founding Fathers. Going even further back. Big pictures of men and women in their house. One of great-great-grandfather who served in Congress. Her great-grandfather was wounded early in the Civil War and continued his career as a lawyer. She told me about the battle scenes of the Revolutionary War and the Civil War in the home's grand library.

She sang a song in Italian. We started laughing when I was telling her what a redneck was (I was).

Brandi sat way back in her "designer" folding chair, our legs touching and just started talking. "You opened up something I have never thought about. Well, I have, but I just have never actually seen it. You have to work, pay rent, buy groceries, buy gas for your car, pay bills, right?"

I had no other choice but to place my hand on the inside of her leg where our legs touched. I said, "That is what I do, exciting things."

Brandi smiled and said, "I don't have to work or pay bills. Yet, you are free. I am a prisoner."

Then she said, "You have opened my eyes." She was serious. Brandi continued, "Everything came together. I can see the future at home. I know what I am going to do. I am not afraid of mother at all now. I *have* to go home, of course."

Out of nowhere, Brandi said, "You talk about Jesus. That was weird at first. I thought, 'How can this guy just talk about Jesus? Nobody says *Jesus* these days. Oh no, yuck, a Jesus person.' Now I see you don't care about what others think. You are the real, David."

I said, "Brandi, right now, life is very real. You showed up while I was looking very closely at what I believe."

Brandi asked the big question, "What about this? Are you okay? Is God and Jesus okay?"

This was *not* the best time to talk about sin.

"Yes, Brandi, of course, I'm good! As for God along with Jesus, this is a big *no*. Huge sin. Three thousand years ago, one thousand years ago, a hundred and today. Having sex outside of marriage is a major sin."

Brandi asked with a whine, "David? Are you sure?"

I said, "Yep."

Brandi was serious, and she had tears, "If things were different, we would stay together forever after tonight."

It was true. I was holding her hand, and these words just came out. I said, "I believe God knows that."

I don't know where the words came from. I may have to answer for them on judgment day.

Brandi started singing about her beautiful shoes and the prince she met. Brandi always sang and made up songs.

I reached up and pulled the end of the silk belt on her robe, and the slipknot came loose.

Brandi stayed for eight more days. She asked about gaps in my stories. She wanted to know every detail. She told me her story of a charmed life. I wanted to hear more. She could tell something funny faster than I could. Say "I love you" in so many different ways. "David, it is true. This is going to be my one true love."

The very next morning, I woke up at six o'clock. Brandi was sleeping so close to me I wanted to wake her. I felt great with three hours of sleep. Wonderful. The auditor was going to be there at seven forty-five. I had a lot to do before he arrived. Then I thought I had better not wake Brandi up.

I had promised Brandi I would be home at six fifteen that evening. She was sleeping sound when I left for work. All I did that day was work. Busy, so busy. Beth came by! We were still just dating and not getting married just yet. I was getting flashbacks of last night when I looked out and saw Beth. I just worked, and we hardly ever went out. Let's see how this goes. She just stopped by. Beth was going to watch something on TV I would definitely hate to watch. That was the strangest feeling, talking to Beth that day.

Salespeople at work kept saying, "You look happy today." That was so incredible last night. I need to do something, the same one that sent me to the doctor that was her nephew. I asked her, and she picked out a good bottle of wine and purchased it while I worked with the auditor. She figured it out from that and the way I was acting. She said, "Good for you, honey." I must have turned as red as the Cabernet. I went to the florist next door and took my time, picking some flowers.

I told the auditor I had to leave at five forty-five. The audit was done, so we walked out together.

When I finally got off work, I was delirious in love lust. I was a little early getting home. What a long hard day. I walked in the apartment. Put the wine and flowers on the coffee table. I had noticed Butch's truck was gone, but Brandi's Mercedes was there.

Brandy walked out of my bedroom; her hair was wet. She was in her robe. She stopped, and looked at me for a full minute. She walked over, and of course, we kissed. She wrapped herself around my left arm and said, "That was incredible. I had no idea something like that existed. Where did you come from? I am still getting aftershocks. I can't stop thinking about last night. I can't read. I get flashbacks over and over. I do not want to scare you. I know I can't keep you. I just want to tell you I love you. You are beautiful, and I love you. I can't help it, David, I will leave in a few days. Okay, I love you. Well, are you okay?" Before I could answer (because I was speechless), Brandy said, "Oh, look, you were so busy today, and you thought about me." She saw the flowers. She knew the name of each one. Common name and the type of flower or Latin name.

I turned her around away from the flowers, looked at her, and said, "You are beautiful, and I love you. I had to steal your line. I can't think right now."

From Here

I was not going to write this. So personal. Today, my last time to read through each chapter. I do want to share what can happen.

We walked the few steps to the sofa holding hands. Brandi sat on my lap, her right arm around my left shoulder. We just held each other. Brandi started crying. And crying.

I held her. Gave her my handkerchief. She took it.

She finally said, "It hurts." She really let loose crying.

I said, "I know, Brandi. I feel it too."

Brandi said, "Oh God, David. This is so real."

"Love so real it hurts. Do you feel better?"

"Yes, wonderful. The pain was a good hurt. I love you so much I hurt. Crying was good. What a *gift*. David, beautiful, David."

"Brandi, I felt the pain. When you were hurting, I felt it."

"I know. We were hurting together. I was crying, and you held me. That was real."

"Brandi, where did you come from? This awareness of love is a feeling of what a pleasure *heaven* is."

Brandi moved away just enough to look at me. "David, the pain is the pain we have on earth to reach heaven."

I looked her in the eyes. "Brandi, we cannot feel this amazing without first the pain."

Brandi responded, "I love you so much I hurt. I cried until the pain was never there. David, now all I remember is this immense love. It was not painful. It was too much at once. I could not take it. Look at my hair. I will get you an ice-cold beer. Relax. I want to get fixed up."

That is what I wanted to keep to myself. Now it is in my book. Of course, I am still holding back.

To Here

We both knew it was going to hurt even more and, of course, decided it was worth it. I learned way more than I bargained for.

The four of us went out to eat and danced twice. I drove to an exclusive restaurant near Lenox Square. We were early, so a table for four was not a problem. Brandi asked to go to Lenox Square. The girls went shopping. Butch and I had a few drinks at one of the many bars. We went to a large record store after that. Some of *my* favorites were in Brandi's stack to take home. Brandi hated Stepenwolf when we first met. Not today. She bought me Beethoven, "Symphony No. 9, Moonlight Sonata," and a few more. Each and every day/hour was important with Brandi.

This was our little circle. We really just didn't know anybody else. It was usually just us four. The last few days only the two of us.

The four of us were sitting around the table one evening. Butch had been telling stories about Vietnam that Lexi had never heard. Some stories he could not finish the first time. The second time, he would finish the horror story.

I finally opened up about the miracle when I dove in the water at Murrells Inlet. I do not tell anyone the complete event.

Now it is in this book.

It was good to tell exactly what happened to Brandi and my new best friends. I even went on and talked about the pain when Dr. Yoder put the weight on the tongs. That is a tough memory. Brandi laughed so hard when I started talking about what I yelled at the doctor. She almost choked to death. Well, she was crying and couldn't breathe. I was concerned because Brandi was coughing and had her hand was up, trying to say stop. When she finally caught her breath, she surprised us with the hiccups. Loud hiccups. That brought the house down.

Brandi said, "Laughing. Laughing. *Hiccup*! Laughing."

That was hilarious *every* time.

When the morning sun was only an hour away from rising, we all held hands together for the first time. I prayed. Jesus was in the room with us that morning. We talked about the pain ahead when Brandi was to go home, and we all went our separate ways. Thanked Jesus for our time together.

The day after the audit was complete, I bargained for some vacation time and took off work. Al Wilkins was fine. I had not taken one day off, outside of a trade, from the day I started work back in high school. Never even late.

I went to see Dad early one morning. He was cleaning out the garage. I helped for around four hours. Mom wanted Dad to take her somewhere, so he had no choice but to take her. I went "home" and cleaned up, and the four of us climbed Stone Mountain. That evening, we watched *Billy Graham and Gunsmoke* on my new portable nineteen-inch black-and-white Panasonic TV.

Eight days later. Brandi could not stay another day because of school. She pushed it to the very maximum limit. Her father sent his personal King Air to Peachtree Dekalb Airport to pick her up. Wheels up at 10:00 a.m. Back to normal for Brandi. Someone was dropped off to deliver the Mercedes home. Brandi had to be at a school event that afternoon.

I left at eight o'clock that morning. It was our agreement. I walk out at eight.

Dekalb Peachtree Airport was fifteen minutes away.

I came home exhausted from Kinney Shoes. It must have been about ten thirty. Yes, I made it a point to work all day that day.

The apartment had the front porch light on. My bedroom lamp was on dim. Both cars were nowhere to be seen. I looked. When I went in, their things were gone. I was exhausted. I locked the door behind me and went to take off my suit. I sat on one of the folding chairs. My bed was perfectly made. A pillow was out of place on this side in the center. Under the pillow was a note.

A lot of thanks for regular things…and then, "Don't ever change. You made Bran so happy." The note was long. Lexi wrote the final part and said, "We borrowed all of the money, $145, that you had left in the cabinet above the fridge for expenses. We spent $20 to stock your place." That is a friend. She knew 100 percent I was fine with that.

As you know, Butch had recently returned from Vietnam. He and Lexi wanted to settle in the North Carolina mountains and raise a family.

Brandi was very smart. She just wanted to go home to get in school.

Myself, I worked so much and went to school; I was hardly ever home. Nothing really. Until Brandi arrived.

This was their home for a while. Brandi left a note. The envelope had a tearstain. The note said, "I love you," eight times. Very serious. Yet she also had to be a clown. So funny. She had put $145 in the note. The rest of what was in the note goes to the grave with me. I never saw them again.

I had never felt so empty. When it hit, there was not enough air in the apartment. I needed to do something, so I went ahead and took off my suit and put on jeans with the same white shirt. That was it. I remember going to the refrigerator. Staring into it for a long time. Closed the refrigerator door with nothing in my hand. Sat on the sofa. The pain was too much. Nothing like I expected. I went back to the bedroom and picked up her note which I had placed back in the envelope. I slowly brought it into the living room. Sat back down on the sofa. I held the note with both hands. After a while, I laid it on the coffee table. I could not open the envelope again. I could not read it.

Ten months later, a certified letter addressed to "Mr. Charles David Cash care of the Kenney District Office" arrived from Butch. Lexi was going to have a little boy. *Now*, her family loves him. Lexi's family was into manufacturing farming equipment. Countrywide tractor dealerships on and on. He and Lexi were so blessed to have met me, he repeated in the letter.

Brandi had not dated at all. She was an honor student at an *Ivy League school. Brandi was studying to be a doctor. She did not go to the big Catholic Church. It was her family's church. She found a very nice Baptist church. *You could find her. Not a good idea. Her mother was not liking the doctor idea or Baptist thing, but she had her daughter back home. Brandi and Lexi talked on the phone every month or so; the friendship had a big plus. Five months ago, the two of us accepted Jesus Christ as our Lord and Savior and were baptized. The three of us are a hundred percent in about Jesus. Thanks to you, David.

Butch signed the letter, and Lexi signed after him. Below that she wrote, "He lives!"

In the letter was a cashier's check for $145.

Butch added that he accepted the job with the company of Lexi's parents. They were moving to Roanoke, Virginia.

I felt like I had a home for a little while.

*I knew exactly where she lived and the school she was attending. I even looked at pictures of her home. Her name was not Brandi. She had a traditional family name. It was four names. After long talks, we both agreed not to write, call, or visit. Unbelievable, until it is the only option.

CHAPTER 10

How Far from God Have I Gone

We Were About To Be In Big Trouble

I ENJOYED BEING WITH BETH, MY GIRLFRIEND FROM HIGH school. We began to be together all the time. Her parents hated it. We were eventually married. Beth was so cool and very smart. I loved her laugh. She was not like any other girl. Beth was happy. We were definitely in love. Her parents hated that. Beth was not big on going to church.

Her father was an atheist. Her mother drank a good bit, and I drank right along with her. Sunday mornings strooong Bloody Marys. Beer all day every day. Beth's grandparents' Ballantine beer all day. I fit right in.

When I gave Beth the diamond, her parents invited Beth's old boyfriend down for a long visit! In the hopes of stopping the marriage.

Beth and I had a nice wedding and a good marriage for a while, almost three years. I blame myself. I worked too much and went to school part-time. I drank a lot. I was going to make it financially. I worked to "get ahead."

Beth's parents looked down on me.

I felt Beth leave before we mentioned *divorce*. She was in a relationship immediately after the divorce. Maybe a little earlier.

I would not even date another girl for over a year after the divorce was final.

While still married, I accepted a job as a full-time salesman and problem solver for a fast-growing commercial cleaning service.

I soon opened my own cleaning service in a different part of North Atlanta. Complete Janitorial Company. It was a huge success. Customers liked the idea of a choice for everything. Mats, supplies, windows in large buildings. Economy to premium service. I was growing. I went into a used-car sales trailer when I was training a saleslady. These guys signed up for premium service. My new girl started selling like she was just supposed to walk into buildings and get contracts signed.

My worst account. An old three-story building. The owner called and complained. Listen, he was two months behind on payments when he called and complained.

I went over with Honest Nate, my supervisor. We listened to his complaints. Collected my past due payments.

Dropped a cancellation of service in his box as we were leaving. I had the best customers. I found the best workers and paid them very well.

After promoting Nate to supervise the business, I was able to "sell like the wind." My supersaleslady and I were taking somebody's business. We went after nice new offices and buildings.

We had new equipment because Complete Janitorial was new.

She had the sales tools. Coffee cups, calendars, notepads, and packs of nice ink pens. We used nice color pamphlets with professional photos for our handout advertising.

Benchmark, a large and well-established janitor company, started going after my accounts. Benchmark advertised "three months' free service." Lower prices. Kickbacks such as dinner for six at Steak and Ale.

Benchmark made me an offer to buy my company. A nice price. Not high enough.

If they did not buy me out, I explained, I was going to war.

I also explained that my customers showed me the advertisements with the free months of service. I had not had one cancellation. Benchmark and myself set up a meeting at their Atlanta office.

I brought with me a sales contract listing all the employees, the accounts, the amounts each account paid monthly, and a list of all the equipment.

What Benchmark would be required to do such as to keep the employees and not ever decrease pay. Extra accounts were offered to employees, never demanded. No increase in or cancellation of service without so much warning (this was expected to be dropped in the first round, big deal over nothing, oldest trick).

Three pages. When Benchmark signed this contract and handed me a cashier's check. I walk away.

My number was much higher. Sixty percent higher. We met thirty percent off my number.

They wanted Nate in the deal. I did not care. It had nothing to do with the deal.

Benchmark was terrible at negotiation.

Nat had worked for them before. Nate made out very nicely.

Benchmark offered me a good position anytime.

I hated that business.

I sat in their office and just chatted.

I received a cashier's check along with the signed contract one hour later.

The owner, Jeff, was down from Raleigh, North Carolina, for this deal. He shook my hand and said, "I believe we both got a good deal. For one, I had to stop you. Two, damn you are good.

You are freaking good. Three, damn, David, you were taking our best accounts. You son of a bitch." Jeff was laughing and said, "We have ice-cold beer."

I said, "I have plenty of time because I am unemployed."

I built that business in fourteen months. My intention was to sell it.

With my lump sum of money to walk away, Beth and I bought new furniture and took a vacation. We still had a good chunk of money we were going to put down on a house.

I was working a lot and going to college for a while. After that, I felt like I was really nothing and going nowhere until Brandi arrived. Now everyone had someplace to go, except yours truly.

You will see a trend in the next book. Much larger companies. Very important.

I had changed jobs, plus the small business, while I was married. Still trying to go to school. Dekalb Community College. It was too late. I had lost Beth. Like I said, I dove into school as soon as we split up. Work and school. I was taking a class in advertising.

Quick story. Through Atlanta in the '60s, the bridge over the interstate, next to the Varsity, was made of stone. Two lanes on each side. An arch of stone over each side. The top of the middle arch rock support was a large rock called the Bridgestone. Sometime in the early 1970s, I wrote an advertising campaign while going to Dekalb Community College. The teacher would not give me my work back. Kept putting me off. I chose a tire company. Back then, potholes and blowouts were the big trouble. Not this tough tire, the strong name "Bridgestone." I wrote a complex and complete advertising campaign about Bridgestone Tires. So tough. I had help from my sister Angela drawing a picture of my tire hitting a pothole. I received an A++ for my grade. Bridgestone Tires showed up when I was on my journey out west, or it could have been while I was in Hawaii…

The company was J. Riggings, men's fashion clothing. J Riggings was a very fast-growing company in a fast-growing industry.

I was hired as a receiving clerk. My job was unloading trucks. Checking in the number of boxes against a purchase order. Lifting boxes working on a loading dock.

The warehouse manager looked at my application. He said, "If you want the job, you can have it." That was it.

From the day I had broken my neck to now, I had been go, go, go. Long hours. Suddenly, I had a regular job. Just like that. Eight till four forty-five.

The shipping manager was an idiot. He was my miniboss. I had his job within two weeks.

I became the department manager in a month.

My department was so clean and organized, and the president of the company noticed.

The warehouse manager walked over, got in my face, and said, "What are you trying to do?"

I answered, "This is the only way I know how to operate.'"

He looked around and said, "It looks good." He was mad.

The Shipping and Receiving Department was beautiful. My shipping "log" was perfect. The Receiving Department was smoothly moving into the distribution area.

I was working late, taping boxes for the next morning. Perfect size for the items coming down the line. Something I had implemented. Not really; it was logical.

The operations manager was walking out the back door. The *big* guy. He noticed my department. He said, "Dave, how are you doing?"

"Doing good, thanks for asking."

"Anything you need?"

I answered, "Are you serious?"

He seemed a little taken back. "Yes, what did you need?"

I know I surprised him. I smiled and said, "I need to be the distribution center manager."

Jim looked at me and said, "You are getting your cart way ahead of your horse."

I laughed. "Okay, tell me you have not talked about it."

Jim smiled, shook his head, and said, "I will see you tomorrow. Good night."

The next day, the warehouse manager came in right on time. To me, that is late. He went up front for about thirty minutes and came back to his desk.

I was slammed, but things were running so smoothly. It was a good thing, because a lot of mistakes were coming up from pricing.

The manager, Don, called my name.

I turned around.

Don said very loudly, "So you are trying to get my job."

Everybody in the warehouse heard him. Everybody was waiting on me.

I said, "Don, I am really busy right now."

Then Don surprised me. He said loudly so everyone could hear this, "I don't blame you, Dave. You deserve it."

Don stayed around long enough to show me what he could to help.

I stayed late and emptied his desk and cleaned it with Windex. I even flipped it over. Cleaned everything.

There was one girl who I quickly obtained a well-deserved long-overdue raise for. She helped me get things perfect.

Receiving clerk to distribution manager in about five months! How cool is that? That is about the time my divorce from Beth was final. I had never worked in a distribution center before. I buried myself in the job as the company grew. It doubled and then tripled in size. We knocked a large hole in the wall and took over the next warehouse that was bigger than our first one.

I rented a nice house when I got the manager job at J Riggings. It is next to a horse stables on the Chattahoochee River.

Life is really that good. I met my neighbor, Chip. Chip lived one mile south. Chip dropped by as I was moving in, introduced himself, and asked permission to use the nice-size pond on our property line to go fishing. Of course, I agreed and met Chip the next day at the "fishing pond." Chip and I were very good friends for years. What a guy. You will be hearing more about Chip.

I was riding horses on the weekend! Behind the house was an abandoned dirt road one mile long that went back to the Chattahoochee River. As soon as I wake up *every* morning, my feet hit the floor. I ran to the river and back. The uphill run heading back was a killer for a few months.

I couldn't stand lying in bed. I hated it. Yuck. Jumped out of bed. Ran my two miles. Exercised. Showered and headed to work. I was always early.

RIVER STORY

Good story. I never slept or wasted a weekend now that I had weekends working at J Riggings.

One Saturday or Sunday, Doug Cofield and I decided to take a johnboat with two paddles and go for a three-hour float down the Chattahoochee. We dropped my car at the parking area which is at the end of the float or ride down the river and headed back up to Buford Dam in Doug's truck with the johnboat to get started.

We had a cooler with beer, water, and some food. We took our shirts off and threw them in the boat. Plenty of sun and shade up ahead.

I had plans for later in the day. Doug was supposed to be somewhere as well. We were feeling good. Doug worked all the time, a very responsible man. We went to high school together. This is a rare time, good friends.

The boat was in the cold water.

Doug mentioned that he overheard a lady say something about the horn. I asked, "What did she say?" He said, "I don't really know if she was talking about the horn going off or not or asking if the horn had gone off." Doug and I took our time. We were there for a while. A lot of people were at the park. Doug asked a couple who were nearby if they heard the horn. They didn't know what he was talking about. We decided the horn would go again by now. Okay, of course, they would blow the horn before they let the dam out.

We both had a paddle. Everything was perfect for floating on the Chattahoochee. Within two hundred yards, it was spectacular. The *wilderness*.

I would guess about two miles or so downriver, we started going a hint faster! Doug and I both knew we were about to be in big trouble. We both agreed to paddle to the side and get out. Nothing but a tall red slope and then trees hanging over the water.

The johnboat picked up speed. We could not make it to the side. We were suddenly going too fast. The water washing up on the bank kept us from reaching land. We were bound to the middle of the river. Up ahead, the Chattahoochee split around a long island. We were forced to the right in the raging river.

It was like going down a huge ditch. The water to our right toward the main land was washing high on the steep bank. To our left, very low and toward the island.

We were racing along on top at a pretty brisk speed.

The boat started sliding down toward the island where there was a lot of debris and fallen trees in the water.

We tried to stay on top.

All at once, we both lost our paddles.

The water to our right was suddenly higher than our heads. We were slipping toward the island and a lot of trees in the river.

Doug was at the front of the boat. Both of us were very focused. No cussing or negative reaction. We flew by at the bottom of the trough going by the tops of trees.

Then the island made a slight bend. The trough was going to hug the island. The top of the river slowed some going through the trees.

Doug, sitting up front, yelled over the roar of the river, "Grab this next…branch." He stood up and grabbed a long tree limb that we were still blasting under.

I had already spotted the limb and had the same idea. When Doug stood up in front of me, I knew he was on the same page. As he said, "Grab," I was already on my way up and grabbed over my head, the same limb.

Our boat decided to turn the back around as we were closing in on the limb. Therefore, I was about four feet from Doug, making me closer to land, between Doug and the island.

The johnboat took off and found the next tree. It rode straight up and became solid stuck with the inside facing us. The water was hammering the inside of the boat.

I was closest to the island. We both were in trouble because I had to overhand walk about ten feet without my feet being drugged out by the water below me. Doug fourteen feet.

We both made it to a place but could go no further. We were still twenty-five or thirty feet from shore, and it was the large base of the tree all the way a foot under the raging water.

We were both balanced/standing on a different branch while holding the one we had grabbed, just near the base, and still just as focused.

Our feet were under the rushing water. Not good! We were talking about what to do next.

Doug's feet were in the worst position to stay. So Doug had to leave. He was about to fall backward.

"Here goes," Doug said and then did an amazing turn and jumped/controlled fall in the water. He disappeared underwater, came up, swam toward shore, and found and grabbed hold of the side. He washed down about forty-plus feet.

The side of the island was fairly straight up. Doug got a lucky hold of the top of a tall green pine that was still attached by its roots. He was up and out in seconds after that.

My turn. I was in a twisted spot. I had one option. I had to fall on my right side in the water and turn and swim. I was closer to the shore. I was pretty much on top of the water washing over the large tree.

I hit the water and was turned over on my back by the water coming over the tree. I was pushed down to the bottom and down the river going through limbs. One place the limbs actually formed a square around me while I was still going backward.

When I went far enough away from the tree, I could turn over and swim up and toward the shore. I believe I was about fifteen feet down because the river was only about half full, and it felt and looked like fifteen feet. I had also been pushed out.

Air! I was already in trouble. I locked my lungs and swam up and toward the shore.

I was getting close when the shore was moving too fast. My hands broke the top four or five times the left hand hit the side. I was seeing sparkles and was about to wash into some tree limbs.

I remember Doug grabbing my right wrist and helping me out of the water.

I climbed the bank and sat down and finally said, "Thanks, Doug."

Doug said, "Don't worry about it. I thought you might have a cigarette."

Doug is the best. I could only respond between short breaths, "Sure, do you have a match?"

My head was throbbing. I was still seeing sparkles. My chest hurt. I told Doug, "Give me a minute. I held my breath way too long. I don't think I can stand up, just dizzy. I'm going to sit for a minute or two." I shut my eyes and put my head on my knees.

Doug said, just loud enough for me to hear it, "Party pooper."

Only a few minutes later, we are sitting on the side of the river watching the water raging high and fast on the other side. I was breathing deeply. The sparkles were few. I think they would stay for a while.

The big swell was still coming down toward this side, an amazing sight.

Just then the johnboat wrapped over 360 degrees around the main tree limb it was up against. It wrapped past itself. Wham.

Our signal to stand up and take turns leading the way.

The island was too thick with vines, bushes, briars, and trees. Our thoughts of a happy-go-lucky walk back diminished.

Doug slapped his pocket. "I have the truck keys." We had to hang off the side of the island for miles. We would try to walk on top. Get scratched up. Go to the side again. The water was rising, and the sun was setting. *What a day!*

At the end of the island, we swam across and made our way to the truck. It was still light, but the sun had set in the valley below the dam.

Thanks, Doug.

Well, you only saved my life that day.

I decided to take up skydiving. First parachute jump at three thousand feet was perfect. Second jump, there was *no* airfield when I jumped out.

I was three thousand feet above a recently timbered pine forest. Nice and quiet. In the distance over a fence, ditch, highway, ditch, power lines, and parking lot is my unreachable airfield and landing spot.

"Sorry, Dave, he should have gone back around."

Long story short, I picked the second ditch as my new landing spot. I broke my right leg. I was praised for a great job in that situation.

~

I started partying with the big shots at work and dating some very pretty girls.

The distribution center was doing fantastic. Cost per item, best in the industry. Zero loss. Everything taken care of. No rough edges. I wrote an article for an industry magazine that was published. The size of our warehouse, as I just mentioned, tripled. My office was very professional and efficient, lots of glass.

I have a new car, I am living well. My parents are proud of me.

I am drinking at the bars. Smoking pot and snorting cocaine are all the rage.

I can always find drugs.

The first woman I go to bed with over a year after the divorce is married. We are the same age. She is smart and good-looking. She is also way up in the organization. We can't stop for a few months. For some reason, I am funny and Superman around this pretty and very smart woman. We choose to cool off.

I am always with other pretty women, most often taking them to bed. Never forcing, never taking advantage of them being drunk.

One younger lady becomes pregnant. Her parents step in and quickly set up an abortion.

I take her for the assigned appointment. She comes out in shock. It was twin girls.

Every time I knew I am sinning against God, it becomes easier.

The voice of God goes away. I am listening to the world.

I go to work, keep drinking, and go to another party with the big bosses. Huge plans for the future. I find another girlfriend. Another favorite drink. More coke.

I receive a call at work from a distribution center in another state. A lot more money. They know all about me. I am the only one on the list. They will pay expenses for six months or whatever I need to help get me there. Round-trip tickets for the plant walk-through. Meet the new boss.

I suddenly hated J Riggings. It was time to play for more money here. They would pay. I would move. I did not care. Negotiation *is* my gift.

The distribution center was very busy. Everything was running smoothly. I was sitting in my office, at my desk, which faces out into the very middle of the action, glass on three sides. I turned to my left where a hall from the warehouse to the office started.

My door was open. A girl I had been thinking about must have walked from the front to my office door. I felt her presence. When I turned and faced her, I was sitting down. Listening to the intercom phone speaker on low of different departments. While I drew up a better receiving form, I was deep in thought. Heather was a deep thinker. Our eyes locked for a second. Heather licked her upper lip slowly. My eyes moved to her lips.

I had been wondering about Heather, if I should ask her out again. I started to ask her to come in and sit down. We had been out with friends a few times.

She was not knockdown beautiful but very pretty. Down-to-earth. Nice figure. Smart. Not a lot of makeup.

I could fall forever in love with her. I actually thought I was a little in love with Heather already. We had recently been on a hike together. Just the two of us. I felt it then.

At that moment, I made up my mind. I ignored her. If I looked back at Heather, I would have stayed.

Today, I think about that turning point. I saw the future. I had some kind of vision roll through my mind. I did what I had to do. I quit my job. I was done.

Broken neck. Eight months in the hospital. Back to school and work. Never a break. School and work. One brief time of what true love is. I gave in to the addiction. Drinking and doing drugs. Smoking weed. Marriage and divorce. Climbing the ladder, drinking. Dating a married woman. Abortion. More money. More sex. More drinking. More drugs. I could love her! I wanted God to help me. I wanted to stop and take her with me. Seriously? Stop, David. You just better stop. David, you are sick. How far from God have I gone?

CHAPTER 11

I Have Got to Get Out of Here

Come As You Are

MADE UP MY MIND AND TURNED IN MY TWO WEEKS' NOTICE. First obstacle, get rid of my car with payments. It was new when I purchased it. Now it is used with a lot of miles. I knew I would have to reach deep into my pocket. In the end, the "new" car was gone.

I owned a dented, rough-looking 1964 Chevrolet Malibu. I performed a major tune-up. Flushed the radiator. Replaced all the belts and hoses. It had four different brands of bad tires. So with a set of new tires, I had full confidence in the Chevrolet. I repaired the dent. Replaced some busted chrome. Worked the interior over. It looked "wow" when I was done. I waxed and polished the fine machine. A light-blue 283 V8 with an automatic transmission, tough as nails.

Lee Floyd, a good friend who had been sharing the rent and doing his part, took over the house I was leasing.

My boss at J Riggings tried to tie me up in a lawsuit. Only because he was in trouble. He can't run the place without me. The president of the company stepped in and stopped the lawsuit. The president of J Riggings also commented on how nice my car was coming along.

My Bible, which is dark-brown grain leather, is most important. "I will read it every day I am away." Let's see how that goes.

I still drink and smoke pot. I brought a white regular-size trash bag of my homegrown weed with me. A good idea. I am in a lot of pain, and I will always be in a lot of pain. I have accepted that I am a drug addict—all the morphine, 162 shots straight into my vein in less than four weeks. I am an addict, I have it bad. I am writing notes most days. I never talk about my time in the hospital. No one cares. Satan wants me back. He can't have me. I leave him in Georgia.

No way do I have enough money for an excursion like this. Hawaii is my destination. I am going out, living it up, blowing my money, managing paycheck to paycheck. I am twenty-four years old.

Just so sick of myself. I can't believe how sickening I have become. Putty in the devil's hands. He can turn me loose to enjoy my sin. Only a Savior as loving as Jesus would want me now. This wonderful Jesus at the age of twenty-four saved me from myself. Pulled out of the devil's grip. I am loving sin, loving it.

Remember when I was seventeen Jesus saved me from drowning? I can walk and use my arms and hands. Again thank you, Jesus. I have been blessed with the wisdom of having had loss and recovery. I was given factual knowledge of a God by being part of two miracles. I have seen a glimpse of heaven. Jesus has sent me the very best people in my life. I have known true love. I have felt the worst of pain.

I, Dave Cash, had failed. At this point in my life, I looked good to everybody but Jesus. My parents and my sisters were proud of me. Work opportunities were good. Satan sure was proud of me. I never talked about Jesus anymore. I worried about myself. New car. Nice clothes. In-style haircut. Cool office. How sick is that?

Taking time, I drove west. Everything was the same until West Texas. I hit it perfectly. I will never forget that first sunset in West Texas, when my reset button was pushed. I had to pull over and stop on the side of the interstate. The sunset was too much to take in. That was the real beginning of my trip

The rest of the journey to the West Coast was to drive, pull over, and take in the scenery. Drive. This is such a beautiful America. I was mesmerized. No hurry, I had no appointments to keep. No immediate destination. So I took a few scenic routes. Camped out. Never looked back.

I drove west till my Chevy Malibu found Laguna Beach, California. This is about the same time I ran very, very low on money. Sleeping in the car. Eating peanut butter sandwiches. Pork and beans with white bread, so good. The coast at Laguna Beach is beyond anything I have imagined. The beauty of California proves God is an artist.

Neighborhoods with small perfectly edged front yards. Great beaches and beach walks. Walkways going up into the ocean front cliffs with wonderful views. Health nuts everywhere, always running. So completely different from Georgia.

I got a job busing tables at Andre's, a high-end restaurant on Pacific Coast Highway in Laguna Beach. Whatever was left of my ego went out the door that day and forever. I took pride in the busboy job, dressed sharp. It was white dress shirt and black or dark-gray pants. I thought ahead and brought some very nice white dress shirts and the right pants in the large trunk of my old car.

I took showers in the beachfront parks before the apartment. I soon rented a small apartment. For I first month's rent, I used the money from work. Plus I sold the rest of my Georgia weed to Bob. Rent was, like everything, expensive. I could see the ocean from the apartment's small porch.

I was soon paid extra to go around to the local vendors and buy the best vegetables and fruit. The head chef would give me a list of what was needed. My years of gardening were paying off. I could pick the perfect ripe anything to be used that day. Avocados were always on the list. Yes, it was that high-end of a restaurant. Of course, they took delivery as well. The street vendors would always send tourists to Andre's when customers asked for the very best restaurant. Pretty smart.

After working at Andre's for two weeks, the number one waiter asked me to bus for him. His story is good. Andrew was tall, dark, and movie-star handsome. Bus people wanted to work with Andrew because of the money, of course. Some of the bus crew had been at Andre's for five or six years. Girls were some of the best at bussing. Still, Andrew asked me to bus for him after two weeks. Nobody could complain. Andrew could do what he wanted.

I told him I was leaving in a few months. I don't know how long I will be staying. Three, four, or five months. He said, "David, that is perfect. We are going to make some good money in those months. Let me show you exactly what to do." Andrew took time and went over exactly how he operated.

He wanted me mostly because I was different. From Georgia, with a strong accent. Plus, I dressed very sharp. We used it up. Toward the end of a meal. Usually during the desert. He would say something to me where I would have to answer. We had it planned. He made sure we never over played. His reservations were 100 percent.

People were leaving me extra tips under their plate, sometimes ten dollars or twenty dollars. Once one hundred dollars was under a plate, all mine. Andrew got money put in his hand, and the customer closed it up. He kept all of it. The tip was still on the table. A lot of money in 1976.

Andrew had the best customers, the richest, who lived in multimillion-dollar mansions overlooking the ocean. Dinner was an event at this restaurant. A business lunch had to be perfect. The client must be impressed, a little entertained. Andre's was the place. Andrew was the waiter. It is going to be expensive.

Let's just say you have a reservation for six. Anything more is tacky. Not happening, unless you are a senator and it is a fiftieth anniversary. Andrew will always know your name. If it is your birthday, he knows. He really cares! If you were in last week and you mention someone not feeling well, Andrew cares. He will ask. This is what people love. All right, a table of six. Andrew will take the drink order. Most people order the usual or a bottle of their favorite wine. He will know when he sees if you always require wine. The wine Sommelier will follow him to the table to address your needs. Andrew does not write down the drink or food order in front of the customer.

Time to take the food order. Six different meals, cooked in different ways, different sauces, six people asking what he would recommend to go with what they ordered. Someone will ask, "Is the abalone local? Can you pick mine out for me?" He will stop and discuss last night's sunset. This whole time, Andrew will have his hands behind his back. Remember, he never writes anything down in front of the guest. When he walks to the back, he will write the order down for the chef.

He would signal me with eye contact when to move in and help. A small gesture or nod in my direction meant different things. My exact timing and being invisible was a must.

Andrew was my boss at work. He was right—we made a lot of money working together. I never sweated rent. I had plenty of extra cash. I could go out, pay my way, and enjoy my stay!

Andrew invited me over to his house for dinner three times. I knew which wine to bring! He and his "partner" had a nice home. The only thing that happened was when his friend/partner was showing me the house. He showed me the master bedroom and said, "This is where we sleep. I mean this is our bedroom." He started blushing, and he said, "I am sorry. I do not want you to be uncomfortable." I told him, "Jimmy, I am just superhappy you guys invited me over. I like the way y'all have the place fixed up." I guess it was the right thing for me to say. Jimmy started talking about "most people using too much furniture."

Andrew was a great host. His partner, Jimmy, finally loosened up and was funny. Jimmy had me crying about my accent. Y'all is much better than "You all." Yes, sire. Oh, man. It was hilarious that night.

Yonder, hey, Dave, where? Over yonder. Where? Yonder. Okay. Thanks. Bahahahaha.

Hey, hey, hey, Dave, are *y'all* "fixin'" to go over yonder? Bahahahaha.

"I never say *yonder*," I said.

"Still funny," was all the apology I was going to get.

Jimmy owned a '69 Mustang convertible. Blue with black. A 302 engine, automatic, twenty-one thousand miles! Bought it new. Paid it off in two years.

Jimmy had at least twenty used bicycles. He repairs and sells them like new for extra money. He also makes very nice-standard wood frames, along with custom frames out of old wood. Great idea with all the art in Laguna Beach. He has two saw tables and a band saw, along with everything else.

Jimmy was also an artist. His work was displayed in town. He showed me some of his art. His style, the California beach and mountains spoke to me! Fantastic work. His artwork sold for three hundred to five hundred dollars. He had to pay if someone else sold it: 30 percent to 40 percent. He was fine. Most people bought directly.

Also, Jimmy worked as a clerk part-time at some big gallery. Just to get out of the house.

On his artwork, he spelled his name Jimi, like Hendrix.

I thought he was just a nerd. I needed a slap in the face.

The three of us talked about everything. Politics, religion, Hawaii, prices, trends, cars, just stuff. The art in their house was a gallery. I understood something about Andrew and Jimmy. They were just regular folks. I like these guys.

Each time, I left their house at around 2:00 a.m. Still ready to stay and talk. Jimmy offered me the guest room. I could not find better friends.

Later, we discussed how the gay life and straight life will always be oil and water. Don't try to force it together. I do not like a lot of straight people. *On* and on. We all agreed that the three of us were the smartest people ever. So *there*.

A week or so after I started work at Andre's, a friend named Bob Smith, a cook, was leaving. He had just worked out his notice.

He told me, "You are the only straight person working on the floor." Bob then said, "Come over to my house tomorrow. I will cook you some real food."

I had no idea until Bob told me. *Every* waiter and bus person was gay. The bus girls were my age and beautiful. So sad. The *owner* of Andre's, Mr. Goldberg, liked me; he always greeted me when I walked in. Mr. Goldberg had a meeting when I was there, right after Bob Smith left. He said that he did not want anyone to say anything out of the way to David. Do not make any gestures or sexual comments. David was not to be touched, harassed, or kidded. Talk with him. Make him feel welcome. Everybody agreed and understood why something had to be said.

Only one guy, Randall, said something out of line. I just never talked to him again. No more bumps into me, or even friendly gay kidding. It needed to be said. I loved that job. Always had rent money on my expensive apartment. I had the best friends. I like everybody but Randall. Never had that at any place I have worked before. Where I liked everybody. I told all my jokes from back home.

On a good night, Mr. Goldberg would bring out decent wines. One of the bus girls and myself, along with a few top waiters, always Andrew, and some others would sit around till midnight, talking. Good times.

I was making more than some of the waiters. I had plenty of time off. Three days a week was standard at Andre's.

Coworkers always ask you what you do on your time off. If you sit around too many times, something is wrong with you.

Surfing, snorkeling, scuba diving, hiking, and even mountain climbing were common answers. Kayaking and shooting some wild river, anything to do with water, were common.

Everybody was healthy!

I learned to surf. Walked a lot. California is beautiful. People began to know me. I was careful. Lots of people were weird, bunch of crazies. Bunch of crazy gays. A whole bunch of weird losers. At night, there were areas that gay men walk around in Speedos and not much clothes. I had to make a fast U-turn once. Wish I could *unsee* that.

Gay nude people trails down to the gay nude beaches were seen from the highway. Tourists were in for a shock. I was told where to avoid. I just learned to avoid those areas like you would any bad area. Even good gays avoided those areas.

I did not see my work friends as gay. Just my friends. That is it, I do not see gay at work.

The one guy who was out of line. He wanted me to know he had group gay sex and bla, bla, bla. I covered my ears and told him to shut up. I did not care. Do not tell me that. I saw that guy as pitiful. No one at work really cared for him.

Andrew heard about it and told Mr. Goldberg. That is why the meeting was called. Most gays at work had partners and a homelife. Mr. Goldburg told Randal no one wanted to hear about his private life. Grow up, shut up.

Andrew and I were such good friends I saw nothing but a friend. We would get to laughing about customers and things customers ask. At after-work get-togethers, Andrew could tell a story. "Jimmy, I mean David." That was his favorite. Customers called me Jimmy because of Jimmy Carter and myself being from Georgia. He could do my accent better than myself. Andrew and I would be crying and laughing together. Everybody after work would be falling off their chairs.

Andrew and I talked about the Bible. As you probably know by now, Andrew is smart. He is a college graduate. He asked a lot of tough questions.

Before I left Andrew accepted everything that we discussed and what the Bible says about Jesus as true. Andrew believes in Jesus. He knows Jesus died for him. Andrew *is saved*.

He had a Bible packed away… Now he reads it.

We went to a Christian bookstore where we picked out a lot of books. Andrew bought all of them. Yes, we discussed the part about him being gay. Some of the books addressed that.

I had a regular place to sit before and after work. After a while, people began to be regular stop and chat with friends. Young boys on bicycles to older couples.

Oddly, I was asked for advice by quite a few of the young men. Twelve to sixteen years old about the gay lifestyle. That many! I told them it was wrong, of course. Andrew heard me talking to a young man. I just kept talking. Andrew was fine. Some boys had gone too far and were living in an all-around bad environment. I know I saved some of the young men. I have a lot of stories about sitting on that wall talking to the best people. Straight, gay, young, old, male, female, and one it was hard to tell.

There was this time near the end of my visit to Laguna Beach. Andrew and I were standing on the beach boardwalk, leaning against the rail, talking about Santa Ana winds, bodysurfing, getting a beer, and watching the waves come in—which, in itself, was unusual. We did not "hang out" on our time off. Out of nowhere, Andrew changed the subject and told me about reading the books he purchased. After reading and studying the books, he was feeling remorseful and bitter about his gay life. He was just looking at the waves and talking. I could not believe my ears and was suddenly experiencing a déjà vu. Andrew was silent for a few minutes. I thought it was my turn to say something.

This just stumbled out of my mouth, "I took my girlfriend to her assigned abortion appointment about a year ago. It was twin girls. I will always be a murderer. Something else: I am a serious drug addict. That's all I think about at times." I paused. Then I said, "Sorry, man, this is about you."

Andrew came right back and said, "David, no, you might just, in a way, understand. I will always be gay, or I can't undo my gay. There's the stupidest thing you will hear today." Andrew stares out at the waves, then continues, "Even if I leave this depraved little town, find a new home, and stop my lifestyle, I will never be free of my desires or…God help me."

We watched a massive set of waves come in.

Andrew continued, "Most of us are happy. I was. Jimmy is. Some are too far gone—personal choice or whatever. A percent may be born that way. I don't know. I never even want to discuss it again. I personally want to make a big change. Stop wasting my life. I am considering going north, inland—Anaheim or the Garden Grove area—taking up golf, working full-time while starting my own accounting business." Andrew took a deep breath and stood up. "Get away from this place."

I stood up, and we started walking. I just casually said, "That is going to be the biggest before and after in your life."

He agreed. Andrew was relieved when he laughed and said, "That's enough of the serious talk."

Come as you are. *You must not remain that way.*

I mentioned money, adding he would need to buy a car. Andrew told me he planned to purchase a new Impala.

I told him, "Nice choice."

He said moving costs and living expenses were no problem. He owned real estate. He had built up $160,000 in GM, Exxon, and IBM stock, and he also had plenty of ready cash in a savings account. Andrew offered, "If you ever need anything, it's yours. I mean it, David."

I looked over at his extended hand and shook it. I said, "Okay, if I could offer anything, I would."

He said, "David, you're better than gold."

A few minutes later, it hit me, I said, "Ashley has her new dance studio in that area." (Readers, you will meet Ashley soon.)

Andrew quickly asked, "Who is Ashley?"

After a very short story, I told him Ashley was looking for an accountant. Maybe the fast-growing "guy that left Rockwell" group could use an extra great mind or an accountant.

People in California are friendly.

Some surfers I did not know showed me how to surf. I rented a board and was trying to learn. These two families with kids and everything for a picnic adopted me for the day. I was with one of the moms. She was showing me how to go from lying down to standing up. Her oldest son started helping her. Then the other husband took over. After a while, the five of us adults swam out together. I stood up for a second. I was praised at how great I did. Their kids on shore even said that was good. I don't know.

I felt like I was a fifth wheel. I could not escape. No way. We had to go back out after I was served lunch. My mom instructor just made me a fresh egg salad sandwich *and* a soft mild cheese with tomato sandwich. Along with that, she handed me a plate with avocado chunks and fresh bread. She said, "Eat. It takes a lot of energy to surf."

Listen to this. There is so much to California. The husbands were a tech start-up company. One had a degree in aerospace engineering. He was working for Rockwell. He left them and went out on his own. Rockwell Man met this other guy right here who wrote software. The young company was already experiencing more business than they could handle. Recently, Rockwell the company began sending them business.

Wait, that is *top secret*.

What a day. I learned to surf and learned a lot about California. I love California.

California girls are beautiful. I just threw that true statement in. California *women* are gorgeous. Plenty of people are at the beach every day. All kinds of games are going on.

Friends invite me over a lot. It is a California thing. Bob Smith wants me over every evening. "Open invitation," his wife says.

He knocks on my apartment four or five times a week. "I checked by Andre's. You were off. Figured maybe you might want to do something." That is the way it is out there. Bob has an extra surfboard. He knows the best hiking trails. His wife can cook.

I pay a monthly rate, added to my rent, for a parking spot just off Pacific Coast Highway. So visitors know I am probably home because of my car. We always take my nice roomy bench seats car.

For one, I have a car!

I decided to leave a clipboard with a piece of paper and the message "Home" or "Not Home" so people would not climb the hundred or so steps to reach my small apartment if I was out and the car was still there. I did not work! My friends would tell me, "I saw the note, but I climbed the stairs and knocked on your door, anyway, just to be sure."

People thought about buying a car "one day" in the area where I lived! It is common along the coast. Not in Georgia. We all have a car. Three drivers in the family. Have three cars. Not in coastal Southern California. Very smart. Bob and his wife did not have a car! I was shocked. His wife was Alessia, Al for short. I called her Alessia. She said, "We thought about getting an older car. Now they have a pollution requirement. The price of gas is too much. Insurance and maintenance." Bob and I just didn't need one. We were saving for a house. Bob showed me their superbicycles. I asked around work about who owned a car. Half of the people did not own a car!

Ashley

When Bob opened the front door to their apartment, he quickly put his finger to his lips. Ashley was a new voice coming from the kitchen. Was Ashley ever on a roll? "God, I can't stand him. All men go for big tits and a slutty dresser. Except Bob, of course. Wesley is a boy with a new toy. I hate all *men*. Men are evil." Her husband, Westey, was a car mechanic at the Mercedes dealership. He fell in love with somebody else. Ashley did not have a clue this affair had been going on for a year. Ashley and Wesley were going to buy a house when he told her.

Bob yelled, "Baby, we have company."

Ashley and I became wonderful friends the rest of my stay in California.

Ashley was a full-time self-employed youth dance instructor for young girls age six to fourteen. She had a first-class business.

A week after I met Ashley, we rented a catamaran for a day. Alessa and Ashley put the whole thing together. Talk about fun! It is a California thing, I am telling you. No lying around. Get outside and go.

Not long after the catamaran, the four of us played Monopoly after dinner.

Ashley had too much to drink. She usually took her bike home. We decided I should drive her instead. When I got to her apartment just a few minutes away, I opened her car door; Ashley was too drunk to walk. I put her arm around my neck and walked her to her door.

She started telling me what a great guy I was. She asked if I thought she was pretty. I told her she was a pretty person and everyone knew how beautiful she was.

We finally got the apartment door open and stepped into the dark apartment. Ashley melted onto the floor. I closed the door, found the switch and turned on the lights, walked back, found the bedroom, turned on the light, and turned the bed down. I turned on lots of lights in the hall and bathroom.

Ashley was sitting up on the floor when I walked back down the hallway to help. I was reaching under one of her arms to stand her up.

She reached for my belt buckle and said, "Let's get your pants off. I want you to help me get your pants off. Come on, I am so ready."

I moved Ashley's hands and said, "Ashley, you are very drunk. Put your arm around my neck so we can stand you up."

She said, "Okay."

I got her up and walked her back to the bedroom.

She turned around and gave me a sloppy French kiss, holding herself up with both arms around my neck. It was over quickly. I walked her over to the bed and laid her on her back.

She said, "Oh yes," and arched her back and said, "Help me take my shorts." She had her shorts off in a flash!

I said, "Okay, you just lie down for one minute and rest, okay?"

Ashley mumbled, "This will be so good for me"—and inhaled—"and *you.*"

I said, "Ashley, even better if you get a little nap."

She said, "Then you will take my panties off?"

I answered, "I promise."

She came back half asleep with "I can unbuckle your pants."

I came back softly with "I will help you. You just have to rest for three minutes." I thought Ashley was finally asleep.

She reached over and found my right hand and just slightly pulled it. "Do you think I am pretty?"

I answer in a whisper about a foot from her ear, "More beautiful than an angel."

She smiled. I pulled the sheet over her. She was snoring very lightly.

I quickly got the plastic trash can from the bathroom and put it beside the bed. I made sure she was facing toward the outside of the bed. I had to pick Ashley up and carefully moved and slid her some.

She had a phone on her nightstand. I was going to call Bob and Alessa. The phone rang. I don't know about this. I picked it up and answered, "Bob, is that you?"

He answered, "Yes, is everything okay?"

I answered, "Yes, Ashley is asleep. But she was totally drunk. I am prepared if she wakes up and gets sick. Can Alessa come on over here?"

Bob said, "She left about a minute ago. We looked at the rum bottle. Ashley rarely drinks, but tonight she drank about a half a fifth of rum along with that wine."

I said, "Thank you. Hang on, Ashley is saying something."

Ashley was saying "I think I'm going to be sick."

I hung up the phone. Ashley leaned over the side of the bed just as I held up the trash can. She grabbed it from me. She would have never made it to the side of the bed, much less the bathroom. She kept throwing up *until* she could not breathe.

She put her feet on the floor dragging the sheet with her keeping herself covered, lying down with her feet on the floor. Poor Ashley.

I waited, sitting on a small stool in the corner of the room near the foot of the bed, until she nodded. I got up, walked over, and handed her a damp washcloth. Traded it for the trash can. I took the trash can to the bathroom, cleaned the vomit out, rinsed it, and brought it back with a fresh washcloth. Ashley traded washcloths with me.

I had noticed Alessa had let herself in and was standing in the living room. Ashley was now balancing sitting up. I saw her shorts on the floor and laid them on the bed. I told her Alessa was in the living room and I was going to leave her here.

Suddenly, I felt like I was too big for this small apartment.

I asked Alessa how long she had been in here.

She told me she got here in time to watch me walk across the hall with the vomit. It looked like I had everything under control. She offered to take over now that the dirty work was done. She called Bob and gave him the update. Alessa went in and stuck her head in to check on her best friend. Alessa came back, and we sat down and waited on Bob. I heard the electric toothbrush going in the bathroom.

"Let's get her something to drink," I said to the apartment.

After a while, Ashley came walking in and said, "Something to drink sounds like a good idea. I feel terrible." She got a bottle of Coke out of the refrigerator. The small bottles of Coke in 1976 were better. Ashley had changed her top and touched up her makeup. She looked away from me. "David, I am so embarrassed. Oh no, I can't believe what I said. What I was trying to do? Any other guy would have taken advantage of me." Ashley pulled out a dining chair and sat down.

Alessa was looking back and forth. "Tell me everything."

I tried to change the subject. "I like your sofa. It sits up. You don't sink down like most sofas."

Alessa said, "Shut up, David."

I knew changing the subject would not work. It did buy me a few seconds.

Bob walked in.

Now it was fruit basket turnover. Alessa caught Bob up. We all either went to the bathroom or got something to drink, like the intermission at a movie. The apartment was definitely smaller. I need to rent a universal room stretcher.

I went for the Coke in the small bottle. Ashley sat beside me and held my hand.

Alessa moved to the dining chair, and Bob sat on the love seat.

Ashley started the story where she couldn't walk to the door and once inside melted on the floor and I was trying to help her up.

She moved quickly to the attempted unbuckling of my pants. Every once in a while, she elbowed me to take over while she drank the iced water she had switched to. Ashley finally started laughing.

Bob said, "It's funny now, but thank you, David. You're a good man."

Ashley's head was on my shoulder. She was holding my hand and my arm. She said, "David, you are a good man."

I needed to hear that.

Laguna Beach is an art area. Plenty of sidewalk art shows. I could write a chapter about California and the places I visited. I was amazed at the nice-size homes with small perfect yards.

The beautiful cars—'55 and '57 Chevys, '65 Mustangs and Camaros, a red-with-white-accent '52 Corvette, a two-tone light-blue-and-white '57 Ford Fairlane. It looked new.

Some were second cars. Some were the only car.

Every Saturday and especially on Sunday, the owners pull the prized possession onto the short flat driveway. Wax, clean, and look at it.

So the four of us would cruise the neighborhoods. It was a thing. Look at the cars in the driveways.

My old Malibu was perfect for that. Bob helped me shine it up for the Sunday ride.

I was getting cash offers.

Seven Model Ts were parked side by side at the dead-end road in an older neighborhood. A man in his eighties kept them in a large "garage" attached to a nice home. Lots of Chevy trucks: '45, '46, '50, and '58. The occasional For Sale sign. Buicks and Cadillacs from the '40s and '50s *driving* around. Neighborhood after neighborhood. Some neighborhoods were not much. Some lots to see.

Oh, I almost forgot—kids selling Kool-Aid, lemonade, homemade cookies, and even tacos!

People from the south of Los Angeles love their cars. Sometimes, this may be the only car in the home. They just don't drive the car to work!

Remember the tech families? I called them a few months later. Ashley and I met them at the same place I learned to surf. Ashley was a terrific surfer. They surfed while I practiced on the surfboard I borrowed from Bob. I thought Ashley might see an opening for her dance classes. It was a very open discussion. Ashley would start with the three young girls who were with us that day. Ashley made new friends that morning. This meeting became the dawn of a business venture for Ashley. By the time I left for Hawaii, Ashley had to add two assistants. Leased a second space near the new friends' tech company. A space which the new tech friends located and negotiated the lease for Ashley.

She was teaching martial arts to the boys and dance classes to the girls. Ashley was going full blast. Big plans for the future. She had upped her rates at the *new* location that was being fed by the tech companies.

All the steep hills finally got the best of the Chevy. Something broke. It was either get it fixed or move on. I chose to move on. A tough decision after five months. I had fallen in love with the friends I had made. Real friends. I sold the car; it had seen its day. Time to go to my final destination. I bought a backpack and a very durable, expensive, lightweight, easy-to-set-up backpacking tent. That same Bible was packed for my jetliner journey. After letting go of the car and apartment, I gave everything else to a friend at work. Except for a nice lightweight jacket I had. Bob was always wearing it, so I gave it to him. I was down to a backpack. I took a bus to the airport. Regular flights from Los Angeles to Honolulu five or six times a day. I called ahead, and there were plenty of seats available. I purchased a one-way ticket.

CHAPTER 12

North Shore of Oahu

Do I Have A Story For You

It was late November 1977. Jimmy Carter was president.
The letter *W* in old Hawaiian city names is pronounced like
V. The state name *Hawaii* is included.

Two chapters about my experiences on Oahu and with the
people I met are enough. So much more to write about. I could
write a book about the North Shore. I just hope people will buy
this book. I need a place to live. With a pool and new airplane.

When I was well inside the airport, it was obvious, not that
many White people. Orientals and Hawaiians were the majority.
The hate for me had already begun... Having no foreknowledge
of this hatred had set me up for a few rough encounters that day.
I was a "Howley" (a f——kin' Howley many times) *Howley* is a
slang term used by most locals for describing a White male. Many
locals hated all Whites. Most just hated White males. A vicious
hate. Blacks, Latinos, Orientals, or anyone with a bit of darker skin
were fine. Pretty much only White. In time, I became friends with
many locals.

I am getting ahead of the story. I am so glad to be writing about Hawaii.

I walked out of the airport and took the bus to the North Shore of Oahu. The name of the bus is "the Bus." It cost twenty-five cents—yep, only a quarter—to go as far as you care to go. I got off the bus in Haleiwa on the North Shore. The airport is on the south of the island. So after quite a lot of stops, the bus traveled steadily over the middle of Oahu with fewer people getting on and off.

The little girls in the family next to me started asking me questions. They were "locals," Hawaiians. Their mother became my tour guide.

One thing that stood out was the pass the Japanese flew through when they attacked Pearl Harbor.

The family was nice to me. The oldest of the girls told me about King Kamehameha. It was useful information. The youngest girl got me a small cup of red Kool-Aid and took my cup when I was finished. The best welcome.

A little over halfway from the airport to the North Shore, the bus stopped at Wahiawa. The high point on the King Kamehameha Highway. A lot of people get off. No one got on. We would be going downhill toward the coast from here.

Dole Pineapple fields mile after mile. Then sugarcane. All of the sudden, I saw the North Shore. I felt like I was coming home. I was ten minutes away.

You can bet I closed my eyes and said, "Thank you, Jesus." I said it in a regular talking voice. My "tour guide" said, "Amen."

The bus was in Haleiwa before I knew it. I found a perfect place to set up the tent and watch the sun set. I went to a restaurant on the river in Haleiwa the next morning for breakfast.

The Haleiwa Grill looked like it was about to fall down. It was leaning inland. Eggs and rice for under a dollar. Everything was served with rice.

When I was broke, that restaurant and a few others served two scoops of rice with gravy, "Surfers Special," for twenty-five cents. I ate that quarter special countless times and was thankful. The two eggs and rice became my favorite…

Haleiwa Beach Park

I was energized and excited to be in Hawaii. The North Shore of Oahu is perfect. Back in the late seventies, the North Shore was still full of secluded beaches. Few people and very few stores. I camped and cooked out on the beach the first week. Swim and hike most days. There was too much to do.

Everything I owned was in my backpack. I toured the Island. Camped at beach parks with showers. So easy. Made friends and hiked the popular trails with people from all over the world.

I finally picked up a free-camping permit for Haleiwa Beach Park. There was a nicely maintained baseball field that the locals use. I could leave my tent set up on the sand next to the water. My new home. At the apex of the North Shore.

I had been on the island for less than two weeks. In the afternoon, the police stopped incoming traffic to the North Shore and were announcing mandatory evacuation orders. Sixty-five-foot waves headed this way! This is what I came to see. I ignored the evacuation order.

I was set up at the Haleiwa Beach Park thirty feet from the water.

I packed my tent and everything I owned into my backpack. I walked down the road through the park entrance and across the highway. There was the base of a mountain. So I climbed up the hill about fifty yards and hid my backpack. It was getting to be about dusk when I walked out of the palms and bushes.

I went straight back to the park and sat on "my bench." This bench was usually beside my tent. The ends of the bench were cement. The back and seat were made of four-inch-by-six-inch boards. It usually took four people to move them.

The ocean had been flat all day. After nightfall, no cars were on the road except police. I saw no other people.

A little after midnight, two policemen drove up in the parking area close to me. I stood up and waited. One of the police got out and walked up the stairs from the parking lot to the beach camping area. He said, "*You cannot* stay. *You must* evacuate." We stood there for about a minute. I explained, "*No*, sir," very nicely. We talked for a few minutes. He got my information, including who to call in case I wouldn't show up at the campsite the following day. The policemen explained they were quite busy and left.

It was a pitch-black moonless night. I could see the lights of Waialua, a small town on the other shore. It was well over halfway through the night; the ocean was still flat. It started picking up an hour later. The waves built. Everything escalated quickly. The roar of the surf was overwhelming. The lights of Waialua were gone. Now I could see the silhouette of huge waves including the tops of the waves that blew back. Rooster tail. All this from bright starlight and a little of the park lights reached out into the waves. All of the park lights had been turned on and left on all night. The roar of the surf now was hard to explain. I was standing on the Park bench.

Now I could see the lights of Waialua clearly through the tubes of the waves.

I was living. All this was going on at about an hour before the first light of dawn. Then a lot of angry fast-moving water washed under the bench I was standing on. I mean a lot of water.

I jumped from the bench to a short seawall. As I did, I looked to my right, and a wave was curling *over* the cement restrooms. This was well lit by the park lights. What an amazing sight to witness.

I ran two or three steps on the seawall and jumped down about three and a half feet to the parking lot of the park entrance road. I ran and looked back. I was halfway to the main road. The bench I was standing on was slammed by the same wave and thrown on the tip of the wave like a toy. Yes, yes, yes. I put on a burst and flew across the road into the palms and up the foot of the mountain.

I saw the light of Waialua through the tubes of the waves. A wave breaking over the bathhouse. On and on, I relived every detail of the bench being tossed in the air.

It was too dark to look for my backpack. I waited for the first sunlight just minutes away, walked up the side of the mountain, and got in my backpack for some *food* and water. I found an almost level spot and popped the tent open. I placed the foot of the tent up against a palm with the tent lying uphill, so I wouldn't roll down the mountain. Crawled in, zipped it up, and went to sleep to the *roar* of the waves. I woke up to the *roar* of waves a few hours later. I had smashed bread for breakfast. I packed everything back into the backpack. Hid it away. I was well rested. Dropped down to the highway.

That day, the police didn't bother me. If you were still there, you were allowed to stay. The water had come across the Kamehameha Highway in a lot of places. The waves destroyed some houses and damaged many others. Sadly, some people died.

By late morning, the tide had moved out, moving the massive waves with it. Now a safer distance. Water was still coming over the highway every so often. Not too bad. Continued doing damage. Not anything like predawn.

It was easy to get rides up and down the North Shore. All you had to do was walk, and locals would even stop and pick you up, always asking, "Did you stay?" Emotions were high. The radio reported the largest waves over sixty feet. I could feel the excitement from looking at the waves and observing the destruction of the hour before dawn. I was up and down the highway all day. It was a bonding thing.

I made some friends that day. One local all-muscle Filipino guy, when he was dropping me off, said I could borrow one of his surfboards! Gave me his phone number. I took him up on the offer until I bought my own board. A lot of the plants around his house were well-maintained pot plants blending in with other plants. Still easy to see. The police did not care. None, zero. Oh, he hated White people.

Something about that day. In Waimea Bay, the parking lot was totally washed out, and the water had washed across the highway toward the Polynesian Cultural Center. I climbed the big rock on the left side of the parking lot. The waves were incredible.

Waves were still fifty-five and sixty feet at Waimea Bay. A few surfers were out. There were television vans with their cameras set up.

I got a ride to the top of the mountain and looked down at the waves coming in. I went as far north as Sunset Beach. What a view. This was beyond belief.

I sat next to some strangers. Others just gathered around where we were sitting. A sandwich shop, just a hundred yards down the road, opened for a few hours.

Someone was passing around some local weed.

Of course, I held up both of my hands and said, "No, absolutely not." I also said, "Another thing: that is not a good idea right out in the open." I got up to move.

Haha, I am kidding. I took a hit. But I did not inhale! Wow, now that was funny.

Okay, stop it, Dave. I smoked some of the locally grown weed. Okay, I had been smoking some of the local homegrown and drinking beer almost every day since my arrival. Man's got to celebrate. Everyday?

A man and his wife who gave me a ride a few hours earlier stopped and sat with us. The couple remembered my name! They brought a cooler packed with beer and started handing them out. It was Bob and Carolyn. Carolyn handed me their phone number. Bob said, "Call in the next few days. It's not like we can call you."

We were so close to the waves. The crashing sound of the waves was on top of me. When you talked, you had to lift your voice over it. The people who stayed that night brought up this day many times over the next month.

The reason I had my own cement and wood bench: I picked up the trash in the Beach Park camping area. Usually, just a few beer cans, but some days, it was a little bad. The park manager gave me the best camping place. He ignored the expiration date on my camping permit. The ultimate was my own park bench beside my small tent. I really did not like the trash sitting there.

A story about the first time someone took my bench while I was gone: a group of surfers. The park manager drove up and screamed at them in broken English to "put it back exactly where it was beside my small tent" while mainly using sign language.

The surfers argued with the park manager. There is one word the park manager knew: *permit*. He started saying, "Permit, permit, permit."

The California surfers were trying to save face. They moved the heavy bench but not exactly where they got it. They started to walk away.

"No Camp, Leave."

The police pulled up.

I walked up and stopped in the parking lot, leaning on the seawall. Watching all this. Everybody was watching this.

The police understood the park manager.

The police told the four surfers to put the park bench back exactly where the park manager instructed, or they would have to leave the park. The camping permit would be canceled. He adds, "It would be a wise choice to put the bench back, young men."

One of the surfers spoke up. "Yes, sir, that sounds like the best plan."

This story would be passed on from camper to camper when anyone started to take my bench.

Some days, I would see where it had been moved and put back.

Matsa

I had an older Hawaiian friend named Matsa. He would stop by and visit me at Haleiwa Beach Park. We enjoyed talking and drinking beer. He invited me over for dinner. He cooked out on the grill, steak and fish. His young wife was in the kitchen, making special side dishes. What a great host and hostess. Their house was magnificent. Wonderful view.

One day, Matsa said, "It is okay with me if you use my name if you are ever in trouble." I responded with "Thank you" and "What good will that do?" Matsa just slapped me on the back, and we kept on talking.

I was told that I was the only White person he had ever talked to. I asked Matsa, and he confirmed that fact was *false*. He was sort of the local *marijuana boss*. He organized local growers and helped fix prices. Firm. No grower could sell below these prices. This was pretty much true across all islands, even if someone wanted five pounds. *No discount.*

This is what happened when California buyers came to Matsa eight years ago—asking and asking for discounts. He would no longer talk to them. He was the only one to approve a big deal on Oahu. There were other local people like him on each island. It was organized at that time. They had to talk to Matsa's "guy" who said *no*. Because he was sick of them not taking his no. Matsa was a gentleman. No discount. He liked not talking to White people. So I was the first White guy in about eight years. Like Matsa told me, "The next White customer is waiting." Plenty of you, not enough Hawaiian gold." Matsa was also the north island crime boss.

Not being born rich or having acquired great wealth, I must work. A full-time job was out of the question. I did very well getting construction jobs through Manpower Job Services in Waipahu. Waipahu is approximately halfway to Honolulu. Usually a forty-minute bus ride on the Bus. At first, I made just enough to get by. One company offered me more money to work during the next set of waves. I quickly told them I could not do it. They were not upset and seemed to respect my decision. I started working directly for them after that.

Sometimes, One Call Construction would drop me off at jobs and give me a helper. Building decks, cleaning up construction work, digging footings, and a lot of roofing work. They would always buy my lunch and were always glad to see me. Whenever I called, it was, "Glad you called," "Perfect timing," "We were just talking about you."

I would take off and not work for a week, ten days, three weeks, or more. Then I'd work for four, five days, a week, or more. These guys gave me a Datsun truck to drive back and forth a few times. I could take hot showers in a couple of the houses. I took off and did not worry about them. Zero. They did eventually ask me to work through a few weeks at a good rate. I chose to do so. I needed a lot of money!

Having been on Oahu for five months at this point, I had a business idea!

Something I always do is help people. Yep, I still do. Anyway, early on, I found people at the end of their road camping out back in the woods near the legal camping areas, rarely taking a shower, stealing from cars and tents. really sad. I was able to get help for some of these sad people.

Here is the story of just one of three people I took to the hospital... Stan was very sick and could not stand on his own. He came over to surf a year ago. The whole area around his tent smelled bad. He told me he had to have some dope. Heroin. I brought him beer for a few days. He would not eat. Stan asked for bourbon. He guzzled the beer. I promised to bring more beer and some weed if he would take a good shower. He had to use soap and shampoo. I went by the church cupboard and picked up some clean clothes. I took him on the bus to the emergency room. Stan was a very sick drug addict. I saw infected needle tracks up his arms from where he had been scratching them.

As we were getting near the hospital, he asked why I was doing this for him.

I said, "I don't know, man. Let's just say Jesus sent me."

This drug addict and thief said while kind of laughing and kind of serious, "You just helped me for no reason. There is no Jesus or God."

I did not feel like getting into that conversation. I just said, "Somebody, which is you, ripped me off, Stan. You stole every-thing, including my new backpack. I saw some of my stuff in your tent. You were easy to find. I did not call the police. I brought you beer, weed, food, and clothes. Your sores are infected so bad that pus is running out. You throw up, drink, and throw up. You took a shower, and you still have dried shit on the back of your leg. Stan, you can hardly breathe, walk, or even stand."

Stan admitted he ripped off all the tents and cars. It all went to the buyers at the same flea market.

I was getting tired of this guy. I said, "You made the decision to go to the hospital."

He was angry. "It was your idea."

It was our stop. I said, "I am going to make sure they take you before I head back."

Stan replied, "I need help getting in. I am sick."

Then he looked up at me. Man, he *was* sick.

I thought he was going to say, "Thank you."

Stan looked at me and said, "I hate you."

I walked Stan in and sat him in a chair.

Stan said to no one, "Yes, I know," like he was talking to a person. Then poor ole Stan was talking to Clifmon or Clif Man? Stan said, "You are messed up, Clifmon." I think his real name was Cliff. He mumbled until he was too sick to talk. I had him checked in.

He was in a wheelchair, and a male nurse was starting to push him down the hall away from me. I had already turned to leave when I heard Stan or Cliff, whatever his name, shout, "All right." Immediately after that shout, I could hear dry heaving and throwing up.

I picked up my pace. Hit the door, gone, as fast as I could.

Living in Oahu was very healthy. As long as it has been since my accident when I arrived on Oahu, I still could not do simple things with my right hand or side—throw a football, play tennis, or throw a frisbee or any kind of ball. My right arm was still uncoordinated and weak. My shoulder blades still stuck out late in the day. The muscles to hold them in always hurt. Back in Georgia, I did the recommended exercises, and I worked out. Nothing helped.

On the North Shore, I swam in the ocean every day. I swam when I come home from work. My work was always lifting and hard work. This lifestyle was really helping. I felt healthy. No red meat. Usually eggs or fish with vegetables and rice. It just happened. You just can't swim, so many times, for eight or nine hours in a day and eat poorly.

I explored the island. Sometimes, I went alone but usually with a friend. I even hit all the tourist places. Took many trips to Honolulu and Waikiki. Lots of hikes in the mountains. I camped on the south side. One place, wow, Hanauma Bay. What a find. Went Snorkeling for three days in a row. Lots of currents! This place was like another world. Octopus, turtles, millions of fish, and beautiful corals. Always went snorkeling out deep and in the currents with a friend for safety. Only ten miles east of Waikiki.

I am jumping around a lot.

As I had a very durable and easy-to-set-up backpacking tent, I camped and cooked out on the beach endlessly. I soon came to realize I had more friends here than I have ever had. Warm Springs became second place. I met people from all over the world. I was invited into a lot of homes. I did not care. In a conversation, I told the truth. I did not care. Like in this book.

An interesting person became a welcome visitor.

I enjoyed thought-provoking conversation with an open mind! I became a better Christian. I would listen to what others believe without judgment.

That is how it works. Most people like to discuss things. Not argue or persuade and push.

My Buddhist Friend

After walking through a large sugarcane field and crossing a dirt cane road and a short walk-through the palms, there was a store. Beside the store was an open-air church. Behind the store was a Chinese neighborhood scattered through the woods and jungle. The church had exceptionally well-polished nice pews. Also a pulpit raised up a couple of feet. A wall behind the pulpit.

No roads that I could see. An old dead-end dirt road with grass growing in it, stopping at the store. It was obviously cut out of the palm jungle for deliveries. I never saw cars parked in this nice area.

A neighborhood with a store in the middle of nowhere and the church. I am sure it has something to do with seasonal work in the sugarcane and pineapple fields.

I would sit in the church on many occasions and sip a cold Chinese beer and eat food from the store. The church looked abandoned except it was so well maintained. Even with all the sun and rain. One day, a man, twenty years of age, walked over while I was sitting in the church. He stopped and stood. Made a slight bow. Explained that he was the son of the preacher of this church. He gave me his name. I gave him mine, and I said I would leave. He said I was welcome to stay, always welcome.

As it went on, this was a Buddhist "church." This man became a good friend. We talked a lot. We both had questions about the other's religion. About God. I mean we sat "in" that church and had the best discussions. I went and visited with him often. He confirmed the seasonal work. This neighborhood was huge in size. It went as far back as to the side of the mountain. Some of the families did have small cars and trucks. There were a few narrow roads.

Black Dog

One Filipino friend brought his wife and very young son and daughter for a Sunday picnic. I picked out potato salad, some rice, and two pieces of meat. There were two choices of meat: fried chicken and what I thought was a small lightly breaded pork chop. I was already eyeing the pie. I was eating the potato salad, having a blast. These people loved my accent. We were comparing stories about where we were from. How life was different.

I picked up the meat, took a big bite, and started chewing.

I looked at the meat and then at my friend.

He put a chicken leg on a paper plate and gave it to his five-year-old daughter.

She walked over, put the chicken leg on my plate, picked up the meat, and took it away.

I swallowed, drank some tea, and asked, "Black Dog?"

My friend just nodded. Tried to apologize.

I said, "No, now I can say, 'I have tried Black Dog.'"

The chicken was fantastic. Everything was very good.

The little girl wanted to sing for me. So we all listened to her. She sang in English and then in Hawaiian.

We were soon on the topic about God, Buddha, Jesus, and what we believe.

His wife was good at conversation.

This is just crazy. I had plenty of beach chairs along with the park bench. Tourists left them on the beach. Because after ten days or two weeks, it was time to *fly* home. I kept a few of the best ones. The beach chairs were not crazy. This is what was crazy. Johnny and his wife, Sharon. What I got myself into!

People would be sitting on my bench when I would come in from swimming, surfing, or maybe hiking. They would usually have some cold beer. I would arrive "home" untie a few nice beach chairs.

This is a different kind of story. Johnny had been stopping by and asking some questions about jealousy, superdeep love, and a marriage lasting a lifetime. So when he showed up with his wife, I was happy to meet her. Till Sharon came a little closer. She was upset. Not unhinged, furious, and outraged. She told me that I gave her husband marriage advice.

I remained calm. Explained I never give advice unless asked. Absolutely never. Her husband only asked what I thought about those things. He talked about them. I listened. We did discuss it some. He never asked for advice. I would discuss anything with her. We must be totally honest.

How could I help? Me, Mr. Divorced and running away from relationships.

"Your husband can stay or take a walk down the beach." Her husband patted her on her leg, got up, and said, "I will leave you two alone." She was livid. I did not see this happening. What did I get myself into? He was moving it. Gone. Just getting it down the beach.

Maybe I will join him. How did I get into this?

"What am I supposed to do?" That is me asking the question to Sharon. We sat. Sharon was staring at the now-distant husband. *Distant* could mean two things.

I finally said, "We may as well talk." I was braced for being hit in the head or something when I asked, "Why are you so mad?"

She came back with, "I always get mad at him. He knew I would get upset." Her honesty with me surprised her. In for a nickel in for a dime, I was thinking. I asked, "Why didn't you yell out or stop him?" She answered, "David, Johnny has changed just a little. All good, I think it is because he drops by and you and him talk. I did not stop him, because I wanted to see what was going on. I asked him, and he told me you and him talk about things that most men are afraid to talk about, like marriage, staying in love for a lifetime. Just seem strange for men. So I wanted to talk to you."

I said, "We also talk about surfing and trucks, guy stuff." We kinda laugh. This feels weird to me. Silence. It was a stupid attempt at a joke. Sharon said, "Oh, God, I don't know. It's just Jesus, David. Look, I mean, yes, we are both thinking about our marriage. Not talking to each other about it. He can talk to you, which is unusual or whatever. I can talk to my friends which is fine for me to do. Not him. Okay, let me start over. All the way over."

Sharon "spilled her guts." She talked. I drank beer and listened. She talked and talked and talked. She finally said, "There he is." I looked. Johnny was still twelve minutes away. Still a mile down the beach.

Sharon kept talking, "I am definitely not mad anymore. I don't want to be the slightest bit mad at Johnny ever again. How stupid. I was my mother. She was miserable and made Dad miserable until he died." Sharon said, "Thank you, David, my new friend." I said, "Sharon, my new friend, I never said anything." She looked at me. I went on, "Besides, unbelievable, you don't say, I had no idea, keep going and other such." Sharon looked at me in amazement, got up, and walked to meet the love of her life.

Winds up. All I had to do was listen.

We were all starved, so Johnny drove us to the Sunset Beach Sandwich Shop, his treat.

It took some work. Sharon decided to get professional counseling to work on some deep inherent problems. Three weeks and seven sessions, *boom*. Sharon was done with the counseling. Johnny went to the last two sessions with Sharon. Then he went to two counseling sessions. They also removed toxic friends.

I was the guest at their house for lunch the next day after the three of us were at "my place." At first, we laughed and had a lot of fun. Deep serious talk started after a while. I was dropped off at the campground just before dark. I was offered a bed to stay over, but it was too early in our friendship. Sharon and Johnny were close friends for the rest of my stay. Dinner at their house often. Cookout at the beach with some friends a few times. Sometimes, they had friends over while I was at their house. Sharon and Johnny helped me set up my house later on when I rented one. They found a church to go to. Made new friends!

Free Bird

I was extra-superbroke. Really happy. Camping at the Haleiwa Beach Park. I had only been in Hawaii for a month or so. A couple invited me to dinner in a few days. A certain date! It was important because they just bought three tickets to the Lynyrd Skynyrd "Free Bird" concert. It was at the Blaisdell Arena in Honolulu. They said I had to go to the "Free Bird" concert because the song reminded them of me. Skynyrd dedicated the last song to Oahu and the state of Hawaii, the "crossroads" of the world. The opening band was not very well-known out there, Charlie Daniels Band. What a show

Kaena Point

Another random story. Three friends and I went on a hike in the mountains. We started early in the morning, across from Mokuleia Beach Park. This is a great place to hike. Lots of waterfalls; tropical plants; and wild fruit such as bananas, papaya, and guavas. Some small groves. Magnificent views of Kaena Point, the most western point of the island. We would be able to see the north and south views of the mountainous point. This was an all-day hike, very steep in some places. Also, gliders cruise the mountainside. Perfect hike with plenty of fruit. We climbed to the top and walked the ridge. Spectacular views of two shores.

Watching the sun, we agreed it was time to head back. On the way down, we came across a small grove of macadamia nut trees. The nuts cracked right open. We all ate some. Um, good. Tasted delicious. Next thing I knew, I was on my hands and knees crawling. Delirious. I didn't know where I was or how long I had been down. I looked up from looking at the ground. Everyone was down. Guess what we learned the hard way. They may be delicious, but macadamia nuts are poisonous until heated or baked to a certain temperature. We all finally got back on our feet. We were glad it was downhill from there. We made it to the bottom of the mountains and out of the forest at the last light.

I was thinking, "I would like to live in a house on the beach."

Time to talk about the business plan. I was not trying to start a Fortune 500 company. Just a supersmall business so I could rent a house on the North Shore, where I could better enjoy the remainder of my stay. I would like a nice-size, steady income and to live in a house on the beach, not across the street from the beach. Be able to help people. Buy a good surfboard. Eat fresh fish every day. I would like to return home with a minimum of two thousand dollars. Looking forward to doing all of this. Especially starting a business.

Waikiki

I have been to Waikiki a lot. I have looked at the "jewelry stands" which sell coral and shell necklaces, along with bracelets and earrings. I made some hard-earned money in construction and put some of it away. Remember, I said I had a business plan in mind. This is what I was working with. I would take further action.

I packed my tent and backpack and took the Bus to Waikiki. Rented a nice hotel suite. I found the perfect place, still expensive even at weekly rates, in a nice area of Waikiki. Just a street back from expensive hotels. Beautiful view. Two rooms, bedroom and living room. One room would have been a lot cheaper. A cheap hotel would have been a lot cheaper and depressing. I was going for a big win. The living room with the desk work area was important. I planned to do a lot of studying and write some letters as well as work. This was a good decision. Money well spent.

The next day, I purchased new Beachcomber Bills sandals. My old ones were looking rough. I bought some in-style surfer shorts that looked better than I thought. A pair of nice lightweight dress pants. Next two white short-sleeved shirts and some cotton Hawaiian shirts. Next stop, the barbershop. Just a trim. Looking sharp.

I was a man on a mission. I also purchased a new, perfect small backpack. Pens and a new notebook. I saw a book about Paul and the book of Romans. Had to purchase that. Food, beer, and coke for the small fridge.

Next day, I called the phone number that was posted on the side of over a third of the jewelry stands in Waikiki.

I took a job selling trinkets or jewelry to tourists.

Standing up in a small booth on the sidewalk, surrounded by other booths selling pretty much the same thing. I made straight 20 percent commission. That is what most booths paid.

Tourists went from booth to booth shopping. I only had a few seconds to get their attention. "This matches your beautiful eyes," "What lovely hair. Try this," "Great tan. This is perfect." I always put a coral necklace or something expensive in their hand. It sounds cheesy, but it worked.

If it was a slow time of day, I walked outside my stand with jewelry in my hands and invited customers to my booth. All kinds of techniques.

A slow mover was Orange Coral. It paid a bonus. I named it Sunset Coral, and I sold it out.

I was making very good money! More than enough to pay for my hotel, new clothes, and fine dining.

The plan was to meet the owner and have him work with me on a North Shore project. Impressive sales would stand out.

I checked to make sure I was getting credit for my supersales. I was *not* just a booth number.

An employee came by every day to pick up the money. We would turn in a list of each item we sold, the price, and totals. We would check this against the remaining inventory. This procedure was never rushed.

The next morning, someone would restock, and we would sign for the new inventory. Okay, I was getting noticed. She said, "David Cash, number one in sales four days in a row." Okay, that must have been my pep talk. Plan is working. Plus I am making plenty of money, plus having a grand ole time.

This same person would always make sure we were not stealing anything. It was always four of this, six of that, two of another. Start of every day, the exact same thing.

Horrible waste of space.

Some things did not sell. Ugly. Some things I would sell out of.

As soon as the inventory clerk left, I took all the "never in a million years" sell down and put it away. I made a great display of the good items. The coral was different even in the same color. I always put the ugly items back in the evening. I had the best-looking booth. Six days of top sales brought the owner out to restock my booth.

He told me I was selling quite a bit more than any other booth.

I told him what I was doing with the ugly stuff.

He told me not to do that. That he had to sell it. I said, "It is priced at three dollars. It is horrible. How many did you sell last week?"

He said, "I doubt very many."

I waited.

Brandon updated his answer. "If any."

I said, "Every inch in this booth is too valuable, pull it out of every booth. Make it a free gift for every purchase over thirty dollars."

Brandon said, "I can't."

I said, "When you walk away, I am pulling it down. I am just being *honest* with you. I would like to have some extra coral necklaces and bracelets to put in that place." I was making sure he realized who he was dealing with. Bahahaha.

He could say, "Get out of here."

Brandon said, "I brought some extra Orange Coral. Will that work?" He could not have said a better color. In a few days, all of his booths had a sign saying "FREE GIFT" in large print and "with $30 purchase" in small print. Things were looking good.

A couple of rough people I knew from the North Shore. I had not seen them in a couple of months or more. Vic and Kelly, they saw me.

They were looking very worn. I let them have the key to my hotel suite. Told them to get a long shower and order some room service. They were definitely hungry. I was not too worried. It was a limited menu room service.

I also told them they could wear my old clothes while they washed their clothes.

I had picked a room on an upper floor with a washer and dryer at the end of the hall.

I gave them a stack of quarters.

I told Vic and Butch we would go out that night.

Vic had very bad teeth and was kind of ugly, very smart bum.

Butch was short and crippled on his right side and cussed with every sentence. Bum.

The two were always getting in trouble.

When I got off work, they were cleaned up and ready to hit the town. They cleaned up very well. Vic had on one of my white shirts I said he could not borrow. I really didn't care. It looked good. We were already laughing. I took them out to a bar that served the best hamburgers. I bought Vic a nice T-shirt with a *big wave* that said Waikiki on it.

They told me it would be a good idea if we brought home a case of Budweiser. It felt good to do that for these guys. They stayed on the sleeper sofa. In the morning, Vic was on the floor. I let them stay all day and another night. I gave them both twenty-five dollars the first morning and asked them to not stop by the booth. They said it would cost another twenty-five each. So funny. I did not fall for the extra twenty-five. Vic bought new Beachcomber Bills. Kelly stayed in the room and slept, watched TV, and ordered room service all day. When it was time to go, they went on and on, "Best time," "I hung the moon."

I felt kind of sad and glad seeing Vic and Kelly walk away. They were camping somewhere.

Just two happy guys.

Back to work. My sales went through the roof. I had short stories for customers when it was slow, always a big sale. Most of my sales were over thirty dollars, anyway. I asked Brandon to stop by my hotel suite. Eight o'clock in the morning. I explained why I needed him at the suite. That was a business suite. I also wanted Brandon to see I knew how to live and was not a slacker.

When he showed up, I had maps of the North Shore laid out all through my living area, desk, and table… I also had the hotel deliver coffee, sandwiches, and doughnuts. Brandon was prepared. He had addresses. Brandon took four nice maps with him. A gift from me. We had one address triple circled. A few double circled. We headed to my stand together still talking. A perfect meeting. No wasted time.

Next day, Brandon bumped up my inventory, and he brought his wife, Lisa. She was 50 percent of the business. Lisa was fired up. Mad at Brandon for not bringing her to the *big* meeting. She thanked me for the beautiful maps. Lisa told me that she and Brandon wanted to do something special for me, anyway. "We hate to lose you selling in town," they said on and on.

These two were opposites.

I was ready to get back "home" to the North Shore. I mentioned the place we triple circled. Sunset Beach.

They invited me over to look at inventory and talk. Brandon had tried North Shore before and been ripped off. He told me horror stories. Sunset Beach was stuck in our heads. We had a place to start.

Brandon went out first to check out the address. Perfect. He talked to the owner.

I sold at the stand for a few more days. After work, I would go to Lisa and Brandon's house, planning and picking out enormous amounts of jewelry. I paid for some; some were consignment. His whole living room and dining room were pegs with jewelry, stacks of boxes, and packages. The selection was fantastic. We were all fired up, excited. All of this inventory eventually went into my room that I will rent at the "triple-circled address."

Brandon would be bringing all he could for the start-up. Every trip was more inventory.

The day came, I had to check out of the hotel first thing the next morning. I would take the Bus to my new home. A room at Sunset Beach.

Brandon and I were totally different. His wife kept him from being a jerk or stubborn. We had a common ground where we got along, with his wife's help. Business and making money.

I lived and worked in Waikiki for seventeen days.

Sunset Beach

I rented a room in the basement of the house directly across the street, which was Kamama Highway, the best view of Sunset Beach. The roof of the house was about level with the road. A huge house with five rooms in the basement that are for rent on a weekly rate. A very big common area. We shared two bathrooms in the basement. In the top secret deal, Brandon and I would rent the front yard! The property at the road was pretty much a drop-off. There were three other jewelry places at Sunset Beach. This would be the ultimate perfect place! Their places were away from the main view because of the drop-off beside the road.

After our final decision on the address, we had planned this. That is why I did not jump and move out here so quickly. We were planning everything. Lisa lined up four truckloads of dirt, shell, and gravel mix to be dumped beside the road on my landlord's property. Plenty of room for my jewelry stand. More than enough.

Brandon brought out a sign on a full piece of plywood. He asked what I think. It was a few years old. It was painted dull yellow with green letters. "CORAL JADE PUKA SHELLS" was painted across it. *Big* letters. Wow. I told Brandon the sign was so perfect, it couldn't be better. He had the rest of the start-up inventory.

The landlord put two deadbolts on my door. It opened into the common room. The window was small and had a bar.

I purchased three six-foot folding tables and three folding chairs. Brandon brought them out.

I picked up my vendor's permit for private property.

The dump trucks arrived. The last load was mainly shell, sand, and gravel. A bobcat was only two doors away. I knocked on his door to let him know we were ready for him. He was done in forty-five minutes.

The morning after, the four truckloads of fill were delivered. I opened it. All this happened in a matter of days.

I covered the tables with the perfect display. Puka shell necklaces were a major, big-time hot fad. In the US, Canada, England, and even in Japan. You better believe I had them. A small pallet of just puka shell necklaces. I had cheap and nice.

Boxes of coral necklaces and bracelets from the Philippines. Big markup!

Beautiful corals: red, white, orange, and pink.

Jade all shapes.

Beautiful display. Everything was priced.

I was back to wearing cutoff faded jeans and no shirt.

I knew I was being stared at with hatred by the other vendors. Their displays and inventory were terrible. I did not care. I felt nothing but excitement.

I made my first sale to the lady I rented from. Then it happened. A tourist bus, not full, because summer had yet to arrive. It was something I will never forget. The bus pulled off the road traveling the north. Like every tourist bus going north or south. Parked right across the road from my stand.

This is important. I had an unobstructed view of the beach and the ocean. We planned it that way. The bus pulled over on the beach side where there was shell and gravel for pulling over. They always rolled past where I could always look out and the tourist can also look out while shopping. I had by far the best view of Sunset Beach and the ocean beyond.

The view was the exact same place we were on the day of the waves. I was looking across the highway at where we were sitting!

Whales jumping! Yes. Breaching; sorry. The first time I saw a whale coming out of the Pacific Ocean, it was a few miles out from Sunset Beach. The water was flat. It looked like a bus coming out of the water! I didn't expect it. Standing behind my booth, looking right at the place where the whale breached. I saw the whales breaching the ocean at least thirty times that summer.

Back to the first tourist bus. Some tourists walk to the beach. A lot of people look around and judge the shopping. My stand gets slammed. Cash only was common in 1978. I took a couple of travelers checks on very big sales. People lined up with large amounts of items. Everyone was saying I had the best jewelry they had seen. Including Waikiki. They were waving people over. My landlord started taking money and was wrapping items and putting them in bags. One man bought fifty puka shell necklaces along with twenty-five bracelets. I had already put each puka shell item in separate baggies.

Everyone was gone and back on the bus in plenty of time. My landlord had waved goodbye with a big smile. She was walking back down her driveway.

I had hundreds, fifties, and a big stack of twenties. Fifties were common in 1978. Of course, most of it was not mine, but a lot of it was!

The Mango Man and his bicycle had magically appeared beside my booth.

Rental cars could park next to my booth. Plenty of room. I made a sign private property. Customer parking.

The room I rented had a long twin bed. And a chair. We just left our door open if we were in the room awake or asleep maybe. It was sorta nice. You got to know everybody *quick*.

A young local, extremely pretty Hawaiian girl kept the common area clean. Her name was Tina. She had a free room inside the main house and did cleaning work for the landlord. I noticed over the next couple of weeks that the guys were taking advantage of Tina. These were mainly California surfers coming and going renting the rooms. Surfers? Except one older alcoholic and another jerk, from France who said he could surf, named Stefon. Never did surf. The jerk took her to bed in the little room! So did the surfers! You could hear everything the walls were thin! Tina was always sad afterward.

She was probably only eighteen, maybe seventeen. So pretty and happy most days. One evening, Tina came into my room. I was lying on my bed, reading with my door open. With all the inventory, it was easiest to just close the door to sit in the chair. So Tina closed the door. I was wearing cutoff jeans. Tina was wearing a swimsuit top and shorts. Tina asked me, "Do you think I am pretty?" I had to say, "Tina, you are the prettiest girl on the whole island. Probably all of the Hawaiian islands, but I have only been on this island." Immediately, Tina got up and sat on my bed almost on top of me and asked if I wanted to do something.

The conversation went almost exactly like this... "Tina, if you would like to sit in here and talk, that would be great."

She smiled and said, "I'm not talking about talking."

I answered, "Tina, I know what you are saying. I can hear you through the walls and doors when you are with guys. I don't do that to a young girl. It is wrong. It is not a proper relationship." Tina said, "I am nineteen." I said, "No, you are not nineteen." She said, "You can hear me doing it?"

Tina slid down to the end of the bed. We talked for about an hour and a half. Tina thanked me. We drank a couple of Cokes I had in the cooler. Tina turned eighteen three weeks ago.

Tina was on her own, working in the house cleaning rooms, starting at the age of sixteen. She told me her mother was in the hospital very sick. That was a lie.

The landlord stopped her from cleaning the common area after I complained about what was taking place. Tina would drop by my stand every so often and help pack up jewelry and talk to customers when a bus was there. I had told her about the Bus that night we were talking.

I was working every day. It did not seem like work. I chained the tables together so they would not be stolen. I would get up very early, clean the tables, and put the cloth down. I would load the backpack with today's merchandise and walk up the driveway to the stand for the day.

The room I was renting got old real fast, especially when Tina quit cleaning.

On the North Shore, rates drop on houses the closer it gets to summer. The surf goes flat. I rented a house next to the beach. It was not cheap. It was two houses back from the beach. No house on the entrance side of my house. It was all beach on that side. A house on the other side of the road would have been cheaper, no way. This house is so perfect. The beach is like right there. It was a two-bedroom, two-bathroom surfer's older house. Landscaping was overgrown. I got right on that. The fence was beat-up. I fixed that. The inside had been remodeled. Very important. Solid doors. Good Locks. Deadbolts front and back. Secure windows. Very nice.

Not much to move. A few clothes. Of course the inventory. My friends Sharon and Johnny were happy to help. They were glad I called. We got started at seven in the morning. They had so much to tell me. We sat at my house, and I listened. Things were definitely going good for them. I told them about my adventures.

We were all just happy together. Those two were so easy to be around. What a housewarming. We went to the sandwich shop and had lunch. My usual, bean sprouts and tomato. Papaya on the side. We walked back to the house and checked out *my* beach. Sharon stayed and visited with Tina. They wound up going to the resort at the North Point of the island and all over the place. Johnny and I walked the beach. Miles down the *beach*. Way on down *my* beach. I had the best beach! We talked and solved world problems. No marriage problems.

For the first time, I did not open the stand that day, did not think about the stand. It was okay. Friends are more important. Also, I did this on the slowest day Saturday. Sunday was the second slowest. I hired some help that week.

Sunday was slow. I had time to think. Really! This little operation had distracted me. It was a necessary distraction. Making some real money, selling nice ocean jewelry to tourists, my little jewelry stand. North Shore, Oahu. I realized I did it. I was living my dream. I had a nice home for a while.

Taking off a full day helped get me back on track. I want to help people. Read and study. Mango Man was not here today. He gives me free mangoes. He insisted. I let him park beside me when a bus came in. Mango Man sold a lot of fruit that way. I learned how I am stuck in my way of seeing things unless I make myself break free.

Mango Man

The Mango Man made his living selling fruit from his bicycle that had a sign on both sides that said, "Fresh Mangoes." When mangoes were out of season, he sold other fruit or opened coconuts. The signs never changed. He lived alone in a small house at the foot of the mountains right behind us. He was probably five feet, ten inches tall and slim. Early thirties, well-traveled, and educated. He had been the Mango Man for seven years. He was to become a special close friend. I was blessed with him. Although we would have never admitted it, back in those *fantastic months*, our paths were meant to cross. Only looking back do I see it.

Mango Man's name is James. I never called him that. He never said the stuck-and-break-free thing. But, *man, oh, man*, I got it. I taught him something. That one thing you see, you don't see it. James finally changed. We both grew. He was more educated than I. Therefore, he thought himself automatically wiser.

If I said something profound, it bothered James. When we were having a deep discussion, I reached a conclusion that was brilliant. James was bothered because *he* was wiser. He would not say anything. He would usually scrunch his eyebrows and look at me and then kind of shake his head.

If James said something brilliant, I would say, "That is very good," or "Well done."

James and I talked a lot—about God, the universe, health, jokes, history, business, and whatever. The deeper the intelligent conversation, the better. We might pick up on one from yesterday. We were both compassionate and caring. We never cussed or had crude women talk. I was not going to take him on in subjects he had studied.

This went on for a while. To where it was obvious to both of us. We were talking about the Creation and the big bang. I went into the creation of time and how some people see the universe with an end or no end. That would go along with time. I was going somewhere with this, and it was going to be okay. Brief. Nothing profound. Just a warm-up.

James interrupted me. "David, hold that thought." He looked out at the ocean and said, "It's gone, David. I do not see it. That one thing." James looked at me and said, "Thanks, man."

Our talks were equal after that, much better.

A Letter from Home

I received a letter from Cindy. My family was planning on flying to Oahu! Mom, Dad, Lavada, and Cindy. I did not foresee that happening. I was very happy about it. I went on as usual until that day arrived.

Tina and My New Home

I was worried about Tina. I talked to her and the landlord. She wanted out of the house. The landlord saw it was a good idea. I started to explain my good honorable intentions to the landlord with Tina moving to my new home.

They both agreed. I did not need to explain myself. They both also agreed I was weird.

The landlord did add "a good weird."

Tina moved in with me, or in my house, the next day.

We had talked about a deal. We talked about it again the evening Tina moved in.

She agreed. *No* men. *No* kids. I am her friend only. She cleaned and cooked, did the grocery shopping, did the laundry, ironed clothes, and kept the house very clean. Tina had her own room with a bathroom. Plus, I paid her!

I started keeping a zipper bank bag in the kitchen drawer with money in it that night.

After giving Tina some money, I went over how the bank bag worked. Tina put receipts in. If she used cash or house items, we had a form for that. Tina wanted money for herself, a draw slip for her. Never a problem. We just kept getting along. Like I said, Tina would be paid, not much. She needed to look for a job as well, in a month or so.

Tina was super-duper superhappy.

I bought a three-hundred-dollar car I had test-driven the day before. I had a home by then. Tina and I got along great. The first day I was at work, she scrubbed the kitchen—the kitchen windows, floor, refrigerator, stove, and cabinets. Next day, she moved on to the rest of the house.

A little after Tina moved in, her sister, Pam, who did not look like her, brought over some things. She showed up on a bicycle with three baskets full of odds and ends.

I knew something was wrong.

Tina was sick. She stayed in her room.

I brought her Coke with ice and soup with a sandwich. She had a temperature! Pam did not have a driver's license, but I said she could drive the car. I knew it was girl stuff. So I sent them on. When I got home from work, Pam was still there. She wanted me to sit with Tina while she went to the pharmacy. I had taken off a little early.

Tina had already given her money out of the moneybag. Tina was proud in front of her sister, showing her she could sign out money. Tina did have STDs.

I did not ask a lot of questions. I paid the doctor's bills. I sent them to a good doctor instead of the crowded free clinic.

Tina was taken right in. She had a female doctor and was well taken care of. A first visit, a visit in four days, a visit in ten days. A visit in a month. Complicated because she had waited so long to get treatment. Poor Tina.

At home, we would watch TV.

Tina would usually sit on the floor and rest her head and arm on my leg. She would fall asleep with her head on my lap or her feet behind my back... Some way or another, she would be touching me.

When I was watching TV or at the desk in the living room, she would get me anything I needed. I think she started reading my mind. Food, books, coffee, water, tea, beer, whatever.

Tina had her sister stay over sometimes. Sometimes, they would have friends over. Four or five young ladies would go back into Tina's room. They would laugh, shout at each other, run back and forth to the fridge, play music, just be girls. If I went to my room to sleep, they would take over the living room and watch TV. Tried to be quiet.

RUSTY

One day at the stand, one of my very favorite people showed up. Rusty. This young quiet man loved to surf. The summer was here, and the good surf was nowhere to be found. Rusty lived on a tight budget and camped all over the island following the surf. Rusty was probably five feet ten, all muscle, with long blond hair and lighter skin than most of us even after being in the sun all day every day. He was supershy. He reminded me a lot of me.

He saved up and made this trip from his home in Kansas. A surfer from Kansas! That's what I thought. Do I have a story for you? Yes, I do! Wait, I have two.

Rusty and I are just walking along a somewhat remote path. Rusty in the front. Around midnight. This is around the second month for me. Rusty has been on Oahu for a while. I like going places with Rusty. He walks fast. We both have our small backpacks and are wearing just shorts and thong sandals, just like most days. We are hitting a steady pace. We have another seven miles to go. We cross a wider trail where six or seven locals are talking and looking at us. We just keep our pace.

When we get beside them, they go after Rusty, hitting him in the head, then just hitting him, and then slapping his chest real loud. The locals were calling him "F——kin' Howley. F——kin' Howley."

Rusty was shouting, "Just keep walking!"

Then they started on me with the same thing, "You piece of garbage. F——kin' Stinking Howley," and popped the side of my head with their knuckles. I was using my arm to protect myself. They were coming down on us pretty hard. One jumped in front of me and hit me in the stomach.

Rusty was shouting, "Don't fight back! David, don't fight back! Keep walking. Just keep walking." They slowed us down.

I never even slightly swung back. So glad. Thank you, Rusty. We kept walking and quickly hit a fast pace out of there.

They were shouting, "Cowards."

This next event happened a few months later. The busy day was toward evening. We were traveling through the palm and jungle woods. Same thing with Rusty in front. We always traveled narrow pathways like this because Rusty was shorter. Rusty and I were taking a very long deep in the jungle path. We were ready to get back to our campsite. Taking this supershortcut. Anyway, we are headed to the campground and feeling good. Had the stride going, making some good time. The sun was shining straight down on the path. It was going to be a beautiful evening. I was so blessed, and was making plans in my head about what I was going to do tomorrow. I was much stronger. I could swim endlessly. Run forever. My left blade was back to normal! Walking and thinking. So quiet and peaceful. We was moving fast. I heard it first. I whispered, "Rusty, what do you think?"

Rusty waited, and we kept on walking. Rusty came back with "It is a lot of them."

I could hear them talking.

Rusty said real low, "This is not good."

We walked into a group of Samoans. Six of them.

On one of the most remote hardly ever used paths on the island. We are in the deepest part of the path. We never see people in the most shallow or beginning stages of this forgotten trail. No trace of it being used. This path is not entirely overgrown! We thought it was mostly forgotten with the new roads and walkways. I think it is a long-lost great shortcut for us. Still! What are the odds?

Things get out of control quickly.

We scuffle. I am on the ground, kicked in the stomach, picked up, and popped hard on the side of my head. They pick on Rusty, the smallest person. Six big Samoans. Known for their *strength* and size, they have Rusty. The fattest guy holds him from behind while another one slaps him. The one slapping him is the shortest Samoan. They call him "Leader." These three are standing on the trail.

The other four have me surrounded just off the path to Rusty's right. Unusual, one of them surrounding me is tall, not that fat. He is in front of me. This is their little game.

The two guys stood me up like a play toy. I snap my senses too. I see many options. Rusty is saying loudly, "I'm fine. I'm fine."

Leader, the short Samoan, is slapping Rusty, then looking at me, and asking, "What are you going to do about it?" The tall guy steps to the left, giving Leader a good view of me. I have a view of what is happening to Rusty. Mr. Leader *punches* Rusty in the stomach and laughs and shouts in the air, "I asked you a question—what are you going to do about-it?" This is hilarious to all the Samoans.

I know these guys *will* break bones. Many bones. They are going to leave us dead or wish we were dead.

We have heard specific stories. Warnings are posted. At the campground, we have been warned by the police.

People who live here told me about Howley's being found beat up with arms and legs both broken. Some dead, others barely alive.

Some Samoans are worse than locals. They don't just hate us; they want us gone from the islands or dead.

At first, four guys surround me—three big, one tall. Two are in front of me, two by my side. Rusty's beating gets underway.

The big guy to my left step away, five feet. Like a lookout.

The big Samoan to my left front steps back to my left side.

One in front, tall man. On each side of me are the bigger strongest Samoans.

The back is still open. Except for the thick forest, palms, and bushes. I am right up against a big palm and bushes. Still, I like this back being open. No eyes behind me. Just the lookout guy about ten feet to my left. Five feet past the man on my left.

I am only about eleven or twelve feet from Rusty.

These killers are organized!

Listen to this. I feel wonderful. I can't be happier. I am superexcited. They are laughing. Rusty is shouting, "Don't do it, David! These guys will kill us." Then Rust would say, "I'm fine. Don't do it, David." Rusty's nose is bleeding; he is slumped over. The big Samoans to my right are laughing. He steps slightly forward to talk to the tall one in front of me. (This tall one has me worried. He can catch Rusty or myself!) If he chases Rusty, he will be standing on the trail, looking for me. I am toast with him standing. Rusty probably is also.

I can't believe my eyes. Tall Guy's neck is a smidgen too long. Oh yes, an iota, a dab, or a mite long.

I am holding back a happy big smile. I have to look afraid, panicked, and terrified.

The Samoans are laughing and shouting. I can tell they are also getting bored.

The one who stepped forward on my right raises his voice to the tall man, "Hey, Breaker, let's break this fuck's legs." Talking about me!

The man holding Rusty had loosened his hold. Leader yelled, "*Holder, watch out!*"

Rusty just barely looked my way. Our eyes made contact.

I gave Rusty a bigger smile than I should have. When Leader yelled, "Watch out," it drew all eyes away from me including the "Watch out!"

Rusty was ready. I looked away from Rusty, and at the back of the neck of Breaker and quick as lighting, I turned my upper body left to swing.

I could picture the guy behind Rusty trying to hold him up. Everyone was laughing loud and hard.

Rusty yelled, "*Help!*" Loud! just as I hit the tall guy in the back of his neck. With all the power from my left arm and body with my left fist, I felt his spinal column crack... I mean a good solid break.

Very important, let me describe that second. As mentioned, I was energized. Fearless. When I saw Rusty was ready, I accidentally gave him my big smile and let him see me look at the back of "Tall Guy," as well as start my left turn.

I did not see Rusty again until this was over.

I kept my eye on Breaker's neck as I turned for the maximum power, a split second. His neck was my 100 percent focus. It was all I could see. I believe my adrenaline hit at this instant. I was going to bust my hand through that neck.

When I released spinning my body right and while extending my left arm, Breaker actually moved back a bit and perfectly positioned his neck for the *blow*. I hit him so hard I could feel my fist smash into his *spine* and keep going. Square in the back of Breaker's neck. It was a solid-crack feeling. My fist felt like steel. I used that same right turning momentum to continue my turn and exit.

I ducked down around behind the guy to my right. He opened up a big space when he stepped forward. I took off. I had an obstacle course of bushes and small palms to get to the trail. I took long steps over everything, which was slower. I was about to blast down the trail to freedom. All I could hear was "Gonna kill you, fucking Howley" on and on. I wanted to take a glance. Somebody tried to trip me. Barely touching me. It did not slow me down. It did widen my path further into the bushes. I did not have any room. Too many palm trees.

I glanced left, making sure Rusty was gone. Not there, "like a puff of smoke in a hurricane." Only a few more strides to the path. I had to get around the left side of a big palm and the thick jungle bush to get on the path.

I was running at the edge of the bushes three feet from the side of the path. Headed toward the edge of the big palm, full speed. The leader, or Leader, the guy I was worried about was not there. I had expected him to be standing in my way. Instead, he dove at me as I ran around the left side of the big palm. About to step on the path.

He reached out and grabbed my left upper arm and snatched me around. Leader was leaning forward, so I kept on spinning and broke his grip.

I glanced to see who else was following me. The tall guy (Breaker) was, in a pile, on the ground. *Not* moving.

The guy who had been to the right of me was the closest. He was the one who attempted to trip me. He was not a problem now. No one else mattered.

Leader tried to grab my right foot as it came around. He gave up when he hit the ground hard from being overextended.

I was going to stomp him in his face.

Nope. I switched from bloodlust to survival in a microsecond.

I was all kinds of twisted and spinning.

I still had massive forward momentum. There was about a three-foot drop over the next five feet. My left hand and knee hit the ground. I pushed off, as my right hand just gently touched the dirt. I had spun too far! And I was up and running.

I lost a Beachcomber Bill sandal. Luckily, it was this side of Leader. I snatched up my sandal, had it on, and was running, one smooth move. The sandal was very important.

Rusty was long gone.

I ran like the wind for a mile and a half when I saw Rusty.

He was standing up leaning over on his with hands and arms stretched out onto his knees.

I ran up and stood across from him and did the same, recovering my breath. When I finally looked up at Rusty, we started laughing. Then we were laughing uncontrollably. Every time we tried to look up and say something, same thing.

First thing Rusty finally squeaked out was, "What were you going to do? Fight all six of them?"

We laughed.

I finally answered between breaths, "I was thinking about it."

That said, we went into laughing fits even more. We could finally say a few words. The other would nod his head and start laughing. We finally caught our breath from running the mile and a half in record time and laughing so hard. When Rusty took off, he didn't just take off running. He knew the leader would be my problem. The leader would have been standing right in my exit path. The instant he yelled, "*Help*," Rusty caught the leader by surprise. Rusty came up and hit him perfectly in his side stomach. He fell to the right side. Away from everybody. Rusty tried to push him into the bushes as he was taking flight.

When Rusty looked at me, that was the signal saying, "I am ready whenever you are." He had a plan. I knew it. He had faith I could get away from the four big *guys*.

Because I didn't do a slight nod or raise my eyebrows. I shot him a big smile.

We were one with a single purpose. Staying alive.

I may as well tell the final story, not really a story, of Rusty. Nothing exciting. I was doing fine at the jewelry stand. Summer was here. Waves were gone. Rusty walked up to my stand with his red surfboard that he kept in perfect repair.

It was always great to see my good friend Rusty. His surfboard was looking shiny and new.

He said, "I thought you might want to buy this for a hundred dollars." It was easily a seven- or eight-hundred-dollar board. Four hundred, worst case.

I said, "Rusty, you don't have to do that." Rusty just wanted me to have it for one hundred dollars. He was headed home. We were so different and so much alike.

He stayed a while and talked. We talked about the six Samoans among other things.

We did talk about what would have happened if the cowards had gotten a hold of me. We finally came to the conclusion. No way, we were smarter than the opponent and were ready for that moment. We trusted each other one hundred percent. It was good to talk about it. I had a few nightmares of being captured again.

Rusty told me that, while he was waiting, he kept saying, "Come on, David. Where are you? Come on, man. Don't do this to me. Where are you?" He was saying this while he was trying to catch his breath. He started tearing up a little when he heard me up the trail and I appeared a second later.

Mango Man was listening to us talk.

I could not believe the surfboard I now owned.

I want to hand the World's Nicest Guy Award to Rusty.

NYMPHA

A few days later, a beautiful lady about my age walked up from the sandwich shop. I recognized her. Nympha. She was so pretty I was still afraid of her. I know her because... I don't know why! I knew her before that. Nympha knew my name.

She wanted to buy some Red Coral. I asked her to wait. I would pick out a really nice red coral necklace. I asked her to choose one to wear in the meantime. Now she wanted the red, orange, and white if I found really nice ones. But she was superfine with waiting. The one I gave her to wear was beautiful! I said she would check back from time to time. I already had an orange, "Sunset Coral," that was stunning. I was saving it. It was at my house.

Nympha could not stand it. She wanted to see it. Had to have it. As I said, Nympha had walked up from the sandwich shop. My house was a half mile or so past the sandwich shop. You would have thought the necklace was going to save her life.

She said, "Please take my car to your house, and bring me *my* necklace." I said, "Please slow down. Go to my house. A friend of mine, Tina, is there. I have a few choice pieces I have set aside which you can choose from. You can pay Tina."

These items I had saved, mainly necklaces and bracelets, were jewelry-store quality. Spectacular. Tina could use a friend like Nympha.

When I finally got off work about three hours later and walked home, Nympha's new BMW was still parked at my house.

I walked in, and they started telling me what a great guy I was. Please. It was all about the jewelry. Not me being a great guy.

They stared showing me Nympha's new jewelry. The girls were both so beautiful and excited. Nympha said the crown jewel was the Sunset Coral and that one puka shell necklace that I had set back. I had to agree. Then Nympha said to watch this and put on a white coral necklace that was so beautiful.

I was saving it to give it to Lavada when she got here. I forgot about marking the necklace for my sister and left it in with the other nice jewelry.

With Nympha's perfect body, dark tan, nice tan breasts, wonderful face, along with the perfect size of the magical jewelry, the effect was stunning.

I was left speechless.

Tina finally said, "It does nothing for me when I try it on." Tina started lifting up her breasts a little and looking in the mirror.

I had to get out of there. I got a couple of beers out of the fridge and left for the beach. I came in when the mosquitos started. I was glad the BMW was gone.

She and Tina went to Waikiki to shop for swimsuits together a week after that. Anyway, I knew Nympha before that. I just can't remember how I first met Nympha.

I finally got used to Nympha visiting Tina, talking, talking, talking. They would play board games that were left in the rental house. Tina would still make my dinner, get me whatever I needed. Talk, talk, get me a beer, talk, fix David a sandwich while talking, talking, talking. The best part was I had "free pricing for each piece of jewelry service." Both of them wanted to open all the new boxes of jewelry when I brought it home. So I made a deal. I bet you know the deal! The two did an excellent job of pricing.

My Family Arrives

The date of their arrival was on the calendar above my small desk at home. Mom, Dad, Lavada, and Cindy would be here in a few days. Angela could not make the trip to Hawaii. Dad and I talked a few times. He would be renting a car, and the family would like to stay in Waikiki. Of course, we agreed.

I told my father about Tina, a young local Hawaiian girl. Friend *only*. Housekeeper. Please get this message across.

I would be meeting them at the arrival gate. I had a list of the most amazing tourist attractions. I would like to go and visit with them.

I had to work at the jewelry stand some of the days they were there.

Cindy and Lavada had pictures of their "Hawaii" trip. Cindy had a perfect photo of the jewelry stand. Lavada remembered Tina well. How pretty and delightful she was. I talked with Lavada a few days ago about the trip.

I have a good story. Everyone was at my house for the first introductions of Tina, and to see the home. Everything was perfect. Fresh fruit and flowers. Tina was very proud. I had the outside just right, of course. Dad noticed and mentioned it to me when he stepped in. The home had lots of room to move around in. We all sat down and got right back up.

Tina was going to show the girls her room. I went outside with Dad. Tina and Lavada hit it off. They were talking in Tina's room. Lavada *had a new boyfriend*. Tina was a great listener. Lavada and Tina came back to the living area and served everyone something to drink. Juice or Coke. Lavada sat back down.

Well, Tina was so happy and comfortable. She sat on the floor beside me and put her arm on my right leg. The way we always sat. No big deal. Except Mom. Her eyes got as big as saucers. The family was all just talking away. So happy to be together. Tina was so nice. She did not speak for a long time. Finally, Tina spoke to Lavada and offered to show Lavada and Cindy around Waikiki and go shopping with them. She knew the places with good prices. Cindy and Lavada liked that. Mom did not like this *at all*. She told Dad it was time to go.

I had already warned Tina about my mother. Tina stayed clear of my mother and the family after that. Lavada and Cindy would have enjoyed Tina and her wonderful company.

My family and I went all over the island.

Cindy enjoyed sitting at the jewelry stand with me. Dad and I had some quality time together. Mango Man and Dad got along great.

On Sunday, Dad drove up to go to church with me.

He arrived early with breakfast from the hotel. He brought way more than enough for Tina and myself.

I was out at the beach dressed for church. Tina and my father had a chance to talk. He wanted her to know that he appreciated her and was sorry if she was hurt in the least.

Tina said I had told her to expect Mrs. Cash to act bad. So she was not hurt too much, just a little bit.

Dad asked if he could pray with her, Tina was excited because I had also told her about my father's prayers.

Tina grabbed my father's hand, and he prayed.

Tina told me later, "When your Father prays, it's like going into outer space. I can't explain going to outer space."

That explanation was the best I've heard in a long time about my father's prayers.

After the prayer, Tina told my father where I always go on Sunday mornings before church.

Dad caught a picture of me that morning on the beach, dressed for church.

Church Service with Dad

We were a little early for the service. I was the only White person every Sunday except this Sunday. A special favor I asked the pastor that morning. He was a little slow to agree.

The song leader, a brilliant man, asked my father to come up front to open the service with prayer. This put a smile on my father's face. He loved to pray in this small church of about eighty people.

While Dad was walking up front, the song leader introduced him, "Mr. Charles Cash is our guest from Atlanta, Georgia.

Georgia is the state directly above Florida. Georgia is on the Atlantic Coast. It is about eight thousand miles Charles has traveled, with his family, to visit his son, David Cash. He has been here every Sunday for the last five months. We are proud to have him as part of our church. Charles Cash, please take your time. You are welcome to say a few words before your prayer if you like."

This is where *my father shines*. He chose to say, "Thank you," and a few other wisely chosen words before he said, "Let's go to the Lord in prayer."

When the prayer was over, I felt as if I would look up and see Jesus standing beside my father. I believe the congregation felt the same way. When My father prays, he may start off asking about something back in Jesus's time or today. A discussion is with Jesus. Dad actually talks to Jesus when he prays. The people in that church on Sunday *morning felt* the presence of Jesus. The preacher stood up minutes after my father returned to his seat and was seated. My dad sat down beside me, grabbed my left leg, and shook it. He was feeling good.

As everybody was leaving, the *little old lady* who always sat in the far-right corner, walked over, and stood in the pew behind Dad and me. She was short from age. I turned around, along with my dad. The little *lady took* my father's hand in both of her hands.

Her granddaughter said to my father, "Mamy wants to ask you something." Two other ladies, along with a gentleman, were standing with us. A small group, along with Dad and me, seven people. Nothing that big was going to happen. Like a *miracle* with fire or anything.

My dad looked at the nice older lady. Before Mamy could speak, her granddaughter told my father. That was the first time she had ever touched a White person. She had never allowed a White person to touch her. Mamy took *my father's* hand up to her face and gently placed his hand on her cheek...

Mamy asked my father, "Ask Jesus to forgive my hate. All my life, I have hated White people."

My father finally spoke. "Yes, I will be honored to pray with you."

Mamy said, "Mr. Charles, ask Jesus to forgive *my* whole life of *hate*." Mamy said *very slowly*, "Pray to Jesus. Tell Jesus I love all people, I love White people, I love them, I love them."

I kid you not. The song leader had walked in the side door and was standing at the front of the church on our side. He said in a voice just loud enough for us all to hear him, "Mr. Cash, looks like you did not travel eight thousand miles just to visit your son."

CHAPTER 13

More North Shore

Ultimate Waimea Bay Bodysurfing

THE JEWELRY STAND LASTED A LOT LONGER THAN BRANDON predicted.

A police car pulled up. An officer I recognized got out, walked up, and explained the citation he was writing.

The police officer's wife owned the jewelry stand diagonal across the road to the right from me. I responded, "Is your wife in violation, sir? Will you be issuing her a citation today along with myself?"

The police officer closed his ticket book and kindly responded, "Have a good afternoon, David." I knew the officer. This was my "shot over the bow." I called Brandon that evening and told him we probably had a week. Two at most... He agreed.

It was over two weeks later. Two police officers with some legal paperwork came to my jewelry stand. A new law was passed. A person must be a home owner and resident of the same county. Must also be this and that. Bottom line, I have to close immediately, or a fine will start today. Fifty-dollar-per-day fine in the first week. One-hundred-dollar-per-day fine in the second week. The maximum fine would remain a hundred dollars per day. A lot of other print on the paperwork. I read the word *jail*. I agreed to close. Summer was over. I was fine. I had enough money. The day off sounded good.

Tina's grandmother—her name is Lani—got out of jail. Lani was in on multiple shoplifting charges. She began receiving welfare, which included an apartment. Tina moved in with Grandmother Lani. Tina started working at the Sunset Beach Sandwich Shop, part-time, during her last month of staying with me.

I will move on with another random story. It is stuck in my head. Stuck in my *head*! The jewelry stand was gone. So were the car and house, gone. Most of my money, gone. Two thousand dollars was buried in the woods.

Money for Home

Boring but cool story. A few days after purchasing the car, I drove out to Mokuleia Beach Park. The most remote park at the beginning of Kaena Point. Many times, zero campers. The desert west end of the island. I parked at the huge dry camping area. Only two tents and one other car. I walked across the road with my tire tool. The one for the tire jack, lug nuts, and the flat end to pop off the hubcaps. My pocket was full of plastic baggies.

I walked down the road till I was at a perfect marker on the road. A lone very tall palm stood at the foot of the mountains. I walked over a half mile in the palm and bush forest toward the palm. Dug a hole near a large rock. Four inches wide and two feet deep. Put all the dirt in the plastic bags. I then put of all the plastic bags with dirt back in the hole. In a certain way. Covered it with leaves. I left lightly marking my path. I checked two weeks later. I could find the rock at a distance, and the place was undisturbed.

About seven weeks later, I had two thousand dollars wrapped and sealed in a small jar. I returned and placed it in the bottom of the hole. Emptied all the dirt out of the baggies on top of the jar and filled up the hole. Covered the small area back up with leaves. Perfect. Nice and safe.

MOKULEIA BEACH PARK

I am so happy. I am camping at the most remote camping area, Mokuleia Beach State Park. No camping permit needed. One very big open park. No palms. Two cement block bathrooms that are cleaned daily. Two outdoor showers.

This state park is found going directly west toward a dead end. Past the polo fields. Beyond the airport or very long air strip. Used a lot for gliders. Nice small airplanes are also there.

To the nearest store, five miles. I have walked it numerous times. I am sitting on the top of a cement picnic table with my feet and sandals on the seat. I never wear a shirt. I am on a table near the east side of the park. When the park ends on this side, there is twenty-five yards of thick palm forest and after that nice homes. The polo fields are on the same side as the homes. I watch them play often. The long landing strip on the right side of the road at the foot of the mountains, I have been there many times.

I enjoy being alone looking out over the ocean, which is flat today. I have been on the island for over a year. Only one other tent in the huge flat campground.

A man from Greece. He is in his early thirties. Taking as long as he wants to go around the world. I am trying to remember. I think his name is Anwan. He says everyone in Greece is *gay*. It is ridiculous. Anwan is learning English. The rich Greek is supersmart and athletic. He can already surf four-foot waves.

I talk with him so he can learn more English.

SNORKELING WITH NYMPHA

A lady was walking down the beach, and she was headed west and came out from around the palm forest that separated the camp area from the houses. She looked over and saw me.

Wow, Nympha. It will be good to catch up. As Nympha got closer, I got nervous. I forgot how pretty she was. I was nervous. When she got closer, I thought we would talk and it would be over quick. But, nooo.

Nympha said, "I thought I saw you camping over here. This is great. I live in a house nearby. I just walked over." I mentioned something about the homes being so nice.

She asked if I wanted to do something. She continued that she wanted to go snorkeling but would not go alone.

I was no longer shy. We were talking and talking.

Nympha said, "When my boyfriend and I bought the house, we had no idea it had such a fantastic reef right out in front! The reef is endless, the currents are stiff and dangerous. Do you want to go?"

I was on my feet and walking beside Nympha on the way to her house. She liked to hold hands and talk. I guess I do too.

We made it to their very nice home.

Nympha's supernice big boyfriend was in the main room when we walked in. Local Hawaiian. He was dressed in a silk Hawaiian shirt, black dress pants, and dress shoes. He was leaving for a meeting in Honolulu. Nympha introduced me as "David, the one I have told you about." Explained we were going snorkeling.

Boyfriend offered his snorkeling gear and asked if I was hungry and then answered for me. "You will burn some energy out there." He raised his voice a little. "Mother, we have a guest."

From upstairs, a voice said, "I will be right down."

We had an open-face sandwich—thinly sliced avocado, medium fried egg, cheese, and bean sprouts, along with fresh papaya in a few minutes.

Boyfriend thanked me for going snorkeling with Nympha.

He said, "She is alone too much, not too many good men like you in the world. Please watch yourself and my Nympha out there."

Boyfriend was out the front door in a rush.

Nympha and I were on the back porch. She was pointing out the different boulders that were sticking up above the water, where we were going. What to do if this or that current was too strong.

Before I knew it, I was underwater and the sea life was better than I could have imagined.

Nympha took my hand every so often. I found out why. It was easier to keep up with each other than constantly looking for the other person. Plus she could control where we are going. We seemed to have about the same air capacity. We stayed out a few hours.

The evening was upon us when we were sitting on Nymphia's back deck. Talking and talking about all that we saw that day.

The sun was about to set when I agreed to meet her the next morning.

Nymphia and I went out three days in a row. Such a large and beautiful reef. I was in fantastic shape. After the third day of snorkeling, Nymphia and her boyfriend had to get ready for a long business trip.

Nymphia was a good friend.

Banzai Pipeline

No parking lot and hard to find, the beautiful perfect waves of the Pipeline are south of Sunset Beach. You could not see them from the highway.

I had visited the Pipeline a few times. I walked beside a small cement highway bridge, along lava rock and sand to the beach area that was mostly under palm trees. I had been there at low tide when the coral reef was just above the surface in some places.

I chose a day when the surf was going to be four to six feet, Hoping I could catch a few small waves at the famous Banzai Pipeline!

I knew I was in trouble when I walked to the beach and saw only locals. The ones on the shore looked at me. I sat under the palms and watched the perfect waves. The sky was perfect. The surfers were all Hawaiian.

I do believe I was fixing "to be in pain."

After watching the waves, I stood up with my board and was about to step in the water. The biggest guy yelled, "You are one stupid f——kin' Howley."

I kept going. Paddled out. I noticed two smaller surfers were out beyond the area. Strange. I let everybody go. Plenty of room. A wave came custom made for me.

Beautiful, I was up on my surfboard that I purchased from Rusty. I had been using it for a couple of months. Nice-size wave for my skills.

Bam point of a surfboard in the back of my head.

I was underwater. I almost blacked out, trying to stay away from the razor-sharp coral. If you get caught in the coral, it could kill you. I was swimming out of the coral and then to the shore. I saw blood from my head wound in the water. I walked down the beach and picked up my board. Glad that was over with.

I grabbed my small backpack with a towel and water. I checked the back of my head with the towel. Not too much blood. I drank a lot of water. Put everything away in the backpack. I was looking *back* out.

The big guy came over and said, "*Now* go, you f——kin' Howley." He immediately hit me in the left side of my face. Some of the people clapped and laughed a little.

I walked to the water and paddled back out.

When I returned, the two small Hawaiian guys were there. I knew them. They would "help" me at the jewelry stand some days. The first one said, "Hey, Jimmy, I thought that was you." (Jimmy was an old joke. People called me Jimmy because I'm from Georgia. Carter was president. Haha.)

I said, "You are not much of a friend. A friend would have spoken up sooner."

The other small guy said, "This Howley is a good *guy*. He is the one that took the shotgun from Lenny."

The first one added, laughing, "Yeah, I guess, he is my friend."

A different surfer said, "Okay, but he should have shot, Lenny."

All the surfers called me Jimmy that day.

I had the best time the rest of that day. And the next day. My younger friends stayed with me at the Pipeline. Showed me some tricks of surfing inside the tube and looking cool. I bought dinner both days.

The boys lived in a welfare home. It was bad. They hated home. I taught them lessons about stealing. I would let them watch my jewelry stand. They would steal jewelry. I would always catch them. I kept a perfect count when I left the tables with them. I had the police nearby when I left the money bag easy to find. I had them almost arrested. One day I left, and nothing was taken! We talked about what trust means and other good stuff.

The two watched my stand and would count the jewelry *and* the money after that.

BODYSURFING

I swim a lot for strength. I like to surf with a surfboard. It is not the best exercise for my shoulder blade muscles.

When I first arrived, I did not own a surfboard.

I would swim out to regular, not-so-popular surf sites and bodysurf. I had some short fins I used until someone took them. Those things were great. I just started bodysurfing without them. I started hitting some ten-foot-plus waves at Kaena Point and doing tricks.

I had the sideways flip perfected. I could look up through the tube. Only holding upside down for a second.

Then I opened the jewelry stand. My upper body and legs were strong from swimming. During the summer, I planned the free fall tricks and the waterfall (triple sideways flip). The waterfall was complicated. Keeping direction and speed.

No one practiced bodysurfing as much as I did. Not even 10 percent as much as I did. I was the master.

When the waves came back, I was out there every day. Surf with the board, and bodysurf.

Waimea Bay Bodysurfing

The waves were going to be huge and perfect for bodysurfing at Waimea Bay. Tomorrow, all day tomorrow. Starting very early. My car radio told me the surf report. I translated it. I was camping at Haleiwa Beach Park. Four and a half months after, the jewelry stand closed down. This was what I was staying around for.

I am in perfect physical shape.

Waimea Bay awaits.

Early the next morning, I park on the left side of the almost-empty parking lot at Waimea Bay. Not near the water, next to the large rock.

The waves are already big. Eight feet near shore break.

I take a skinny joint, called a pinner, and break it in half.

I climb to the top of the rock and smoke the smaller half of the joint. One and a half hits. Watching the waves come in for about twenty minutes. Absolutely perfect. Not busting into itself. Making big splashes. *No.* These are large clean long curls near the shore! Very rare. With good closeouts.

Ultimate Waimea bodysurfing.

I have my spot picked out. As I am climbing down, someone else is climbing up. I will see him in the water later.

Going by the car for a long drink of water and to get rid of my sandals, I head for the water. First one in. An hour later, five other people. The waves become twelve feet. Standing tall. Perfect tubes. Nice rides. Good free falls. Free falls—I make them into an art.

I look around six people and then back to five. Six including myself. The apex of the waves are straight as a wall! I can drop back into the tube, go to the top of the wave, and blast out. Have time for a 360-degree sideways roll. Still ride immediately to the top and free-fall to the bottom and come out the back side. Over and over. Something new. Riding upside down. I can look through the water to the sky. I come out of the tube on my back and see the sky. I roll over, picking up speed heading down; turn up; find the top; and go for the free fall.

Later the apex has moved up. It is now curved. I have something new in case anyone is watching. I come out high and fast. My first sideways roll is perfect. I immediately follow with a second and third roll as I speed forward and drop down. My waterfall is perfect. (If I take it to the end and go around, too much swimming.) On the last roll, I cut straight into the wave and came out back. Yes, I did three perfect rolls as I sped forward. The first controlled roll, I accomplished just as I exited the tube of the wave. With the next two speeding forward while rolling sideways down the face of this clean monster wave, it appears as if the forward edge of the tube is following me.

And, yes, again! I am glad you asked. This difficult and amazing feat has never been witnessed before. Okay, I don't know about that.

I did the waterfall twice!

I have my duty. I come out fast down, up, down, straight up through the top. I rise some good distance above the top of the wave. My back to the beach. When I am at the peak, I salute. I salute the ocean. Yep. Not much time. My legs are not straight.

Right after the salute, I begin to fall to the left. Must be twenty-plus feet of air below me, as I am behind the wave now. Halfway to the water behind the wave, I have to go into a cannonball.

It is a very good salute.

Only four people now, including myself. I will go up and down, up, down, up—free fall jackknife. Yahoo, having fun. Another half hour or so goes by. The waves are getting sloppy. I can tell by the last free fall and the back of the waves, these waves are eighteen feet.

I am about done. Swimming all day. Looks like me and two other guys. Those guys must have started a lot later.

I had to go in. Exhaustion hit. The last wave was almost no tube. I took the wave all the way in. My legs trembled when I stood on them. I let the white water push me on as I wiped my face.

The beach was packed! The crowd stood up, clapped, and cheered. A nice large video camera was set up. The camera turned to face me.

The crowd parted to let me pass. A few people stand up and clap. I walked through the crowd and turned to look at the monster waves I was just in. It was so massive. I could not believe I was out in that.

A microphone was placed near my face. Everyone gave the thirty-year-old blonde lady room. She said, "I have never seen anything like that before, Mr...." Wendy had a name tag on.

I said, "My name is David. I had no idea so many people were watching."

Wendy replied, laughing, "Today and tomorrow is one of the annual bodysurfing championships. You were putting on the best show. David, rolling down the wave. Unbelievable. Can you tell us something about it? How do you do that?"

I am thinking, *This is weird. I only wanted to bodysurf.* I reluctantly answered, "Today, Waimea delivered the best bodysurfing waves of the year. Those perfect waves were a lot of it." I shook my head, put both of my hands up, and mouthed, "*No more.*"

Wendy said, "Everyone would like to thank you for the show today. Well done." With that, Wendy turned and faced the crowd. The loud speaker popped. Wendy announced, "The best bodysurfing I have ever seen. Let's show David how much we appreciate fantastic bodysurfing!"

Tina was suddenly standing beside me, waving at the camera. The crowd was busy watching the remaining two bodysurfers and huge waves. I heard someone clapping and shouting from the big rock I was on earlier. It was packed with people. I recognized him!

Tina was really proud of me. We drove to the sandwich shop. Tina told me she could not believe it when I popped out of the tube in the big championship, rolling down that wave. We could not believe what just happened.

"When you shot straight up through the top, midair salute to the ocean," Tina said, "half the people saluted. People stood up. You had to fall twenty feet." Tina went through a lot of my "rather breathtaking" moves.

People kept asking, "Who is that guy?"

Tina would tell people that he was the guy that had the jewelry stand at Sunset Beach. Many of the people remembered me. Nice guy.

I dropped Tina off at her grandmother's apartment.

Tina asked me to come by the sandwich shop at three o'clock on Wednesday. That is when she got off.

I readily agreed.

When I got back to Haleiwa Beach Park, exhausted and feeling remarkable, the sun was on the way to setting. What a day. What a day. What a day.

The next day, people kept dropping by my campsite. "I saw you on TV last night." The island had a local UHF station just for surfing.

The Birds

Studying the Bible for hours at a time. Praying going back and forth to my Bible.

I was at the west side of Mokuleia Beach Park. Sometimes, I would sit at a table. This time, I was in the front of my tent, facing the water, sitting cross-legged, reading the red words of Jesus. I had just prayed. It was still morning.

The car and surfboard were both long gone. I was also fasting. My prayer was the usual. His will not mine. I had just gotten over a powerful addiction craving which *we* fought—Jesus and myself.

This is incredible. I could feel the spirit. I felt the need to put on a shirt. A nice *one* that Dad purchased for me when we were sightseeing. I was camped only a few feet from the beach.

Deciding to get on out and enjoy this day, I stood beside my tent on the dry grass. I looked out over the water toward the horizon. I saw what looked like a tornado, but it was a clear day. It became a very large tornado!

I walked down on the beach to the edge of the water. I looked both ways on the beach, no one. The tornado got closer, and I realized it was birds. The Birds would circle down to the water by the thousands and then go up very high, maybe a mile high, by the thousands. Circling.

The circle on the water with birds sitting, approaching and leaving, from side to side, I can only guess, a quarter mile wide.

The top was well over a half a mile wide.

The top was thin where it flared out similar to the top of a screw. That is where most of the sound was coming from. So loud and magnificent.

It was very, very tall and flared out slowly until, at the top, it started to flare out quickly, as I mentioned.

Without anything to judge by. The size of the top and bottom might have been larger.

For some reason, it was inspiring, uplifting, as well as exciting. I had to stay at the edge of the water. The huge funnel was full of birds.

I could also hear them. With the breeze coming in that morning, the Birds sounded like they were all around me. The Bird Tornado slowly went back out.

That's the story of the Birds, and I'm sticking to it.

After the prayer and seeing another wonder of God, I felt as exceptionally strong. My mind was clear. Wow, I remember being so happy and full of energy.

Not alone at all.

I told two respected local Hawaiians what I saw. They *both* knew exactly what I was talking about. It is more than a legend. Well, of course. It is called "the Birds." It means luck for a fishing crew to see them. Very rare. They had never heard of anyone on shore seeing "the Birds."

Digging up my two thousand dollars that same day, I left Oahu and headed back to Georgia the next day. I gave away my tent. It was still in great shape. I went by and visited a few friends,

Matsa, broke his rule, and gave me a discount on two ounces. He claimed it was not a discount at all. Only payment for taking the shotgun away from Lenny. We had a good laugh.

I mailed some postcards from Waikiki. Took me long enough.

After purchasing new socks, shoes, long pants, a billfold, and a jacket. I had only used the money left from selling the surfboard. I headed to the airport on the Bus with the two thousand dollars that I retrieved from the woods and a paper shopping bag with all my belongings was less than half full.

CHAPTER 14

Back in Georgia

"I'm Sorry, Did You Think It Was Love"

Back on the mainland. At the Los Angeles International Airport (LAX), I walked out and saw six stars through the haze. I seriously thought about going back to Hawaii and giving it another year. Maui this time. Tickets were cheap.

Time to get back and see my dad, and I love my grandmother Ma too much. I had a big surprise for Ma. The bus used Longview Drive, the road in front of her house. That is where I was getting off. Right in front of Ma's (Maw's) house.

I had five hours before my bus headed out. I rested in a stairwell at the airport. In the stairwell, I looked back at the past twenty months.

I pulled out my well used Bible with some notes and fell asleep. When I woke up, there was still enough time before my bus left.

The ride across the States was what I needed before I returned home.

I gave the Bible to an old man named Westley, who sat down beside me. I was staring out the window.

He asked if he could borrow it. He was so happy reading the Bible I loaned him, nodding his head and smiling.

I finally found out why.

He said, "Shord do preshate your Bible. I never had one that nice." He went on, "Daddy did. He read to the family every night." Westley was a talker. He went on, "I am going to stay with my oldest son, his wife, and six children, who are six of my fifteen grandchildren."

I asked him "Do you have a Bible, Westly?"

He said, "Sure. Read it every day."

He showed me the most-used Bible I believe I have ever seen.

I noticed we had something in common. Not a mark on any of the pages in the worn Bible. I will not mark in my Bible.

My dad does make notes in his Bibles. Many preachers mark in Bibles.

I don't. Beside the point. I asked, "Why did you ask to borrow mine if you have yours?"

This man said, "Well, Mr. Cash, it was very odd. Just now, I was reading Ezekiel while waiting on this bus and noticed part of the book of Ezekiel was missing. I was staring at the middle of the book of Daniel. The rest of Ezekiel and the beginning of Daniel was gone. I do not know how long those pages have been missing. I have not been in that part of my Bible in a while." Westly went on and on about the travels of his Bible and what studies he had been doing.

My, soon-to-be-his, Bible was a very nice Bible. I kept it in good condition.

Thieves don't seem to mess with Bibles. Westley opened his Bible, and sure enough, Ezekiel 27 went straight to Daniel 11. Other pages were about to fall out!

I also gave him twenty dollars along with my Bible.

I watched his son and stepdaughter hug him and pick up his luggage through the window of the bus.

I wonder about the little things like that. Westly just happened to find those pages missing that morning. I had a nice Bible to give him, that had served its purpose. What were the chances he would sit beside me? Today, that bus? So many what-ifs.

Did Jesus intervene? I am serious. Do things similar to Westley and the Bible happen to you? He needed a nice Bible to enter a new home. My Bible? Just asking.

I wish I had Westley back. Country White trash girl, cowboy hat and all decided I was lonely. She was chewing gum and thought she was pretty. Talking, telling one lie after another. Yep, this is more like the bus ride should be.

I couldn't believe I was sitting beside a "real Nashville star." The contracts had been signed. Her boyfriend left. Took the brand-new truck! Her agent was sending her money. But she needed a place to stay. If you know what I mean. "Where did you get that tan?" "How far are you going?" "You sure don't talk much." She would not shut up.

I had to just tell the *stupid redneck grayhound girl* the truth. I was part of the Billy Graham Crusade. We should talk about her soul and the decisions she was making at her young age. That worked. I had a nice non talking person after that.

I had given the driver Ma's address. He knew the exact house. This had been his route for nine years.

I was going to pull the cable anyway so everyone knew the bus was going to make a stop. The bus driver blew the horn. Ma was opening the door as I walked up.

She is the *best grandmother*.

I knew I could relax a little before all the commotion.

We talked. Ma fixed me some iced tea.

She was so happy I arrived at her house.

Ma could not stand it any longer.

She called my parents' house, and while looking at me, she said, "Guess who I have over here."

Mom and Dad only lived a mile away.

They drove over with Lavada, who happened to be at their house.

Mom went and bought some beautiful T-bone steaks and cooked them right then.

The whole family was over in a matter of an hour.

My steak took up the complete plate. I had not eaten red meat in over a year. It was *magnificent*.

What a great time. Hugs and more hugs.

I went to church with them on Sunday.

My fame was over in a week.

Dad let me borrow his truck.

I went to J Riggings, where I was working when I quit and took off twenty months ago. Everybody was still there. Lots of handshakes. The ladies were hugging me a little longer than usual. They all looked and smelled very nice.

The operations manager sent his secretary out. She asked me to hang on until Jim could speak to me. Then Tim Moon came up and told me, "Dave, you were right, man. You were right about everything." He gave me a big hand shake and a guy hug. We were talking when Jim came back. Tim and I made plans to meet in a few hours at the same bar as before. Jim was very glad to see me. My old boss, in between Jim and myself, was way across the distribution center. He was always taking credit for my ideas.

Jim, of course, shook my hand. He said, "Dave, we really missed you around here. I had no idea the amount of work you were doing as a manager. Thank you for stopping by. It is good to see you. You are looking well, I must admit."

I responded, "Thank you, Jim. It feels good to step back into the shop. I really love this place."

Jim said, "It showed as soon as you left. You managed this center extremely well. Dave, we had to hire three people to replace you. That is what I wanted to tell you."

Wow, I thought. I could only respond, "Thank you, Jim, to hear my work was finally noticed. Thanks. Very much."

That was a confidence booster. I went back to the house I was renting before I left. Everything was the same. My old-bedroom things and mattress set had been moved to a different bedroom. I just moved right in.

Stopped in next door to visit Chip. He was surprised. Happy. Pulled a Fosters "oil can" out of the fridge. Ice cold. He had a girlfriend at the time. So sweet and pretty. She said Chip wondered what happened to me, if I would return. Chip said, "Before we get started, let's smoke a little of this reefer I just bought."

I said, "I brought you a souvenir." I tossed a half ounce of the best pot in the world onto his coffee table.

Chip said, "I am going to cry." He picked up the bag, smelled it, and handed it to his girlfriend.

I said, "I am glad to be back and see the place." Chip cut the bottom off a Zig Zag. Julie, his girlfriend, rolls the perfect-size joint for this quality weed. "Mr. David, tell us just anything about this most amazing venture."

I took a long pull off the cold Fosters beer. Yep, Chips place was something. Old, unfinished wood, comfortable.

I was the reason for a big party.

That and everybody was looking for the Hawaiian weed to be passed around.

I had the weirdest feeling. A lot of friends showed up. We had a keg and plenty of food. Suddenly the feeling. Nothing had changed. It was like I had never left. I looked around. It hit me. I had changed. Everything else was the same. I knew I had to do something soon. I took a side trail.

A friend walked up to me and said, "Don't worry about a job. Just go to work with me. These guys will hire you." Commercial construction, hard work. My friend was smart; he knew I had more of the Hawaiian smoke.

I found a good-looking girlfriend. It was at a party at the river behind the house we were renting. I drove my '64 Pontiac Tempest down to the river once the party was well underway. This girl stood out. Single and supergood-looking. That day, she even had fresh flowers in her hair. Her name is Jesse. She was talking to another guy, standing very close to him. I took a second look, almost impossible not to. She must have read my mind. Jesse glanced my way and noticed me looking at her. Then she put her hand on the arm of the guy she was talking to.

That guy, Richard Kardos, was a sleaze bucket. He was as interesting to talk to as a chicken. She was playing a game with me.

I quit, too much trouble. I walked to the riverside. Forgot about her. A lot of people to talk to.

Her place was a lot closer to work. I still kept the other place. We had so much fun. She had a five-year-old son. We drove to Miami to visit her friends along with her "best friend."

Her friends in Miami had nice offshore boats. One owned a beautiful restaurant. Wonderful fresh seafood. Everyone had their own business. We went fishing every day. I was catching fish soon after arriving. She knew a lot of the nicest people.

I was welcome and treated like one of them. If you ever need anything, never hesitate to call. Was told to me often enough.

What a vacation.

Back in Atlanta. Her "best friend" got us incredible tickets to the sold-out Rolling Stones concert at the Fox.

Her friend traveled with the band!

After the concert, we went to the hotel where the band were staying. Her friend took us to a large suite of the sound manager, who was the one that supplied us with the tickets. It was just the four of us for a little while—the sound manager, who was dating Jesse's friend, Jesse, and myself. Jesse's friend asked how we liked the seats. We were in the center, about one-quarter back from the front. There were no better seats. Empty seats on each side of us. The head technician said we always took care of Jesse.

The suite was very large. It started getting wild. People poured in. Mr. Sound Tech broke open a vacuum-packed brick of primo pot, pulled out a drawer from the dresser, handed it to me with three new packs of Zig Zags, and said, "You know what to do!" I responded, "Fast as I can."

I rolled and rolled and rolled. He ordered room service, a case of Heineken and Becks. It was ice cold served in a bunch of round buckets of ice. Someone ordered room service. Two people came in to quickly remove old buckets and trash. Monster tip. Both took a few joints. As the cleanup guys were leaving, a cart loaded with club sandwiches and apple pie showed up. I grabbed one of each. Both were better than ever. Two guys came in quickly to remove old buckets and trash, replace towels, and get monster tips. Each gladly received joints. More beer arrived. A cart of thick hamburgers with fries.

I had already quit smoking and drinking. I had to drive. I found a Coke to drink in the suite's bar. I kept rolling perfect joints till I was way ahead. Mick Jagger was in the hall when we left. Just kidding about Jagger. What a night.

Before I realized it, I was living with Jesse. She was the perfect girlfriend. Dinner was always ready and very good. Clothes was clean. Plenty of sex. Always a party to go to.

This girl played a trick on me. She asked if we were going to get married. I said, "Yeah, probably, someday." She got pushy and got all lovey, in a moment of weakness, soon after getting a haircut. I had just taken a shower. I said, "Soon, yeah, that would be nice."

Problem was I was ready to get out. So me saying, "Soon, yeah, that would be nice," meant I was about to ask her to marry me.

She planned a party. Did not tell me until the day before. All my friends! A preengagement party! All her friends. It was an all-out fancy deal. Her girlfriends were so happy for her. My buddies said, "Dang, David."

That night, I arrived home from work early to her place. Her car was not there. I realized I had pretty much moved in.

While she was at her parents' house, I mean this was the day of the party. I grabbed my clothes. I left a lot of stuff because I did not want to get caught. My electronics stayed. Records and tapes. I didn't care. She could have all the "stuff."

I just wanted to leave. I was *gone*.

I was told later. She could have killed me, but she told everybody she broke it off. No one believed her. No one believed I asked her to marry me. Her old boyfriend was there. He was always there.

Many months later, I was contracting by the square foot, working for Metro Insulation. I walked into a restaurant bar on lunch break with one other installer. Jesse's father was there at a table, drinking. I tried to avoid him, but it was too small a place. He was a very nice man. I ordered a beer and sat down. The two of us. The other installer had his own truck, so he ate and took off.

It was meant to be. He cleared up just about everything. Mr. Brown was an alcoholic. He was lonely. Ready to talk.

I did not "get" Jesse. Jesse chose me. Her weak boyfriend took her to the party at the river. She went to meet me, the guy who did not care. Mr. Confidence did not need a new car to impress the girls. Threw girls away like old chewing gum. Stan used quote signs to say "this good 'Christian man.'"

I had heard enough. So I said, "Stan, you are really telling me your daughter went to the party with her boyfriend to meet me, her second husband? Her boyfriend told her this crap about me."

Stan was taking a sip of straight whisky. He raised his eyebrows just slightly.

After a few minutes of silence, Stan remarked, "Dave, I'm sorry. Did you think it was love? That cursed-with-good-looks daughter of mine has been through so many men! Party after party. Now she is twenty-four? She is looking closely in the mirror. You passed inspection with her friends in Miami! I heard Jesse on the phone. They all love you. You can party with the best. I know Jesse wants a husband. All her 'friends' have one. She believes you will be interesting and make some money. A good catch. She can help you with some connections, I don't know. David, I wouldn't trust her as a wife."

Two more drinks showed up. I asked, "Stan, why are you telling me this?" Stan had the answer, "Dave you are a good man. You laugh hard. You tell the funniest jokes. You are too honest. It would be great to have you in the family. But I am glad you got away while you could. Jesse is fine. She has already found her soulmate, that special someone." I said, "A toast to the best almost-father-in-law."

I knew I dodged a bullet when I grabbed my clothes from Jesse's and took off. Stan confirmed it was a large-caliber hollow point.

I was falling right back into what I had left. When I left Jesse's that day, my first stop was at my folks' house. The only one at home was Mom. It was good to talk to her about what I just did. Yep, my mother was the best one to discuss things with. I left there feeling much better.

CHAPTER 15

Abandoned House on the Edge of Town

My Life Was About to Change

THERE IS AN OLD THREE-ROOM TENANT HOUSE ON FORTY acres. It sits back about a quarter mile off the corner of Highways 141 and 120. What an intersection. Back then, only one full-service gas station stood at the intersection. Highway 141 is a popular street, road, or highway. It starts in Buckhead near Lenox Square and winds its way north to Cummings, Georgia.

Back to the house, it is completely full of trash. A hoarder spent twenty-five years stuffing it jammed full. The hoarder also piled junk along the sides of the house. The man died years back. That's when the yard and area around it became a local illegal dump. Endless construction and landscape debris, along with household garbage, have made this project just not worth it.

Walking up to the house, you immediately see, besides the endless garbage, it needs a roof. The original old wood shingles are visible where the dry rotted roofing has blown away. The full-length front and back porch floors have rotted away. Therefore, the main front door has chunks of cement blocks lined up as steps. Busted windows, boards missing, and the paint has peeled in huge chunks of white paint down to the natural wood.

The house has no plumbing.

Like many tenant houses, this house has three rooms and two front doors. Walking inside the ceiling of the house is twelve feet. In many places, the trash is up to the ceiling. A narrow foot path runs through the middle of each room. At places, I have to turn a little sideways through stacks of brown grocery bags, endless newspapers, magazines, old blinds, broken chairs, moth-eaten clothes, children's plastic and broken wooden toys, and parts of furniture.

Along each side of the house, as I mentioned, is a place for glass, rusted pipe, miles of cables, bicycle frames, bicycle tires, bicycle handlebars, rusted wheelbarrows, broken kids' wagons all gathered in the right area with years of weeds, bushes, and small trees growing around and through them. I promise, not one thing of value. You can see the house has been open and gone through many times over the years it has sat full.

The largest room, also the common room, has a fireplace. The trash was stuffed higher and fuller in this room.

No one wants this place. There are other old houses.

I liked the house. This is it.

Jimmy Carmichale, a fairly new friend, understood. This old house was small. Perfect for one person. Even Jimmy said, "Don't do it, Dave, no way, not worth all the work." He went with me to visit the owner a few times.

That is Mrs. Findley, the owner, seventy-five years old. She drove a twelve-year-old light-yellow Lincoln Continental with only sixteen thousand miles. Mrs. Findley always dressed nice. She had about twenty cats and cooked dinner for them every day.

I could not believe such a beautiful, large, and well-kept home, not far from downtown Duluth, Georgia.

It took five visits, but we eventually worked out a deal.

She had already decided to tear the place down. The place was "disgusting," she said repeatedly. It was going to cost a lot, but it was such an eyesore on her property. Right there on that very popular intersection. The fire department would burn it down for free. The city would haul off the debris for a large price.

She could, at first, not comprehend what I was asking to do for free. She then did not believe I would do what I said.

My now-friend Mrs. Findley tried to talk me out of it. "It has just way too much garbage. The house is probably rotten with all the big holes in the roof. Well, okay," she finally said, "I have nothing to lose."

I rented the place for twenty-five dollars a month. Part of the deal is that I had to bring her the rent and give it to her every month. Plan on a visit. If she was not at home, come back when she was. I couldn't mail the rent. That was our deal until six years later when the sweet lady suddenly died. That is when the deal ended.

I gave Mrs. Findley a check for twenty-five dollars. She insisted on two free months. So on the bottom of the check where it says "For," I wrote the appropriate month, three months out. On the back, I wrote the simple lease conditions. This check had both our signatures as a check normally does. I kept it for the entirety of my time at the house. The canceled check was inside one of those clear invoice envelopes you see stuck on the front of boxes. I had a new one and stuck it inside, next to the front door.

When I drove back up to the house, it hit me that I just rented a trash dump. It looked a lot worse. I had been putting on blinders as to the amount of endless garbage.

I went to work immediately. My 100 percent focus was on the inside of the house. I had abruptly quit my construction job. The manager was fine. I was always early and worked hard. Worked late when asked. He wrote my check and added an extra fifty!

All my belongings were in a cheap luggage bag and eighteen-by-twenty-inch cardboard box. My Florsheim shoe selling clothes were on hangers. I had my '64 Pontiac Tempest. Everything I own, again!

I was sort of in hiding. I wanted to be left alone. I had arrived back in Georgia from Hawaii and slipped right back into a big ego. I was with a girl I didn't plan on getting married to. Going nowhere. Never reading or studying. Sorry, you know the story.

At first, Jimmy Charmichale was the only one who knew about the house or where I was. I did not ask for any help. I purchased a new wheelbarrow and borrowed Jimmy's hand trucks to use inside the house. I told my father about the house. I had been borrowing his truck. This is what he loaned me when I first arrived home from Hawaii. A little Chevy S-10. I gave it back as soon as I was able. He loaded it to me, again, after I broke it off with Jesse. Jesse and I shared a car. Plus I used a work truck. Just like him. He answered, "Anytime, son."

I also borrowed a small trailer from Chip. Load after load, I cleared the inside of the house. Around the clock, in four days, the house was empty, not clean but empty. Dad helped the last two days. Chip came over on Friday. A lot of manpower that day. Chip was really getting into the project and did not leave till dark. He was a machine.

Dad came up late Friday and helped after working all week at General Motors. He was itching to get in on this project. As you already know, we work well together.

Chip said, "Hello, Mr. Cash," and kept on working. My happy father made a lot of measurements and wrote them down. He also was making some sketches. Worked for only forty-five minutes and took off.

My father was back early Saturday. He brought some of my mother's biscuits. Six with sausage and four with butter and fig preserves. A thermos of coffee.

The two of us worked outside on the worst piles of construction debris. Roofing, wet Sheetrock, and more roofing and more Sheetrock on and on. Dad and I cleared huge mounds of garbage. We also swept the house out very well. Scraping where needed.

We stopped with the garbage about one o'clock to build a stand for an old porcelain kitchen sink Dad brought with him. It had been sitting in his garage for about ten years. We built the stand out of new two-by-fours my father always kept for something like this. When we dropped the flawless old sink in the frame, it was perfect for the old house.

We also tore out all the old deck and frame from the front and back porches. It was rotten and unsafe.

Dad and I framed it with new roughhewn two-by-eight pine. My father precut the framing of the front and back porch last night.

Smart, he had electricity at his house. Dad also brought a used piece of five-eighths plywood. He had cut it last night as well, to fit on the front porch, at the front door.

It looked good, and people could step on the front porch and walk up to the front door. My father had also cut a three-foot-wide, half-inch piece for the back door.

A lot done in one day.

Like I said, Dad and I work well together.

Sunset on Saturday, I could see what we had accomplished in about a week.

My father offered me his truck for the next week. I took him up on it.

During week, two I picked up the PVC and some five-gallon buckets of quality wrong-color-mixed paint. I delivered gravel to my front yard, as well as river rock. Tore down a couple of old real estate signs that week and carried them home for the porch deck. Picked up a *new* Sears hot-water heater (on sale, damaged).

I borrowed money from my dad so I could go ahead and buy the new roofing. He insisted on the loan. I did not ask. I had the money, but it was going fast.

Friday night, I drove into Chamblee and returned Dad's truck... I started to say something. My father told me he knew how much I appreciated it.

I took a hot shower at my folks' house. I had to be at work tomorrow, Saturday morning. I was broke. I would be able to make a 50 percent draw against my pay after I would work tomorrow.

During that week, I had my father's truck. I wrote myself a list to make best use of the truck. I also had to stop myself from picking up the endless junk. I must move inside and start serious cleaning.

I took long naps in the backseat of my car instead of going to bed at the house I was staying in. That way, I would wake up and go to work. I told them to rent my room a week ago. It was rented the next day. Someone was using my room for free, anyway.

At the back of my mind, *Now I have to get some water hooked up!*

The ceiling, walls, and floors were all made of one-by-three tongue and groove wood. In very good condition. The roof only had one leak! How? It was a wonderful job of wood shingles under layers of old roofing. I guess. The piles of newspapers soaked up all the water! No damage to the floor. It drained out a small knot hole in the ceiling onto the ten feet of newspapers. Zero damage to my new home. Hard to believe.

After scraping and sweeping, I mopped the floors with water and a little bleach using water that I brought in five-gallon buckets and one-gallon jugs. I opened the house up to dry.

The front yard was a long, wide black mud puddle. I picked up three loads of gravel that I mentioned for nice parking. Made a good walkway into the front door with that load of river rock. That made a big difference in the way my new home looked.

A few days after the floor drying, I mixed up about four or so gallons of water base primer. I thinned it some. Made three gallons into four. I used a mop, mop bucket, squeegee, and big paintbrush. I very quickly painted a thin coat of primer on all the floors, painting the primer a little up on the walls. The floor loved it. It just soaked the primer up. It dried fast.

I had the power turned on, and the phone hooked up. I purchased a mailbox and made a work-of-art post to put it on. I moved in the day after the primer was put down. I was already sleeping/camping there. *Now* I carried a bag inside. A box. I also carried in my Florsheim shoe-selling work clothes on hangers. I sat on the floor. Home.

A Story about Bees

Listen to this. I never knew, heard, or even read about bees doing something like what I am going to tell you.

I was sitting on a seat cushion that was left over from my broken-neck days. I was sitting on the cushion which was on the floor. I was leaning against the wall next to the main front door, admiring my new home and also looking out the window to my right. The wall straight ahead had the hole where I would hook up a woodstove. Across from the front door was the door leading into the large common room with the recently installed kitchen sink. The common room had a fireplace.

Back to what I was going to amaze you with about Bees.

I believe those were wasps, maybe hornets. I say wasps.

I was looking out the window and noticed one of the panes was broken in a way that it fell part way and left an opening about an inch wide and pretty long. I had noticed this broken windowpane before. This time, a solid-black wasp crawled through the opening and took flight inside my empty living room.

Empty except for myself and my medium-size suitcase.

The wasp was black, long, and thin. I had seen them often as you might have. The wasp flew around the room staying in the top half. Then in the top third. Then the top of the room. The wasp flew full speed into a spider web.

I watched it as it seemed to struggle.

It was moving its wings and legs.

The nest was bouncing wildly.

The wasp stopped.

I thought, *What was that all about?* I looked over to my right as before, and another wasp was outside on my broken windowpane.

The wasp that was in the nest started bouncing and moving more wildly than before.

To me, it looked like it was getting more tangled.

Then the wasp did a grand finally *jurk, jurk, jurk.* Bouncing very wildly until the wasp broke loose and fell to the floor, very tangled up in the spiderweb. About this time, the other black wasp crawled in the broken glass and took flight. It also flew in circles around the room. Round and round.

I look at the other wasp on the floor. That one is lifting its wings and moving its legs out, using its front legs to gather the spiderweb strands.

I notice the second wasp is circling higher. I believe I know which spiderweb the wasp is going for.

It flies past it, goes around again, and then, at full speed, flies into the one I know it is going after. The wasp starts using its wings and legs, getting more and more web tangled. It looks so tangled the web is bouncing.

I look back at the one on my newly primed floor. This little fella is working away. It has a tiny ball started at its front with the shorter front legs. The wasp is using its mouth pinchers and front legs steadily working to pull a continuous strand of web off. It is working its wings and legs trying to follow the strand.

Never seen anything like this. I am mesmerized and watch the wasp on the floor for a few minutes.

He is going at a steady pace—pushing the wings and legs out as needed; pulling with the short front legs; and, with the help of his pinchers, winding the strand into a ball.

I look up at the Wasp in the web. I notice this time it is *not* getting more tangled. The wasp is pulling more webs apart with its wings and grabbing strands with the back legs. The wasp does get more tangled as it pulls more web, moving legs and wings; the web is swinging. The wasp stops and jerks.

My friend on the floor is steady working.

I look back up.

The second wasp is now *jurk, jurk, jurk, jurk, jurk, jurk, jurk.* Looks like this one is in trouble. The wasp stops and hangs in the web.

I glance back at my friend on the floor. He has the steady pace going. The ball is the size of a BB! It looks too big.

The movement catches the corner of my eye. *Jurk, jurk, jurk!* He has me worried.

The wasp falls and hits the floor hard. That has got to hurt. I watch as he lies still and then begins to use his front smaller legs and mouth pinchers to clear an opening.

I forget about my beer. It am so busy around here.

I look at my new friend, Wasp Number One.

He is finishing up. The ball is a size BB. Can be a touch larger than a BB!

I watch as he takes the ball in just his four back legs.

He flies around the room. Gathers the ball close to him with all six legs. Now, of course, heads toward the window. At the last split second, the wasp turns sideways to clear his wings through the narrow glass.

I watch him fly outside and away.

I watch the other wasp finish with his ball of web and depart.

Another wasp was on the window. I went ahead and let him in.

After that wasp left, I fixed the hole with some tape. And swept the ceiling.

The wasp started arriving in the other front room that I was not planning on using for a while. So I gave it to them for a few days, went in, and checked on them from time to time.

One wasp was stuck in the web.

I checked for hours.

Yep, this guy messed up.

I took my step ladder and cut the spiderweb just above him. Let him drop on a paper plate and lie him on the floor.

Five wasp friends showed up to help the wasp in trouble.

When I walked in, one of the wasps flew up a few feet and hung in the air a foot from me. That wasp let me know who was boss.

I could come and go after that.

The five of them worked together. The one who was caught in the net slowly livened up and started helping. The little feller made it.

After that, I swept the webs and patched the place the wasp was getting in.

I called Duluth Water and hooked up with City Water. Digging a 150-foot trench two feet deep to the side of my house was steady work.

I had already purchased a 150 foot of one-inch PVC as my main water pipe. First, I hooked up the kitchen sink.

Wonderful, "waterful," I made up a new word. Waterful. Water inside the house.

Next, the hot-water heater. Hot and cold water and a very professional job, I will say.

I was shaving at the sink, washing off right next to the kitchen sink. I hooked up a hose so I could shower on the back porch. Warm water outside. Soon after that, I framed a shower. Used plastic for the sides.

After vacuuming the walls, I painted the living room walls light gray because that is what was in the wrong-mix-quality paint. The common room was a light mint green for the same reason. The other front room, I decided I would not paint the walls. I washed them.

I was lucky. Five gallons, dark brick red for my floors. I painted a dark brick red the front and back porches. Two coats. The porch post, the mailbox post. The other front door. My car, just kidding. Exterior latex wrong-mix color.

Randy, a contractor friend. I worked for him off and on when he was low on help. He drove up with a fiberglass shower stall. A stand-up shower stall. Randy got out of his truck smiling and said, "Do you want this?"

I was about to do a backflip and ask how much.

Randy was doing a remodel. He usually cut these out because it's easier. He remembered I framed a shower area. All I had so far was thick plastic for the sides. Randy took this one out in one piece. It was a pain. It had to have been. Randy backed up to my porch and gave it to me!

I tried to give him fifty dollars.

He was insulted. *No.* Randy finally took the fifteen-dollar beer money for the guys who helped get the shower stall out in one piece.

We drank a few dark St. Pauli Girls as we moved the fiberglass shower stall into the room I had already framed for the shower stall. I already had the plumbing ready. Randy took a six-pack of those ice-cold dark St. Pauli's with him.

Last thing, Randy said, "Your place looks like a picture you would see on a postcard...the way you drive up at an angle and the big oak tree at the end of your driveway." When I told the guys where I was taking the shower stall, one of them said, "You mean the dump! I wish you would have taken a before-and-after picture."

The next week, Chip drove up pulling a twenty-foot sailboat! Big grin. He asked me, "Guess what I just bought."

It was forty degrees this morning, and we were headed to Lake Lanier. It warmed up to seventy degrees.

The two of us took the boat out. Raised the sales. Opened everything. Checked the boat out. It was a calm day. Chip had a nice basic sailboat. We took it for a run and made a list.

We had a four-man "team." All winter long, no traffic on Lake Lanier in the cold months.

At the beginning of the next spring, I went with Chip to the Outer Banks, North Carolina, for a week. We stayed with his father. He lived on the beach his whole life. Traveled the world on ships. What a wonderful week. Chip's Father was so kind.

He gave me a belt buckle. Hand-carved ivory. He had display cases of things he collected. He bought the belt buckle in some foreign land. It wound up being worth $1,800. Chip said his father never gave him one. I was more than happy to give the belt buckle to Chip.

Going to work at Florsheim shoes. Thursday, Saturday, and Sunday straight commission, making more than the store manager. I was about five months living in the *abandoned house*. I had to stop major work on my home and work in residential construction along with the shoe sales job at Lenox Square. My pockets had become way too empty. I owed my father money.

I was hitting the sweet spot. I was saving for a lot of things— new chainsaws, a nice woodstove, some new tools, a new window air conditioner, another nice suit for work. The list went on. I had a list of books for a home library. New tires! A radiator and car insurance just hit. Sorry, about complaining.

I felt at home. I loved coming home with the hot and cold water.

Dad brought the old rounded-top refrigerator he kept out in their garage. It even looked perfect in this old house. With some sandpaper and Rust-o-leum spray paint, it looked very nice.

The kitchen and dining room are fine. Two-burner hot plate. Four slot toaster. Old table with four chairs. Remember, this is the biggest room in the house. It has a fireplace.

It happened. *My home is finished.* The outside is light brown with dark-brown trim. I have a few flowers planted along the front. A beautiful well-kept yard. Zero trash around the house. My home is perfect for a postcard. I have a bathroom with a septic tank that I have dug by hand. The *new* toilet, I just had to reach in my billfold and purchase it. I went ahead and bought a good one. As for the septic tank, I used old cinder block and cement pipe that Mrs. Findley gave me. It was in her backyard. A cement slab that was dumped here for the top. This septic tank would handle a small building.

I now have nice carpet in the front and back rooms. A new woodstove, chain saw, window air conditioner. I like the new twin extralong mattress I purchased. I purchased a full extralong as well because a lot of people tend to like my place and stay.

Peace and quiet.

I built two bedframes. I purchased three new very simple cushion chairs. Five chairs that go in and out, the front porch usually. Living very simple. Living alone is what God planned for me. Back to reading and studying.

I still drink and smoke weed off and on. The superaddiction to drinking and or need for strong dope hits hard about once a month.

Sometimes, I may get a sickening reality. This is how it starts. When it first starts, the last thing I want is liquor or drugs because I feel sick. The reality keeps opening up. For instance, if I am walking out of the grocery store, I know to keep walking. It is not a panic attack. It just gets too real. Just too aware.

Suddenly, the sick feeling goes away. I have to drink a lot of alcohol. The switch is flipped. I must shut the thoughts down. So the brain hits the switch for the next fix. It wants the drug. It always lasts for a few days. If I am drinking a beer or have not drunk in a week or two, I must do some serious drinking, do cocaine or something. I must have strong liquor.

Living alone, I have read and exercised trying to get through the supercraving. I will wake up at 3:00 a.m. sometimes, mad because I emptied the house of strong alcohol, even though I went to bed without a thought of drinking. Instead, I began to do sit-ups and push-ups. I never see or feel it coming. It just hits.

My main craving is that I need morphine. I need something. The craving is strong. I had it a lot at Warm Springs, at home in the side room, in my apartment, at work in the shoe store, day or night. In Hawaii, twice in a row, the need was so strong I could taste drugs.

I paced, prayed, and exercised, only to get blackout drunk on the third or fourth day a few times in the *abandoned house*. This is after being totally nothing for many months. Continuous craving. Lasting days. I have never heard of that.

Believe me, I have had so much "unsolicited" advice, the worst. I have asked for advice, the best.

Just north of Duluth, a church has had a sign-up for years. Some of you readers may remember the sign: "Problem with Alcohol. Meeting Here. Every Tuesday and Thursday 7:00 p.m." I tried that for a while. Supernice people.

Every day, I get up early. As soon as I wake up, I jump out of bed. Yes, even if it is freezing. I always exercise, shower and shave, and dress nice. I believe we are supposed to always try our best to be clean and dress well. Also try to be clean spiritually. Your body is a temple of the Holy Spirit, who is in you.

I have a home. Friends are coming over, sitting on the porch. They always bring twelve packs of beer or a couple of six-packs of bottles so much that I have it double stacked outside my refrigerator full of beer. I work two or three jobs. Friends with young children love my place, the nice yard, and the woods. I plan food to cook out. I make it a point to take off a day on the weekend whenever I can.

Mrs. Findley drove up one time with six kids running around the house.

One little girl saw her and wanted to show Mrs. Findley she could do a somersault.

Mrs. Findley was so happy seeing the children. They all wanted to show her something.

With six or seven cars and trucks parked in front of my house. The little girl's mother volunteered to turn the huge Lincoln Continental around for Mrs. Findley.

Mrs. Findley walked through the house, and the children followed her.

She refused a chair on the front porch.

I offered her some tea.

She said that was the fourth offer, that she would like to be on her way. Mrs. Findley said, "I just love all the children playing. When I see friends in town, they tell me how nice the place looks from the road. They tell me they like what I have done with the place! "David, you have done more than we agreed to. The place is so nice. I am going to have to charge you more rent." She started laughing. She was so quick with that joke.

I started laughing and gave her a short hug. She hugged back real hard.

Her big yellow Lincoln was pointed in the right direction. A couple of kids ran up to hold her door and say, "Bye." She drove down the long driveway. My first inspection?

Most of my friends are married with a kid or two. Or on a second marriage with a kid or two from the first marriage. Not that many single people out there. I am setting up for the possibility of a long run at being single. Looong run. I live in a place most ladies would not like. I do not have a new, or even a nice, ride. I am broke. I am an addict. I have nothing to offer. Bad luck with women.

Really don't deserve a good one the way I have acted. I need to get back on track. I don't know what I need. I am working and working.

My addiction has taken over again. I started drinking too much. Now I want cocaine, weed, and alcohol. All at once. I have an excessive need. I went to the library and read information on addiction. Before I broke my neck, I never wanted to drink or do drugs. I am such a bad addict now. I have a need so excessive I cannot overcome it. It is stronger than I am. It reminds me of that powerful need for morphine only fourteen years ago.

I never wanted to do cocaine. If someone says "cocaine," I want to have some. If I have some, I want a lot. I can't get enough. I never wanted to do cocaine. I never wanted to be a drunk—nice name, an alcoholic. I drink beer. Liquor goes down too fast.

So I will live alone and try to control my morphine addiction that gets worse.

I read theology books, books about Creation and such. I love reading history and science, and sometimes, I can't read when the major cravings hits. Jogging helps. I have tried to find another person with the same problem. Similar is not working. Anyway, moving on.

Another story. I was over at Chip's house. He lives in a nice old house. He has become a successful insurance adjuster. He had in the last few days returned from a long trip to Florida writing hurricane damage. He returned with a half-pound of cocaine. The best and purest I have ever had.

Two dozen or so of us were having a party at Chip's house we started around lunch. I brought over three cases of beer iced down in coolers. Heinekens and Michelob for later. We all had some of Chip's coke and had a nice time. The city people go home. I refilled the coolers late that evening and added some ice. I also bought three more cases of beer. Six cases total. Put two of them in the fridge. Finally, I got to sleep during the day's sunrise.

Chip called about two o'clock on Sunday afternoon. "Hay, man, we are cooking up some hamburgers and steaks. There is one thing missing."

I said, "I have the beer."

Chip said, "Okay, you're invited. Hurry. We are out over here." He hung up. No alcohol sales on Sunday in Georgia. I knew the Saturday party was a warm-up party.

I open the large trunk to my '64 Tempest. The coolers are moved to Chip's front porch. The beer out of coolers is taken care of with the utmost care. Most of it is iced down. What a relief!

Eight of us are enjoying filet mignon cooked medium with Tater Tots and thick slices of tomato and potato salad. Plenty of big hamburgers with all the fixings are also being consumed. The food is finished. The girls are in the kitchen with the case of wine. Chip is chopping up the coke and passing it around. Ice-cold beer and doing lines.

I realize this one girl has taken up with me or keeps following me around. Now we have become a "couple," I guess. She is regular pretty, which is the best kind of pretty. Then she smiled and wow pretty.

She will probably run or disappear when she finds out I am broke. Plus, I don't have any money. That was not a typing mistake.

Oh well, I had a girlfriend for the party. She told me the guy who left with the couple was her date. The couple is her best friend from high school and her husband. Now the guys over there would not leave her alone. They kept hitting on her. She didn't want to leave just because of them. She told me her name is Julia. She already knew my name.

It's getting to around 2:00 a.m. Chip lay me out a monster line. Bigger than a new carpenter's pencil. The lines had been getting bigger all night, and it was the purest coke I had ever experienced.

For some reason, I looked down at my left pocket. My left shirt pocket was jumping with the rhythm of my heart. I did not know it at the time that line would 100 percent kill me. I wanted it. I even took the straw and said, "Thank you, Chip." I still almost hit it. Half up the right, half up the left. I was feeling superhuman. I had already done more, way more cocaine than I had ever done before. Well, it was over two days. Today alone, I was at a new personal high. I had already "snorted" at least a thousand dollars' worth today, ten hours. I could feel my heart slamming in my chest.

Instead, I put my hands up and told Chip, "I've had enough."

Chip raised his palms, took a half step back, and halfway shouted, "Hold the press!"

My friends laughed.

Chip cut the big fat line into about ten lines.

I continued to drink ice-cold beer. It seemed to calm me down and feed my addiction.

Julia, God's *perfect gift*.

I headed home with a cooler of beer and a sound-asleep Julia. Julia loved my house. I gave her the room I kept for guests. I had the room fixed up with books, a reading chair, an electric heater, extra blankets, and, of course, the supermattress. Along with yard tools and construction tools, very clean and neat together in one corner. Okay, chain, rope, bucket, and wheelbarrow.

We didn't get to my house until a couple of hours before daybreak. In the morning, she lay in bed on the great mattress while I sat in the chair and we talked. I was still up. I made coffee for her and a bacon-and-egg sandwich on light toast. I cut it in small pieces, covered it for warmth…

Julia called her mother. Told her I was a different kind of person. That she had her own room. I didn't take her home until the next day. Julia started fixing up my house. Made her room *her* room. Moved the tools *out*. Really cleaned the kitchen area and asked me to help move things. Called her mother three times.

I was withdrawing. Drinking regular beer.

She was very understanding. Not going to leave me alone. Not going to show me to her mother like this.

I finally slept in fits of insomnia that night.

Julia slept great in her room. On the wonderful mattress and everything fixed up so nicely.

She told me about sleeping so well on her mattress in her room at my house. Most of the way to her house.

Her mother, Nancy, liked me. Nancy was forty-four to forty-five years old.

I soon found out Julia had just turned twenty-four. I thought so. Nancy told me her daughter hadn't brought a boy home since high school.

They both cooked fresh vegetables and corn bread. Beans and greens. Healthy food. Fed me. I stayed at Julia's and her mother's home for three days. No drinking at their house. Her mom was twelve years divorced and twelve years sober. No drinking was perfect.

The grass was overgrown. They had two old lawn mowers. Also a basic Briggs & Stratton Rototiller... What really caught my attention was a 1970 White Pontiac Le Mans with a cracked driver's window and two flat tires. Definitely been setting a while.

I was getting excited. I thought, *Two wonderful ladies to hang out with, and you are all happy about working on lawnmowers and a car.*

I kept my mechanic tools in the trunk of my car. I had to run to get some fresh gas, thirty weight oil. I went ahead and bought two new spark plugs. I had one of the lawnmowers ready in a couple of hours.

Her mom had me set the blade a little high. She and Julia started cutting grass and picking things up in the yard.

I decided on the Rototiller next. Very basic. It was the oldest and had been sitting for the longest period of time. I went around and soaked it with 3-in-One oil. Took the carburetor all the way down and cleaned every part in gasoline. Found the problem. Fixed it. I put the tiller back together with the new part I made.

It fired right up. Bunch of smoke at first. After I made a few adjustments, Julia was waving at me, hands over her head. I waved back, topped off the tank, and "walked" the tiller over to their perfect garden spot.

I went around the perimeter of their garden area and then back and forth. When I turned around after about an hour, Nancy was standing beside me with a glass of iced tea. She took over tilling the garden.

I was getting the sweats and sick from three days of no drugs and no alcohol. I took a shower and changed into my best clean "car working on clothes" that I kept in my car.

Julia could see I was not right. Pointed to her bed, she came back with a glass of Coke and ice. I was asleep. It was only about four thirty in the afternoon.

I woke up right after dark, walked through the kitchen, waved, and went out the back door. To a dark place next to the woods. I threw up and threw up. My stomach heaved on and on. I waited and threw up some more. Then dry heaves till I was out of breath. The bottom of my stomach wanted to get rid of more. I wanted to get rid of it. I kept going till in one big heave my stomach and muscles jerked my body over. I threw up a lot more of something. The very last vile sickness in the very bottom of my stomach and guts. After spitting my mouth as clean as I could, I backed away, pulled my handkerchief out, and wiped my mouth. Tears were running down my face. I was breathing the fresh air.

I heard Nancy say, "Damn, Dave." Only time I ever heard her cuss.

I cleaned up again.

I had two "mothers" mothering me. Soup, crackers.

I did as told, no choice. Slept in Julia's room. Old sad, bad mattress.

She slept with her mother.

I went to work on the Pontiac Le Mans the next day.

Under the hood was a disaster. Someone had worked on this and left it in worse shape.

I called my father.

He knew the1970 Pontiac Le Mans and the 250 six-cylinder engine that came from Chevrolet. He had the book on that motor.

I didn't need it. I said, "I know we had two of those motors. I have worked on them with you." I took my pen out, and my father told me the spark plug and distributor cap location from his memory. Dad said, "Be sure to check the coil on that model." He nailed it.

Long story, short. The Le Mans was running in a few days. It was the coil. I did a major tune-up after I had it running. There was a box in the trunk with a new water pump, so I put it on.

Big also, the car smoked a little out the exhaust, so I added the original Teflon additive to the fresh oil. Oh yeah, you have to follow the instructions. Change the fresh oil as soon as treatment is finished. It stopped the smoke, and you could hear it pick up rpms and run even smoother.

Nancy gladly paid for all the parts, including a new heavy-duty battery. The car needed a full set of tires. It did not even have a spare tire. Some brakes, alignment, and such.

After making it back and forth to work at Lenox Square for a few days, we cleaned out my house of beer, bourbon, vodka, and everything. Julia and I took it to Chip. A lot of alcohol.

He was happy. I had the beer iced down. He could also see the change in me. He asked Julia, kidding, "What did you do to him?"

We stayed at my house for two days and nights. Julia insisted we hide the car around the back, read books, and slept. I finally fell into a deep sleep. It was raining and cool. So I had a fire in the fireplace.

I made the written list. Breaks. Front shocks. Front alignment. The universal joint was bad. Along with whatever the shop might find, I told her I would wire up the Universal Joint so we could drive it. I asked Nancy about taking it somewhere. Nancy was all in. She already knew what kind of tires she wanted! She had some money saved to buy a car for Julia. Just not near enough. I called a few places. I ordered the tires ahead of time. We chose a place in Doraville for the repairs.

We took it in the next week, dropped it off in the morning, and picked it up at three o'clock. Michelin rain tires. Parts and labor were so cheap. The tires were not.

We had to buy some things from a local junkyard. Driver's window, some door parts, and trim items. The spare wheel and tire.

Julia and I scrubbed it with compound and waxed it. We used blue Rit Dye on the faded cloth interior.

As the next month passed, I swapped out their kitchen faucet for a nice one Nancy ordered out of the Sears catalog. I borrowed Jimmy Carmichale's truck and put some much-needed gravel on the driveway.

All of these things were the least I could do. Julia saved me from myself.

Julia and I loved to read together in her room at my house. Julia would lie in her bed. I would sit in the chair beside her. We never read junk. Always history, science, and theology. We would trade books. Julia wanted to be alone. Just us. We always parked our cars beside the house. It appeared no one was home.

Julia started saying, "I love you," while we were reading.

I would say, "I love you," and keep on reading. Sometimes, I would go first.

Julia came along at the right time. I would have stayed drunk and on drugs!

We visited my mother and father in Chamblee.

I showed Dad the Le Mans. I had just scrubbed and pressure-washed the motor again. Removed and painted many of the parts under the hood.

It was a showpiece. We all enjoyed talking about the car. Mom thought Julia was the best girl in the world that day. Back in the house, my dear mother had coffee or iced tea ready. She had a cake in the oven that smelled good. Mom even pulled out pictures to show Julia. Well, they were having a good ole time.

Dad and I talked about Bible things.

Julia and I made it back to my house after dark. Julia was asleep. I went in and turned her bed cover, quilt, and sheet down. Turned her night lamp that she liked on and the electric heater on a timer. Just the way she liked it.

She had me pick her up on my back and carry her in.

What a perfect day, we both agreed.

Julia wanted another special breakfast—served in bed so she could sleep in. This happened a lot! Julia was not a morning person. I made three tomato-bacon-and-fried-egg sandwiches. I cut the sandwiches into quarters. I had to make it exceptional. I made my "exclusive" white gravy and white bread! By now, I knew exactly how Julia liked her coffee. We went by Kroger last night on the way home from Chamblee. Fresh orange juice. Not a crumb was left of the breakfast. That morning, Julia asked me to marry her!

We talked about it for the rest of the day. Oh, I wanted to. She knew how much I loved her and would marry her.

I was a drug addict and alcoholic. Relapse is in my future. Not much of an income. I needed a good job. I had been going into Florsheim shoes to work while we were going together. A high school education gets a person nowhere.

She must go to college. Study, not have children so soon. She argued, together we could accomplish all those things.

At the end of the day, I chose to sacrifice my happiness.

She was going to school. Not have a bunch of babies and stay home.

That was the last night she stayed at my house. I gave that fine mattress with the box springs to her. Took it up to their house and set it up.

With the Pontiac ready, Julia was soon going to college in North Georgia and studying till late.

I buckled down working in town selling shoes and also working construction. Wasting my life away.

A few months later, I started a new job. I was working so many hours and out of town with Sun Data.

Our busy lives pulled us apart. Not that it's any of your business, I never slept with Julia.

Unbelievable how God will send the right person. Exact perfect timing.

She saved me. She told me it worked both ways.

That night we met, she was depressed. So sick of men hitting on her *and* her mother. Julia worked as a waitress. Some of the older men would say ugly things about her. Guys her age would say nasty things. She was sick of it. Julia stayed home and slept all day and cried a lot. If she went on a date, guys wanted to feel her boobs on the first date or do it.

Julia had stopped going to work. She told me, "My mother drove me to work. I sat in the car with her. I could not go in. Mom went in and talked to Mrs. Baker, the owner. Mrs. Baker said she would call her daughter to help out for the lunch rush. I asked Mom what happened. She told me that she took care of me today. 'If you want to quit, you can do that yourself.' Mom and I ate at the little Mexican place in Duluth that was always extragood. After lunch, my mother called and told the restaurant I quit. We drove on to Doraville and did some shopping. I bought some nice clothes and shoes. I had so much fun. The next day, I was sleepy all day. Work called and asked me to come back. I hung up on them and started crying. I felt worthless."

Julia would not leave the house. Her friends were worried about her. If a friend stopped by, Julia would tell them she was fine, just wanting to be left alone.

That was not at all like Julia! She cherished every single friend.

Julia was sleeping all day and night. Reading junk. Watching TV. Crying for hours. This went on for six months. She had pills from the doctor. Nothing changed. Julia could not go past her front door!

One day, she tried on the clothes she bought six months ago. She forgot how good they looked, so she put on the new shoes. It was a good thought. Thinking about how her mother called and quit the job for her.

Her mother walked in from working. Nancy was surprised. That was it. Julia went back to sleeping and crying.

Six days later, Julia was getting dressed in the new clothes again! She was beating herself up. "How can I back out? I am so sleepy."

Her mother talked Julia into going out with her best friend and husband to a party. "You call me to pick you up if you get too tired."

Julia insisted if she had not met me. She would have gone right back to sleeping all day, the same as you would have kept drinking.

Julia told me I really was a gentleman. She said she saw it at the party. I stood out. The lady at the party whom Julia asked, "Who is that guy?" according to Julia, told her, "You are perfectly safe with David. He is the last gentleman."

Well, Julia has never lied to me.

The *Atlanta Journal and Constitution* was a good paper back then. Reported the news.

Two days after the little get-together at Chip's house, the *Atlanta Journal* had an article about *eight* people in Atlanta and the surrounding area dying of cocaine overdose, mainly from inhaling (snorting) the drug. The article went on to talk about the quality of the cocaine. It sounded like a sales pitch to the drug community.

What I saw was the *number*. The number would have been *nine*. That is all I was. A number. If I die of cocaine use in the surrounding area of Atlanta, I have to die on the good stuff. It is usually the other way.

That was a wake-up call.

When the supercraving hits, I can pray. I love to pray. Jesus is good to me. I talk to Jesus and feel him next to me. This works for me. It may not work for you. I am not trying to convert you from your beliefs. It could happen. I hope you find Jesus. Whatever. This is a true story. Okay, that is all. When the supercraving *hits*, I, maybe not you, must do this immediately.

I start talking to Jesus like he is standing next to me. Well, Jesus is not going to talk back to me immediately. That makes it a prayer. I am talking *to* Jesus. Jesus is so kind, because he listens to my prayers. I do not want to be boring or greedy. Asking for the same thing over and over. My love of Jesus is so strong I must tell him. His will is best for me. What I want may interfere with his plan. I need to tell him how much I need him. Satan wants me. I do not want to do what Satan asks. I need Jesus. I am so happy to have Jesus to talk to when Satan attacks me. I see daily unique prayer is important. Jesus wants to help in many ways. He likes me talking to him.

My Life Was About to Change

I drive all the way into Lenox Square three days a week. I work running stock and selling shoes. I receive straight commission from my sales. Easiest thing in that area of Atlanta to sell is Florsheim shoes.

I am doing okay. I need some money. I also work in construction. I make good money subcontracting for Metro Insulation by the square foot. The area supervisor and I insulate my living room ceiling for the wholesale price of insulation! I help him insulate his parents' garage that will become a guest bedroom. That was my excitement last week.

I also do Sheetrock work. Work on a crew in residential construction. Another day of wasting my life away.

A person I have not seen in about two years, out of nowhere, drives up my driveway and tells me of a job, hands me a business card, and is gone in less than five minutes.

A sort of friend drives up my long driveway. The drive is diagonal to my house.

I see him halfway up the gravel drive. I often sit in that chair where I can watch the driveway. I walk out.

He opens the door to his beat-up truck with the window down but only places his foot on the truck's side rail.

I can tell Greg is not going to get out of his truck. I walk closer.

As I am walking toward him, he tells me about a job his parents want him to take, but he doesn't want the job. He doesn't want any job. He says, "If you go down there and see these people, it would be doing me and my folks a favor."

I tell Greg, "Thank you, Greg. I will go check it out. Yes, I will be glad to."

Greg went ahead, got out of his truck, and stood beside it. The motor is running, and the door is still open.

I walk on up to him.

He hands me a business card with an address circled. Greg tells me, "Thanks, Dave, you are doing me a big favor," as he is getting in his truck. That is it. Greg leaves very quickly.

Just like today, back then in the *abandoned house*, I always dressed clean cut. Every day, I shower, shave, dress neatly, polish my shoes, and iron my clothes. I am fairly sure Greg wanted to send a clean-cut person to Sun Data, because of his parents.

The president of the company was the owner of the card I was holding. I found out Greg's parents were close friends with John Crilly, the president of SunData and his wife.

My life was about to change. This came my way just as I was ready. My addiction was under control. The house was finished. I had plenty of firewood for the winter. I had completed all the work on the '64 Pontiac Tempest. The interior of my car looked new! It was ready. Just drive it. Even the location of Sun Data *is super*. At this job, I would be able to use my qualities, and the right people would see them. I did not see this until later.

I am not so wise a man as to see God's plan when it is happening.

MY GIFT IS NEGOTIATING

Fresh haircut, dressed sharp wearing khaki Levi Dockers and blue button-up shirt pressed with nice creases. I wore my brown Florsheim Royal Imperial slip-ons. Feeling good. Actually, this is the way I usually dress. Except the shoes.

Today, I am a man on a mission. In my shirt pocket is one ink pen and I am holding two one-page résumés folded *to fit in* an envelope. I had *no* envelope.

Small lobby with four chairs and a sliding window.

"I am here to see John Crilly." When asked if I have an appointment, I answer no. I show them the card. When the receptionist asks for the card, I respond, "Yes, I would like to have the card back." I am not giving up anything. I never want to sell another shoe or carry packs of shingles up a ladder.

Minutes later, I am sitting in the office of a nice-enough guy. John Crilly starts telling me a lot of things that I laugh at because he is laughing.

Then I just start laughing and talking.

Years later, I openly accepted the fact that meeting John for the first time and the ten or so minutes the two of us were laughing and talking was clearly the most valuable "before and after" event in my life.

John finally stops laughing and tells the receptionist to find the vice president Dan Hindrix. All this for a warehouse and truck driver job. Seems that has been a sore spot for this rather new fast-growing company.

The vice president tells an off-color joke about women.

I don't laugh.

Silence.

I quickly come back and tell the best joke of the day. Follow up with another *killer joke* while we are laughing. Great recovery.

Well, the "interview" is about over. My résumé is spot-on.

I knew I was hired.

The VP said, "We need you to start tomorrow morning? We pay eight dollars an hour. You've got to be here by eight."

I let that settle and answered with "The very best I can work for is eleven."

John and Dan looked at each other. Silence.

I added rather plainly, "I understand."

It was silent. So I was getting up to leave (barely).

John Crilly said, "Eleven dollars an hour will be fine, Mr. Cash."

I said, "Thank you, looking forward to working here."

The VP said, "Let me show you around."

So easy.

Dan was sitting on the edge of his chair.

The two kept nodding at each other. They said, "We need you," and "You've got to be here." A few more clues.

When I named my price, I had taken over the interview and was suddenly in charge, not John and Dan.

John Crilly saw it and respected how I had handled the interview.

John and I became friends that day.

Dan Hendrex walked me through a fifteen-thousand-square-foot warehouse full of IBM equipment.

That first walk into the warehouse, I knew I was in the right place. I could use my brain by just learning what I was looking at. What was it used for? Who used it? What went with what? I remember Dan asking if I had any questions. I answered, "Too many."

Dan liked that answer.

The next morning, I was put in a truck loaded with expensive IBM data-processing equipment. The equipment was wrapped in shrink wrap. The addresses for delivery were on bills of lading in order on a clipboard. Different states only as far north as Virginia. We were to pick up a full truckload of equipment at three different addresses.

In the early '80s, the size of computers was large and on wheels, except for workstations. CPUs (Central Processing Units) were on wheels and tall. Printer, tape drives, and data storage units were also on wheels, weighing hundreds of pounds, table and counter high.

Sun Data sent Brainless, Contrary, who believed he knew everything; Bad Breath, who talked all the time; and Retarded Person with me. He wore a curled-up-on-the-sides cheap straw cowboy hat and cowboy boots.

Someone, it may have been Dan, told him he was in charge!

He had the Sun Data American Express credit card with his name on it.

It was a rough week only because of the idiot. Sorry, no offense to idiots.

In the truck, he talked about his wife letting him "poke her," droning on and on lying about how smart he was. How much money he had. Airbrain flirted with waitresses at every truck stop. Truck stops were the only place to get diesel back in 1980.

Airbrain showed off like he was a big-time businessman in the computer industry. He would always say, "It is hard to find good help. I have to do it myself. Out here delivering and picking up IBM… (bla, bla) IBM…(bla, bla) computers…data (bla) data (bla, bla)."

At every stop, I would go to the back of the truck and secure everything, tie it down, and check all the straps.

If people were around, Mr. Airbrain would walk out and yell at me, "What do you think you are doing?"

I was in the back of the truck, and it was easy to see what I was doing. I responded, "We need to check the straps whenever we get a chance."

Airbrain does this at almost every truck stop. He yells, "Listen here. You don't touch anything. Now get your ass out of my truck. I will fix that mess you have made." Good old Airbrain trying to impress people he doesn't know Gets in the back of the truck and unbuckles all of my work and redoes it. He yells, "It is a damn good thing I came out here in time…(bla, bla). To see here (bla). In the back of *my* truck." (Hertz Rental big letters on the side.) He finally jumps out and pulls the door shut and yells, "Son, you could have bankrupted me. That IBM data equipment is mighty expensive. Now get in. I'll drive."

This would be funny if it were not for all the damaged equipment. With a full load, Airbrain ran over a curb that was very high. The hole after the curb was deep because tractor trailers had made it. I could hear the big expensive CPUs, large printers, and big data-storage devices crashing around. Our truck bottomed out "*bam*" and "*scraped*" on the curb as we kept going.

I suggested we stop and check the load.

Of course, he was silent.

I said, "Pull over."

Airbrain said, "It's fine."

I said, "Pull back into the truck stop, or I will beat the crap out of you."

Airbrain said, "What?"

I shouted, "You heard me. Now pull over, or I will fuck you up."

Airhead pulled back in the truck stop. Airbrain started to say something,

I grabbed his collar. I bounced the back of his head real hard on the curved metal of the truck, behind his head, where the window was rolled down.

I explained, "Don't say a word. I am driving us home. Don't speak to me. You can nod your head or use sign language. Don't you dare speak to me ever." I took the keys out of the ignition. I went around and opened the back. It was bad. It took a while to get things strapped down.

When I was done, Airbrain was sitting on the passenger's side, looking out his side window.

We were in a twenty-four-foot box truck. We were headed home with a truckload of smashed up equipment.

I backed the truck up to the dock at 11:00 p.m.

My hope for this job. Learning from the bottom up. Is not going to be thrown out the window by Airbrain.

The next morning, when I walked in, I receptionist caught me and asked me to wait in John's office.

I stood up.

John walked in mad. "The equipment is smashed up. I was just called back to look at it."

I said, "Mr. Crilly, I am not surprised. That friend of your wife's husband is the reason it is smashed. Sir, I did my very best to protect the equipment. I would check it every time we stopped, pull the straps tighter, made sure the load was packed tight so there wouldn't be one scratch. Mr. Dummy would undo my work and redo it his way and run over curbs. He can't drive a truck. He has an attitude, and he undid my very good packing and strapping because someone might have told him he was the manager. I take great pride in my work, Mr. Crilly."

John Crilly said, "Is that right?"

I said, "I wouldn't let him around anymore equipment."

John said, "Did you hit his head?"

I answered truthfully, "His head hit the truck."

John said, "So you are just going to throw your buddy under the bus and blame it all on him."

I responded, "He is not my buddy. It is one hundred percent his fault."

I am glad it was not my left arm and hand.

That is the last time I, to this day, respond with violence.

John quickly said, "I believe you. I need you to make another trip. Need to be in Texas as fast as you can. The damaged equipment is being unloaded. It will be repaired and installed in Austin, Texas, in two and a half days."

I said under my breath, "I love this job," and then apologized, "I did not mean to say that out loud."

John said, "It's good. We will send you out alone."

I said, "I can make that drive straight through."

John Crilly handed me my Sun Data American Express card and said, "I could use your help in back today, getting that equipment cleaned up. We have a lot going on."

I responded, "Thank you, yes, sir," and took off through the offices then the staging room full of technicians and IBM equipment. The equipment was opened up and being worked on.

Then I walked through the double doors to the warehouse and made my way to the back.

Nobody was working! I asked who was in charge.

A stoned guy said, "We need to take the... Fuck, man, take a break till I figure this out."

I went back to the staging room and found Phil, a technician working on a System 3 CPU. I told him the short, quick story. Phil was to become a good friend for many years.

He was smiling and said, "This is the CPU your best friend bounced around the back of the truck." That was pretty funny.

Phil gave me my own work order. "Walk with me in the back."

The guys were suddenly busy.

Phil introduced me to a different person. Showed me all the equipment on the work order. Stood and talked with me. Told me he would meet me in Austin the day after tomorrow. Then Phil said loudly, "Dave Cash, any problems at all, do not hesitate to let John or myself know." Phil walked back up front.

The man close by whom Phil introduced me to said, "Let me help you, Mr. Dave." The two of us began working. The others slowly began to... Well, I don't know what those guys were doing. We built a new crew in the next few weeks.

Just to let you know, the next book starts right here. After the first chapter, I signed up and completed a sixteen-month course in computer technology, soon after starting my own business. Later I became a deacon in a local church. I financed and built two churches in Guatemala. I have my new state-of-the-art airplane and am living in a three-million-dollar beach home. I've traveled to well-known and remote places in the world. I have lived both wonderful and very rough lives. Twelve years ago, the money was gone. I rent a room. I miss the airplane. I will tell you the true story in the many books ahead. I will be writing for other interesting friends. So much to do. Remember, life is about the people.

NOTE 1

During that time, I saw something. The time I died. I could only remember one fragment of this while lying on the beach. This fragment kept coming back until six weeks later, when the complete trip to the edge of heaven was revealed again. I do not know why I forgot most of this, and it was revealed in its entirety later.

This is the fragment: people I knew who have passed away are in a bright white room. They are looking out at me. I wanted to go into that room with them.

NOTE 2

This is what I saw when I died. What came to me completely later was this: It is totally dark except for a tiny dot of light, and I am rapidly moving toward the light. As I get closer, the lighted area gets bigger and bigger. The light I have been traveling toward is the very bright white background of a wonderful place. I notice something moving in the light. It is people.

People I begin to recognize. The people stop and look toward me as I get closer. The very first is Grandmother Cash on the right side of the light. She is younger, maybe thirty years old. I can still easily recognize Grandmother Cash. I cannot see her feet. I can see just down to her knees. There is a short wall. Grandfather Cash walks up on the left side. White long-sleeved shirt and black pants.

He looks about forty. His hair was a little gray. He is bigger than I remember. Grandfather Cash is so happy. He waves just once but can't stop smiling. I can't stop either.

Some other people walk up between them. Three of my aunts that are so old and small. Now they are beautiful, with long hair and old timey long dresses. Standing tall. I am looking at Grandmother Cash. Her big eyes are happy. Her smile is contagious. She is so beautiful.

A young man eighteen or so walks up with a gentleman about thirty-five years old. He is dressed in older-style clothes, well pressed. He also has a short beard. He looks like my dad! I believe it was my great-grandfather.

In the distant background, people are just casually walking by in white light. I believe there are about eight or nine of my relatives gathered toward the front looking at me through the large open "window." The farthest edges of my vision are still black, so I am not all the way there. If I get any closer, I will join them. I want to join them. So close.

I have forgotten about my troubles on earth. This is where I want to go. I want to join them in the light. I am as close to being in the same room. Just a little more. My forward movement stops. I look at them in heaven so happy. Grandmother Cash nods her head and gives me a small you have to go back now wave. They all are smiling. A few more wave farewells. I'm so happy as I start to back away because I have seen a portal into heaven. This explanation does not come close to how I felt just seeing what I saw for just a minute. I wave back. Everybody smiles, and a few give me a small wave. The light rapidly shrinks in the distance

EXPLAINING TO MY FATHER WHAT I FELT. ALREADY DELIRIous, now fully in withdrawal. I was unable to explain everything during the first hour. I was trying very hard to get the message across by shaping my sentences. Making every word important. Comparing what I was feeling with the pain of love? I guess. David was one messed-up young man.

I imagined my message from inside the beginning of my withdrawal was important. At first, I believed there were no tongs, and I was sitting comfortably on the bed. Soon I realized I was hooked up to tongs and lay back down.

My father wrote everything I said down. It looked nothing like what you just read. First, I arranged the complete sentences. After that, I had phrases and words to work with. Trying to keep the phrases and words somewhat in the order my father wrote them down. Then it was similar to a box of extra words. I placed everything together like a puzzle.

I had to add a lot of regular words. Just kept swapping and changing things. If I had to come up with a percentage. Only about 70 percent of this is from my father's notes. I finally just took the liberty to finish it. I had worked on this off and on for months, and it still needed some work to read smoothly. I could see what I was trying to say. So I added a little more and wrapped it up.

I had this in a spiral notebook along with Dad's notes! My wife, soon-to-be ex-wife, threw all my notebooks away in 2009. I was able to 90 percent rewrite "No Morphine" from memory and some old notes I fortunately had.

Dad told me the words became "fewer and far between. I finally thought you were going to sleep. I put the notebook away and sat down."

I believe the message, I thought so important, has been achieved.

*T*HIS *HAS SOME ADULT CONTENT.*

This was an illusion, vision, or nightmare. I believe this to be the last nightmare during my withdrawal from morphine. I told a lot of this to my dad in the days following my withdrawal from the drug. He wrote down what I told him. Continuing to recall bits and pieces of this *visit to hell,* I added more when I learned to write with my left hand at Warm Springs. It was like putting pieces in a jigsaw puzzle.

The complete withdrawal from morphine, which lasted for ninety some hours, became one very real vision connected to another. Each dream was real. In color. I could feel pain. I could also see great distance and fine detail. I could hear a motor running and radio playing in a car when the car was in the dream. Real people outside the hallucination could become part of the illusion.

This first part is my dream previous to meeting Satan. I include this as it shows me coming out of the withdrawal. This dream is logical. Not like some of the horror I escaped from or became a victim of in previous illusions.

CONVEYOR BELT

Standing on a conveyor belt going into a huge grain thresher, I could see the blue sky above. The grain thresher in my dream had more threshing bars, and they were larger than normal. The thresher bars are flying around at supersonic speed. I can constantly hear them. The conveyor belt leading into the thresher must have been turned up to the fastest speed setting, because I began panicking, running on the belt, moving slowly away from the threshing bars.

Jumping up, I grabbed the top of the side of the belt area. Just in time. When I grabbed the top and started to pull myself up to get out of the grain thresher, a huge mound of grain and straw began coming down the conveyor belt. I thought I was safe and began pulling myself up, to climb out.

It was not going to be. An evil Mexican man with a beard wearing a floppy hat, who in an earlier nightmare had been chasing me, looked over the edge from above. His face and beard were bloody from our previous encounter. He was about six or seven feet above me standing on some hay bales. I managed to get my arm over the edge of the side of the grain thresher.

Now I could see a field and an old barn with a tractor parked out front. The barn and tractor were about fifty yards away. Right next to me were the bales of straw stacked beside the thresher.

The man started throwing chunks of cement blocks at me. Each one made a blasting sound when it hit the thrashing bars. I caught one and threw it right back while hanging on with my left arm and hand over the side of the grain thrasher. More straw and grain went past under my feet on the conveyor belt, but it was on fire.

I finally remember why I am leaving this dream in the "Hell" chapter. The next-to-the-last illusion. The conveyor belt stops. It is as if the illusion is paused! The fire stops under me! I catch on fire. I am in the worst pain. I am burning. I start screaming. The flames are in front of my face because my body is on fire. A hand comes through the flames. A lady with a white hat appears, and no more flames. The pain goes away. I can't move my arms or legs. The lady with the nurse's hat gives me some water with ice. So delicious. She says I was screaming. I tell her I was on fire. And I say to her, "Thank you for the water." The water has ice in it, so I say, "I really like the ice in the water." She says to me, "You haven't talked to anyone in days. This is good news. I will tell the doctor." I ask her to help me! I don't want to go back. She is gone. I return to the illusion.

The Mexican was mad now. He yelled at me. It was because I threw something back. He got a pipe and started punching me in the head and back. I almost made it. The Mexican used the pipe to pry me away from the side. Still throwing chunks of cement blocks at me. I let go of the edge and fell flat into the conveyor belt. My feet were gone so fast I hardly realized it... I looked up just as the pain hit me of my feet being cut off and saw a bale of hay just about to hit me. I was doomed to the next nightmare.

It was immediately after that I took a trip to *hell*. Separation from God.

Hell

In the next instant, the illusion changed. I was comfortable, looking out the window in the back of a new, nicest luxury limousine. Being healthy and very rich, I had a lot of experience in this life for a man who was thirty years old. Feeling unhurried in the limousine, I looked at my watch, anyway. A simple silver-face Rolex. I had on a wedding band. The tan summer suit went with my lightweight calfskin loafers. White shirt, no tie today.

The driver slowed down, looked into the rearview mirror, and said, "Just up ahead, Mr. Cash. Your wife and girls should be here soon." The driver saw me look at my watch. He followed up with "We are a few minutes early, as you always like, sir."

I was looking around the place; it was a neighborhood of small shops and a few larger full-glass-front stores. Recognizing the French words and many other clues, I was in a small city in Southern France. These were well-kept older buildings with cobblestone streets. Narrow walk-through areas to large alleyways that were made into streets with fountains a century ago. Beyond that, more shops and vendors, alongside living areas and side streets. The driver pulled to a stop.

How nice. What a spectacular day. I told the driver I could manage the door, and I opened the limousine door and stepped out. I was across from a corner store with an all glass front, selling dishes and glassware. This was where I was supposed to meet my wife. Beyond that was a pastry shop. The vendors were opening up. I stood up and closed the door.

The limousine is gone. Now across from where I am standing is a large hole in the road and sidewalk. To the right of the large hole are people sitting on the curb. Black, White, Latino, and Oriental. Eighteen half-dressed people who are just sitting on the curb until they get to a huge boulder. Going left from the big hole, people are sitting all the way, side by side, until the road turns. The people sitting turn with the road.

The place was sweltering. The stench of sulfur and something dead made it hard to breathe. The buildings were stained from mold, plastered with grime and empty of merchandise. No trees or vegetation. I walked across the street and through one store with a dozen half-dressed sad looking, grimy people sitting on the floor leaning up against the walls. They were all staring at the floor in front of them. They appeared to be of low energy, or maybe it was exhaustion. No, that was not it at all! It was hopelessness. I recognized that look from Godless people at a funeral. Despair. Grief. Pain. Sorrow. And, yes, the empty feeling of hopelessness. What kind of place is this?

One female looked up and watched me walk through.

When I reach the outside large alley that is now a street, I see two men kicking three naked ladies. The ladies are filthy, lying on the grimy brick pavers. The ladies are covering their heads with their arms and hands. The women are yelling for help. People walk slowly by and glance over. They keep on walking. One guy stops and talks to the men that are kicking the ladies. The three men began arguing. Now the three ladies get up and start to fight each other. No blood anywhere. They are sweaty and so filthy. One of the men sees me looking. All he is wearing is a T-shirt. He sort of yawns a big green two-tooth hole in his dirty face. The two other men walk slowly away.

The alleyway is crowded with wrinkled people who are wearing little covering, others just in the nude.

I begin to panic. I want out of here. Please, God. The prayer goes nowhere!

The smell of *hell* is revolting. It smells like burnt flesh, old fish, and sulfur. Again breathing is difficult. Everyone and everything is filthy.

Everyone looks wicked, foul, and repulsive. The sound of sex and shouts from rape are everywhere. Depraved, unnatural, and perverted.

I look away, but nastiness is everywhere. I hear shouts directed at me, "Look, look." I squint my eyes so I won't see the vileness around me. I take off my suit coat, roll it up, and secure it under my left arm.

Finally, a side street that will take me back to the main road I was on earlier. People sitting along both sides of the street. Once I return to the main road, I quickly look up at a wall with a large gate. The wall that spans the horizon ahead in the distance is not there when I am in the limousine. Was it there when I got out?

The middle of the main road is somewhat clear of people. I see no vehicles of any kind. Something else, no human waste! No food packages! Lots of adults, no evidence of any path to a "bathroom." Don't see it or smell it. It stinks bad enough. No regular trash. Not one trash can.

Again, people are shouting for me to look at them. "Look, look." I will not look. Screams and more screams. A man is getting beaten with a rock! His skin is torn. No blood is coming out! No fluids. The man is screaming. The woman with the rock stands and looks at me. I shouldn't have looked. I turn, look forward, and jog toward the large gate that is about one and a little more miles away.

Many times, arms and hands reach out to grab me. My suit coat is snatched away, gone. The people start grabbing at my shirt and pants. I break into a run and easily shake them off.

When I reach the large gate, an oversized door opens. I walk through. Big difference. So nice and cool.

A lot of well-dressed people are standing around. I am talking about three hundred, maybe more. They look like regular folks.

Of course, I am thinking, *This is not good, what I just walked through. Am I in hell? Is this the receiving center for hell?* I am definitely confused. I am ready to run.

Then I heard in a preacher's voice, "No, no, no, Mr. Cash. You are my very *special guest.*"

I turned toward the voice. A man about fifty years old, losing his dark-blonde-and-gray hair with a receding hairline. He was wearing jeans, a golf shirt, and penny loafers without socks. He had his hand extended. I reluctantly took Mr. Jeans and Golf Shirt's hand.

I said, "As you must already know, I am David Cash." I paused, glanced around, and continued. I asked, "This is *your place?*" I gently tried to take my hand back.

"Oh yes, Charles David Cash." He released my hand. "Your name is not in my book...*yet*. Tried my best, tried my best, I did. Plenty of time left. Love a good challenge. Hahahaha."

The laugh was not delightful, you would say. I knew exactly who I was talking to, just like you reading this probably know who I was talking to by then.

I did not understand why I was there. I didn't know if I was in a hospital. *Is it real? Am I dead!* Satan was confusing me. So I asked, "Kind sir, I believe you failed to formally introduce yourself." As I mentioned, it was pleasantly air-conditioned in this area. Very nice. It seemed the people standing around had no idea what was going on. Well, nor did I. The gates were magnificent. The beautiful wall left and right reached the horizon. The sky was perfect. The music was magnificent. The floor was gold!

I forgot the question I had asked when he answered, "I am sorry. My name is Joe. Everybody calls me Brother Joe or Pastor Joe. Glad to meet you face-to-face in my place. You can just call me Joe. Where they can't hear us, let's go." Joe said very loud, "Fine churchgoing folks." Then he shouted louder, "Mighty fine Christian people! Mighty fine, mighty fine churchgoing Christian people! What a joke. Folks, I meant mighty fine folks!"

A cloud passed through the church folks' area. The music started playing "Amazing Grace." Angels appeared when the cloud dissipated. The angels with beautiful wings started shining and raising their hands.

That was the last thing I saw as we walked back through the same door I had walked through a few minutes earlier. The door in the gate. On the air-conditioned side, the gate was magnificent, pearly and shimmering. Yes, on the air-conditioned side, the gate as well as the wall were something to see.

We walked back into sweltering nasty heat. The smell hit me like a punch in the nose. There it was, just a big steel-framed wall with all the gears, pulleys, and cables for the gate fully visible. Actually, quite a work of engineering.

Joe was laughing so hard. He was trying to say something. So I said a rhyme for him, "What a joke, folks." Joe pointed at me, crying and laughing, stomping his foot. He finally calmed down. First thing Joe said while still laughing was, "Angels don't have wings."

His voice began to get deeper. "Hahahahahaha. Satan is my name. Brother Joe, Pastor Joe, how cheesy. Hahahahaha, I will preach them all into my vile home, hahahahahahaha." Now Joe sounded like he had a deeper voice. "My name is Satan. I am the preacher, the 'spiritual leader.' I go to church and look down on the poor person or the addict. Fat, puffy, uppity Christian. They do the same, worry about themselves only. It's okay to read the Bible a different way, hahahahahahaha. Little cheating, lying, worthless fucks in for a surprise. Hahahahaha, lie about giving to the church. Hahaha, one of my favorites…these people have rejected, of their own free will." JoeSatan went into a laughing fit, talking about Jesus in a way of hate I refuse to type.

JoeSatan, sounding bigger and larger, said, "See the man with his dick in his hand?" That is not all big JoeSatan said about the man. It was so vile. Satan does not hold back. Satan loves cursing God.

I said, "Yes, I did not need to see that. Satan told me he was a TV and radio preacher out of California. The man was a pervert and a glutton, preaching for the money. He helped send a lot of people my way. He will go to hell stage two very soon. I just wanted a bunch of his followers to see him here."

When I looked back to where "Brother Joe" was just a few seconds ago, there was Satan looking like Satan.

I spun around away from Satan to run. Only, in my haste, I tripped on my own feet. Satan leaned over me. I fell on my side. I scrambled on over, crawled, and tried to get up and run. I got halfway up and started running. The heat went up, up, up, and up! I finally got myself straightened up to run. I shot out of there running faster than I have ever ran. The whole place started screaming. High-pitched screaming becoming louder and louder. It was too hot and getting hotter!

Satan walked up beside me and said with a voice I could easily hear over the screams, "Going somewhere? I mean really? Hahahahaha!" Then the screams slowly stopped as throats became too dry. He sang the most perfect song. The devil has a voice like a roaring fire along with an echo of an ocean cave. I was entranced for just a second.

> You are in my world now, sinner,
> People never in eternity leave.
> You're a most nasty offender,
> In the very nicest place in hell.
> Something you must see,
> A few vile tricks I have up my sleeve!
> The first one I believe,
> You'll never be free
> From the vile disgusting smell...

On and on, the devil sang. We all know he loves rhymes. When he sings, it is mesmerizing. (Please watch out on regular earth. Demons can't rhyme like the devil. So you will hear demon-possessed people repeating things over and over and over! Let's say seven to nine words. They will sort of talk-sing them. Anyway, that is a different subject.)

As I said, I never ran as fast as I ran in hell that day. Satan walked at a steady pace beside me. Satan was laughing so hard. "Where in hell are you going to run off to, David?" Satan's breath stank of old milk and fish. He bent down and said with his foul breath, "We are almost done." I stopped my futile running. Satan was standing twenty feet in front of me. The old devil walked up to stand beside me, talking as he walked, "Let's welcome the new guys—the judgmental, 'better than thou,' the 'I'm saved because I go to church' group."

Satan is huge, with hair that's black like coal. His skin is yellowed, patchy, and pulled tight around his bones. The eyes are deep seated and the color of red wine. He stands ten feet tall. The temperature gets even hotter. I am sweating profusely. There is no water!

We are in the middle of people sweating. Sweating, the first sign I have seen of moisture. The temperature is like standing in front of an open oven. I hear the occasional high-pitched scream. Everyone is holding their throat, crawling, or just lying on their side. Eyes closed, breathing slowly because even breathing through the nose hurts the dryness on the throat.

"Ever been that thirsty?" Satan is looking at me as my throat has gone dry. I can't answer.

One door is as wide as it needs to be. It swings up, and the complete complex from the air-conditioned side slides all three hundred plus people forever into hell. I was watching all the mechanisms working to bring the regular fine church folk into hell. The music stops. The door simply slides closed and seals the fate for eternity of the people who just did not get it.

They had the extra time and money. They said they did help! They never helped anybody. Someone needs to say the obvious; the pregnant teenager was a slut.

Finally heard enough, told the alcoholic he needed to just quit drinking.

The group we play cards with knows a lot. In fact, a lady in church who lost her son to drugs should have raised him better.

We do not want to sell our old church building to Black people. (I refuse to type the word.) It used to be a decent neighborhood.

If you have been divorced, you are not as good a Christian as "me."

I've been going here longer than you, so it's more my church.

The deacon's wife was married once before. That ain't right.

I promised not to tell, so if you promise not to tell, I will tell you. The guy who wears the same sport coat and tie every Sunday left his wife and kids twelve years ago. It gets better. He went to prison for a year and a half because of drinking and driving. Almost killed some people.

Gay people have to stop being, you know, before they can come to church.

I don't know about that. Depends on who it is. Walter donated a lot of money.

That altar call, you felt the Spirit move you. Your wife bumped your elbow. Wow, it felt good. You really wanted to rededicate your life, read the Bible more, pray for forgiveness, go on a mission trip, one foot in the aisle. Get rid of the old stubborn self. Live a new life as a real Christian. Ask Jesus forgiveness. A tear ran down your face, looking up.

You did not want to go up and kneel beside the superfat lady, the pregnant girl with tattoos and that old Black drunk. Definitely not with that White lady that has her black grandson with her. Yep, the wife saw it also. What would people think?

The angels become horrid demons; and each of them, one at a time, with one mighty jump, jumps up and lands halfway up the wall. The demons have alligator skin all over. Large heads. One face is mutated human shaped, another alligator face with a short snout. Each face is horribly different from the others. One at a time the demons look around the crowd before they make the powerful jump. They only lightly steady themselves with their front claws as the demons look for someone to tear apart... The front claws are as big and long as a young woman's forearm, deadly sharp. Four claws on each powerful front hand. The front arms are long and have a bat-type skin underneath for gliding. The back feet are like very large human hands with the most unusual claws. This is what grabs the wall or gate so securely the rest of the body is free to do battle. The claws are only as big as a man's thumb. Listen to this: the claw is curved metal strong as titanium. The demon's pride and power, his monstrous powerful back legs. Each demon climbs the rest of the way to the top. Once on top of the wall, the large demons look down to keep watch. I almost forgot, these demons have a tail. A few feet long, it is slick and deadly in a fight. The tail is always moving.

Satan starts laughing, roaring, and howling. Satan is disgusting. He spits when he talks. Fleas run around his nose, and he stinks. Dark-brown sharp teeth. He breathes through his mouth. His long tongue goes out and back in quickly every so often. The devil has a lot of bugs and scorpions crawling in his hair. "Hahahahaha hahahahahahahaha. This is my favorite part." Satan spits when he gets excited. He spits a lot. It runs down his face and onto his chest. He stumbles his words on his spit... He spits this out, "They all thought they had been good enough their whole life, hahaha-hahahahahahaha, so they would go to heaven. Every one of these [expletive] deserves to be here. Look down on people. Judge that person. No, you didn't kill anybody. Hahahahahahahahahaha."

Satan is watching the newcomers as they start to scream. The wrinkled people quit choking. They get up and sort of rush the newcomers. The wrinkles are organizing!

Satan said in a deep voice, "Mr. Cash, you have seen enough. My deal is complete."

One of the newcomers is throwing up. Bugs and rats rush to the vomit. The other new people one at a time begin to throw up until they all go into multiple dry heaves and then choking.

I yell, "Satan, what deal?"

Satan says, "Wait, wait. Look, this is the best part. Shut up, and look at this."

The rats and bugs are finished with the vomit and scurry underground. All of the sudden, the choking stops, and the naked wrinkled people pounce on the newcomers. Newcomers take off running in all directions. Satan is laughing. His nose snot is running into his mouth.

The wrinkled people are chasing and, what looks like, raping a few of the new women. I can't look. The new men run, but it is not their game! I see organization in the wrinkled people... The new church folks are going to lose. One of the new men is being kicked in the head, while five or six wrinkled men and women are pulling his clothes off. I don't want to know about this. A woman is spread out nude. She is screaming. The people around her are mocking her scream by screaming louder. So horrible. I refuse to tell you more. New people just found out: in hell, a person cannot pass out.

I cannot pray, "God, help her," in this place.

Satan loves depravity, hate, and violence. This is his world, or so he still believes. I guess that is what the people wanted me to see when they were shouting, "Look." Wrinkled people are running off with the new people's clothes. Only cloth. Most leather and metal never make it into this side of hell. The scene back at the gate is unexplainably disgusting.

Satan wears a loincloth made out of ladies' most private parts, on which he has a belt that carries a whip. He takes the whip and snaps it a half mile, grabs a newcomer that has been running, and brings her back to him. She is cast under his foot. Screaming. Satan snatches her already-torn dress off and says, "It is so hot in hell, my dear. You will not need this dress or this bra or these." The lady is now nude. She has gray hair, is just a little overweight, and has too much makeup.

Satan is telling me all this, even though I can see. Satan tells her to stand up. She does as she was told. I do not believe she had a choice. The devil slaps her down and says, "Get up." When she does, he says, "Beverly, Beverly, Beverly whore, I like the way you operate. Always the perfect church person, hahahahahaha, judge people, fuck a few people. Unfaithful bitch. You are better than that person. Well, do you see that person here? That person is not here. You are not as special as you thought. You are a slut. By the way, there is no sleep in hell. No satisfaction. Those people cannot be raped. No full erection for men. Just frustration. Constant thirst and hunger. You are stuck with demented people. No orgasm. None. No beauty. No night. No beautiful sunrise. No food. No one cares in hell." Satan just slaps her about a hundred yards away, and that is it. The devil himself says, "In the first part of hell, Beverly will feel that blow to her body. No bones are broken, and she will not die." Beverly is in hell. The devil says this like a poem,

Constant sameness. No rain.
No different day. No less pain.
No latter next week. No feeling better.
No gentle breeze. No kindness.
You will not wake, because you never sleep. This is hell.
No comfort. No love. This is my home.

This is my domain, where I sit upon the throne.
Throughout centuries of hell, you'll never get used to the stink.
The first hundred years creep slowly by while you think.

"I can look forward to it getting a lot worse when this one hundred years is only a curse." I yelled, "Satan, you heard me!"

Satan laughed and laughed. He finally laughed, saying, "David, you want to say, 'Thank you for the lesson on hell.'"

I screamed, "What deal?" I have got to get out of here. I also must know about the "deal" he is talking about. I asked firmly, "Tell me about the deal."

He bent over and looked close at my face. Two feet away. I couldn't stand the ugliness. Snot a foot long hanging from his chin mixed with spit. Bugs. He smiled. The horridness was too much, so I closed my eyes. The smell improved. I opened my eyes, expecting to see the vileness of Satan.

I did not expect this.

Satan had turned into what looked like an albino, standing about ten feet away from me. He was about as tall as I am but with enormous powerful muscles. He was just the opposite on personal hygiene. A very clean Satan. No bugs, no spit when he talked. White skin and hair. His skin had an occasional sparkle. His white hair stood up on top. Three inches wide, four inches tall, it flared out a bit at the top. The sides of his hair were long and pulled back into a ponytail that was braided down his back about a foot. Not a hair out of place. His eyes were still deep burgundy. His teeth were shiny orange. His fingernails and toenails were clean and shiny. He wore a small black tight speedo swimsuit.

Satan did a quick backflip with a spin.

Everyone in hell went blind.

Most just sat down right where they were. Some of the wrinkled people started feeling around for a place to sit down. Some held hands for a few steps. Some walked with their hands in front of them.

None of the people came near us. Like a barrier around albino Satan and me.

Satan jumped higher, doing more spins and flips all the while singing, "I am spectacular, remarkable, astounding, so dazzling, wondrous, and magnificent." He stopped and calmly sang, "I have lots and lots of tricks. A lot of ways to make you join me here."

The devil said, "I must show you around the first stage of hell a little more." Satan made it obvious he was avoiding my question. "Remember now, this is just the first stage. The first stage is so big and dry. We are only at receiving. In a few years, people move along. It is all the same the further you go. Stage one. Same day. It never changes."

Satan stopped and started again, "There are three stages." Satan stood straight when he said, "I thought of that. Three stages." He put his hands on his hips and proudly nodded. "Would you like to see the next place, where the wicked go after they have been here in my first stage for about a hundred years?"

The devil took his left hand off his hip, stretched out his arm, pointed at me, and said, "You, David, may just go straight to stage two on the first day. Many go straight to hell stage two." He thought that was clever.

Satan continued as he starts to pace back and forth, "Oh, it is where some of my most horrid demons live. The fire and cave keepers. The god-forsaken prisoners are separated from one another in the next level. Alone for eternity."

I couldn't stand this arrogant white devil. "Shut up," I yelled. I cut him off. "No, Satan, I will not be joining you in stage one, two, or the worst of hell. I have listened long enough. The deal. Tell me about this deal you made. Could I get the answer?"

With so much thunder and cracks of lightning, hell turned pitch-black with more lightning. I saw the blinded people with each lightning bolt.

All was quiet, and I was standing a few feet across from the most beautiful woman. She had no clothes on. I was alone standing face-to-face with her in the quiet woods, beside a stream, with a small waterfall. We were alone for a few minutes, so I looked away.

On the other side of the stream, to my left, was a dogwood forest on a steep hill. It was in full bloom. The petals were very slowly falling in the water and floating down stream. On this side of the stream, the land was flat with some large boulders along with assorted and scattered hardwoods as far as I could see.

When she spoke, her voice was wonderful. I turned and looked at her.

She said, "David, I got you out of there. I was scared that we would both perish. Finally, I have found you. We are both safe now. You are an intelligent man. I know how brilliant you are. Come here. Finally, Satan is gone."

She said in the most inviting voice. "Please touch my breast. Please, we don't have long. Just the nipple. Kiss my nipple, and place your hand where I long for you. Oh, David, I need your touch. We need to be close. Come closer, David. I may never see you again."

I was dazed. I had never seen a more beautiful woman. But I said, "Satan, the deal *now!*"

Did I ever make the devil mad? All hell began to quake! The woods dissipated; and the blind, hot, sweaty, wrinkled people were back. It was much quieter when they were blind.

Naked devil woman was shouting, "Listen to this, you piece of shit. You are an addict and will fall to alcohol and die drunk. Cocaine David, sounds good. You love cocaine. It will kill you. The deal is I can tempt you with everything I have—sex, money, drugs, alcohol, all the nice things money can buy." She was so proud of herself. "Whatever is in my bag of tricks, I will win your soul with it. God will lose to me. You lose your soul to me. I want your soul, David Cash. The deal David. The deal is I have to show you a small part of hell. After that, it is open season on your soul. Now. Yes, the deal is now complete. It has been completed. I was going for a quick win, take you in your sleep."

Satan, the beautiful woman, it seemed so naturally, turned into a snake. She looked and moved perfectly like a snake, only she was thirty yards long. She put her snake face very close to my smaller face. Satan the snake said so softly that only I could have heard it. Still in the lady's voice, she said, "This is going to be so easy."

All I could say was, "I don't know about that."

Satan the lady snake coiled up, turned, and looked around, the tongue going out and in. Then she slithered toward the gate. As she got close to the door on the gate, I saw the snake become Brother Joe.

Joe turned around and waved just like a regular guy. Satan Joe turned and opened the door and walked through.

That was it. My trip to hell.

After my trip to hell—it seems!—I went to sleep. After which, I woke up to sunshine coming in my hospital room window. Well, over three and a half days had passed of my withdrawal delirium.

LAURA TOLD ME HER HUSBAND WAS DANGEROUS. A GODLESS awful man. She was surprised I was allowed to stay. A miracle Laura claimed. Only once did she tell me the story. Two days before her death.

Laura's beauty wasn't all he wanted. There was an add-on. Laura spoke other languages fluently. Understood many more.

He took her everywhere. All over the world. She met presidents, dictators, and leaders of small countries. In the US and around the world. Movie stars. Powerful people of industry. Many politicians.

Laura was his showpiece. Beautiful, imposing, and entertaining. Laura could dine or just talk with heads of state. Powerful along with the glamorous. A way of life. For a while.

"After three girls and no boys, Robert was done. He began using me, and that was it. He never loved me. Never. I knew that after the first year. A grand wedding. When the wedding was over, Robert was on the phone. I was a prisoner. Outside my room were trained guards. He is a criminal. His father is a criminal. The worst. Robert will have you killed if you breathe this.

"*Promoted* means 'killed.' Example, 'We promoted him. He was promoted.' Robert was too high up to be promoted. He sells girls. Lots of young girls. All the small countries around Russia. He advertises for young ladies who want a rich American husband. The girls pay a small fee. Many are very pretty, and rich men here pay him massive amounts.

"Robert has pictures of the girls. Some are as young as fourteen! All of the average girls are sold straight into businesses servicing men. He sees the young women as inventory. Customers keep coming back. If needed, Robert resells the same girl once she becomes pregnant, or the customer wants a different one! No reason necessary. Robert is protected. The law cannot touch him."

Laura told me all of this and more. When she finished talking, Laura asked me to pray for all those girls.

That was it. This is what Laura told me. I wondered if it was true.

I could not imagine a person being that bad. Evil had not entered my small world. Drunk husbands were the worst I had ever known. I would hear about a murderer on the news.

This one man was doing something far worse than murder. I had been in the room with that kind of evil.

My brain protected me. This story of Laura's husband and the young women soon slid far back into my memory.

THIS IS IN THE BACK OF THE BOOK BECAUSE I DO NOT WANT a story about Lenny in my book.

Lenny drives an old rusted green triumph. The car has no top. He wears dark circle sunglasses all the time. With orange red hair and red face, he thinks he is Mr. Cool. Lives on welfare and anything illegal. Selling pot and ripping off customers are what he is good at. Never does anything for anybody.

First time I met Lenny, I was sitting on a cement table at Mokuleia Beach Park. Lenny pulled up into a parking place, got out of his car, walked up, and sat down beside me. Lenny asked me, "What are you going to eat?"

Having been on the North Shore for a couple of months, I had seen Lenny before. From what I saw, I had no use for him.

I answered, "I don't know."

Lenny asked, "Are you hungry?"

"Now that you mention it, yes, I am."

"I have been watching. You don't have anything to eat."

I just looked at the ocean. I wasn't hungry till he showed up. "Yep, I am hungry."

"Do you have any money?"

"No, not a bit. Are you worried about me?"

"In a way, it bothers me. So I guess I am worried about you."

I told Lenny, "Good, thank you. You can worry about me, because I am not going to worry at all."

Lenny looked straight at me, told me I was messed up, hurried to his car, and ranted on and on. He told me a thing or two and left.

What was that all about? I thought. *Now I am thinking about food. I have about a hundred dollars. Guess I will get something to eat.*

JOHNNY AND LOTUS

Lazy Johnny, Slow Johnny, Boring Johnny, Lifeless Johnny, or anything similar, we all know it is Johnny. "Happily married to Lotus" Johnny. I don't know them. I know of them.

Johnny is thirty, a local Hawaiian. He is lazy, etc. "Would not hurt a fly" kind of person. Lotus, his wife, whom Johnny is crazy about. Lotus is probably forty. She is half Hawaiian and half Japanese. Lotus has a flat butt and a little bit of a belly hanging over her swimsuit or shorts bottom. Small breasts.

Okay, the stupid story. Lotus drives up to my jewelry stand and parks in the landlord's driveway. Lotus jumps out of her new dark-blue Mustang. All excited. "David, oh, David, thank you for being here. Oh, David. Matsa told me to drive straight here. He told me you would go get Johnny. Oh, David, Matsa told me you would take care of everything, not to worry. Oh, David…"

I announced, "Do not say, 'Oh, David.' Where is Johnny?"

"Oh, David, Lenny kidnapped Johnny. I will watch your business. You go get Johnny. Lenny has Johnny at Lenny's house. Oh, David."

I said, "Okay, Lotus, move your car. These two young men will take care of the customers. You may help them."

My car was parked down the driveway. As I was leaving, her car was already moving across the highway. One of the two boys said through my car window, "Oh, David."

I knew one of them was going to say it.

The other one said, "I think she likes you."

I just said. "Watch her."

As I was pulling out, they were yelling, "Oh, David, bye, oh, David." I really like those two.

Lenny lived two miles away. Across the street from the beach. Nice view. I had not seen the stupid devil in months. I guess a month before Waikiki.

His house is easy to spot, the dark-green triumph under a two-car carport.

I pulled in and parked on the driveway and walked up to the screen door. Walking up and looking in, I noticed there was not very much furniture in the living area.

When I arrived at the door and looked in, Lenny was sitting in a small cushion chair directly across the room from me. Right beside Lenny in a similar chair, against the other wall, was Johnny.

Lenny had a shotgun pointed at me. No one told me about a shotgun.

Lenny said, "Did you bring the money?"

I responded, "I just came here to get Johnny. No one told me about you having a shotgun. I was not told to bring any money."

Lenny was trying to be cool. "This is none of your business, Mr. Cash. Now go on."

Lenny walked to the screen door and held the two barrels in my face. Through the screen.

I said, "Okay, I came to pick up Johnny."

I looked past Lenny and at Johnny. "Johnny, stand up and walk out. I am here. Lenny is not going to shoot you."

Johnny stood up.

Lenny yelled, "Johnny, sit down, or I will kill David!"

Johnny sat down.

This was stupid. Lenny, a certified nut, was picking on the weakest person. I just wanted to get back to work.

I started to walk away. Lenny quickly opened the door, walked out, and yelled, "Stop! Where are you going?"

I stopped and turned around. Lenny put the double-barrel in my face. I said, "Get the gun out of my car. Get your finger off the trigger before the gun goes off."

Lenny said, "I will keep my fingers on the triggers."

I asked, "How much for Johnny? I have boxes of hundreds, fifties, and twenties. The jewelry stand is a cash cow. Your finger on the trigger scares me."

Lenny said, "Two thousand. Two thousand."

"That's it? Come on, man, if you will just move your finger off to the side, we can all three ride and grab your money."

Lenny replied, "I will sit in the back."

"No, I am very nervous, clear the trigger. I am not going to try anything. I would only get shot. Which is what is going to happen with that old shotgun. It could have a hair trigger. Lenny, two thousand dollars is nothing to me."

"Where is all this money, big shot?"

"Move your finger, my friend. We will ride out to Kaena Point. I will show you one hundred and forty thousand dollars in cash. Move the finger so I can lean back against my car. This is too stressful. You have been holding the gun with your finger ready for too long."

Lenny slowly placed the barrels of the shotgun just a tad away from the middle of my eyebrows.

After that, Lenny said, "Put your hands up."

I put my hands up.

He moved his finger off the trigger.

I snatched the shotgun out of Lenny's hands.

I was mad because I needed to be at work. Lenny was stupid. I took it out on Lenny. I decided not to hurt him.

I took the twenty-gauge shells out of the crappy shotgun and checked the triggers. Very hair triggers! I hit Lenny on the right side of his head. (I changed my mind.) He could have blown my head off! His sunglasses fell off. He loved those sunglasses, paid a lot of money for them.

I stomped on Lenny's precious sunglasses.

I told Lenny to go inside and apologize to Johnny and send him out to my car.

Lenny said, "Yes, sir. I will do that."

I said, "What else?"

Lenny was speechless.

I said, "I only hit you once."

Lenny actually bowed and answered, "Thank you, David. Very kind, thank you, and I really mean it."

I said, "Okay, be sure you apologize to Johnny."

Anyway, I had my fun, insulted Lenny some more, and finally left. I was back at work, gone for maybe thirty minutes.

After making sure it would never fire again, I gave the shotgun to my landlord. She asked for it. Wanted it for display.

My young helpers at the jewelry stand told me Lenny had that shotgun with him everywhere he went for the last, maybe, four months. It would be on his car dash, at one-ounce-pot deals, by his side to visit people and take it to parties, at the beach, cookouts. Everywhere Lenny went, he had that shotgun.

Low-class story. Not worthy of my book. I stuck it in the back because it was brought up in the book a couple of times.

It was also brought up for a couple of weeks after the episode. I heard this, "Thanks for taking the shotgun away from Lenny." Friends, along with people I did not know, told me that. I also was told this a few times, "He was going to eventually kill someone."

Johnny borrowed eight hundred dollars. Lenny started adding daily fees. The loan was three weeks old. The amount was still only a thousand dollars that day.

Johnny's parents were well-off. They just bought that new Mustang for Johnny. An estate sends Johnny money every month. His parents gave him the house he lives in years ago.

I asked him, "Why did you borrow money from Lenny?"

I know, of course, why. Then I asked myself, "Why did I ask?"

Johnny answered, "It was a surprise for Lotus. She is so good. I hope you find a Lotus one day."

Why, oh, why did I ask? I did not want to hear any more.

He went on. "I thought Lenny was my friend."

We arrived back at my stand in time to save me from hearing about the surprise for Lotus.

My two young friends and trusted helpers were happy I was back. Lotus talked nonstop, tried on jewelry, and made a wreck of the stand.